DISCOURSE AND TRUTH
&
PARRĒSIA

MICHEL FOUCAULT

DISCOURSE & TRUTH AND *PARRĒSIA*

EDITED BY
Henri-Paul Fruchaud and
Daniele Lorenzini

INTRODUCTION BY
Frédéric Gros

ENGLISH EDITION ESTABLISHED BY
Nancy Luxon

The University of Chicago Press • Chicago and London

The University of Chicago Press, Chicago 60637
The University of Chicago Press, Ltd., London

Published 2019
Printed in the United States of America

28 27 26 25 24 23 22 21 20 19   1 2 3 4 5

ISBN-13: 978-0-226-50946-4 (cloth)
ISBN-13: 978-0-226-50963-1 (e-book)
DOI: https://doi.org/10.7208/chicago/9780226509631.001.0001

Originally published as *"Discours et vérité" précédé de "La parrêsia"*
© Librairie Philosophique J. Vrin, Paris, 2016. http://www.vrin.fr

Library of Congress Cataloging-in-Publication Data

Names: Foucault, Michel, 1926–1984, author. | Fruchaud, Henri-Paul, editor. |
Lorenzini, Daniele, editor. | Luxon, Nancy, editor.
Title: Discourse and truth and parresia / Michel Foucault ; edited by
Henri-Paul Fruchaud and Daniele Lorenzini ; introduction by Frederic Gros ;
English edition established by Nancy Luxon.
Description: Chicago ; London : The University of Chicago Press, 2019. |
Includes bibliographical references and index. | English translation
of two seminars given in 1982 and 1983.
Identifiers: LCCN 2018057647 | ISBN 9780226509464 (cloth : alk. paper) |
ISBN 9780226509631 (e-book)
Subjects: LCSH: Freedom of speech. | Philosophy, Ancient.
Classification: LCC JC591 .F67 2019 | DDC 323.44/301—dc23
LC record available at https://lccn.loc.gov/2018057647

♾ This paper meets the requirements of ANSI/NISO Z39.48-1992
(Permanence of Paper).

CONTENTS

ABBREVIATIONS OF WORKS BY MICHEL FOUCAULT

CCS *Qu'est-ce que la critique?* suivi de *La culture de soi*, ed. H.-P. Fruchaud and D. Lorenzini (Paris: Vrin, 2015)

CV *Le courage de la vérité. Le gouvernement de soi et des autres II. Cours au Collège de France, 1983–1984*, ed. F. Gros (Paris: Seuil-Gallimard, 2008)

CT *The Courage of Truth, Lectures at the Collège de France, 1983–1984*, ed. Frédéric Gros, trans. Graham Burchell, English series ed. Arnold I. Davidson (New York and Basingstoke: Palgrave Macmillan, 2011)

DE, II *Dits et écrits II, 1976–1988*, ed. Daniel Defert and François Ewald with the collaboration of J. Lagrange (Paris: Gallimard, 2001)

EW, 1 *The Essential Works of Foucault, 1954–1984. Volume 1: Ethics, Subjectivity and Truth*, ed. Paul Rabinow (New York: New Press, 1997)

EW, 3 *The Essential Works of Foucault, 1954–1984. Volume 3: Power*, ed. James D. Faubion (New York: New Press, 2000)

GSA *Le gouvernement de soi et des autres. Cours au Collège de France, 1982–1983*, ed. F. Gros (Paris: Seuil-Gallimard, 2008)

GSO *The Government of Self and Others: Lectures at the Collège de France, 1982–1983*, ed. Frédéric Gros, trans. Graham Burchell, English series ed. Arnold I. Davidson (New York and Basingstoke: Palgrave Macmillan, 2010)

GV *Du gouvernement des vivants. Cours au Collège de France, 1979–1980*, ed. M. Senellart (Paris: Seuil-Gallimard, 2012)

GL *On the Government of the Living: Lectures at the Collège de France, 1979–1980*, ed. Michael Senellart, trans. Graham Burchell, English series ed. Arnold I. Davidson (New York and Basingstoke: Palgrave Macmillan, 2014)

HS *L'herméneutique du sujet. Cours au Collège de France, 1981–1982*, ed. F. Gros (Paris: Seuil-Gallimard, 2001)

HS (Eng) *The Hermeneutics of the Subject: Lectures at the Collège de France, 1981–1982*, ed. Frédéric Gros, trans. Graham Burchell, English series ed. Arnold I. Davidson (New York: Palgrave Macmillan, 2005)

MFDV *Mal faire, dire vrai. Fonction de l'aveu en justice*, ed. F. Brion and B. Harcourt (Louvain-la-Neuve: Presses universitaires de Louvain, 2012)

WDTT *Wrong-Doing, Truth-Telling: The Function of Avowal in Justice*, ed. Fabienne Brion and Bernard E. Harcourt, trans. Stephen W. Sawyer (Chicago: University of Chicago Press, 2014)

OHS *L'origine de l'herméneutique de soi. Conférences prononcées à Dartmouth College, 1980*, ed. H.-P. Fruchaud and D. Lorenzini (Paris: Vrin, 2013)

ABHS *About the Beginning of the Hermeneutics of the Self: Lectures at Dartmouth College, 1980*, ed. Henri-Paul Fruchaud and Daniele Lorenzini, trans. Graham Burchell (Chicago: University of Chicago Press, 2016)

SP *Surveiller et punir. Naissance de la prison* (Paris: Gallimard, 1975)

DP *Discipline and Punish: The Birth of the Prison*, trans. Alan Sheridan (London: Allen Lane, 1977)

SS *Histoire de la sexualité III. Le souci de soi* (Paris: Gallimard, 1984)

CS *The Care of the Self*, trans. Robert Hurley (New York: Pantheon, 1986)

STP *Sécurité, territoire, population. Cours au Collège de France, 1977–1978*, ed. M. Senellart (Paris: Seuil-Gallimard, 2004)

STP (Eng) *Security, Territory, Population: Lectures at the Collège de France, 1977–1978*, ed. Michael Senellart, trans. Graham Burchell, English series ed. Arnold I. Davidson (New York and Basingstoke: Palgrave Macmillan, 2007)

SV *Subjectivité et vérité. Cours au Collège de France, 1980–1981*, ed. F. Gros (Paris: Seuil-Gallimard, 2014)

ST *Subjectivity and Truth: Lectures at the Collège de France, 1980–1981*, ed. Frédéric Gros, trans. Graham Burchell, English series ed. Arnold I. Davidson (New York and Basingstoke: Palgrave Macmillan, 2017)

UP *Histoire de la sexualité II. L'usage des plaisirs* (Paris: Gallimard, 1984)

UP (Eng) *The Use of Pleasure*, trans. Robert Hurley (New York: Pantheon, 1985)

VS *Histoire de la sexualité I. La volonté de savoir* (Paris: Gallimard, 1976)

HIST *The History of Sexuality. Volume 1: An Introduction*, trans. Robert Hurley (New York: Random House, 1978)

PREFACE

THIS EDITION PRESENTS A SERIES of lectures given in English by Michel Foucault from October to November 1983 at the University of California, Berkeley, under the title "Discourse and Truth."

Until recently, this series of lectures was unpublished in France. A first English version, which did not precisely present Foucault's actual words, was published by Joseph Pearson in 2001 under the title *Fearless Speech*.

Preceding this lecture series is a public lecture on *parrēsia* that Foucault gave in French at the University of Grenoble in May 1982. This lecture was published for the first time in the journal *Anabases* 16 (2012).

The texts for these lectures have been established in the following manner:

> For the lectures at Berkeley: from the recordings held at IMEC (Institut Mémoires de l'Édition Contemporaine) and at the University of California, Berkeley, with the assistance of Davey K. Tomlinson in establishing the transcription of the English version.
>
> For the lecture at Grenoble: from a single recording held at IMEC.

We were also able to consult the written lecture notes for the lectures at Berkeley and at Grenoble that are held at the Bibliothèque nationale de France.

The texts for the lectures were established in the most literal manner possible. We have only, where it seemed useful, eliminated some redundant phrasings or corrected the construction of some awkward sentences.

In particular, we would like to thank the Bibliothèque nationale de France, for the invaluable assistance it offered in allowing us to consult manuscripts from the Foucault archives before these were made available to the public. We also would like to thank Stuart Elden and Joseph Pearson, from whom we were able to learn the seminar title under which the lectures on *parrēsia* were delivered at the University of California, Berkeley.

Henri-Paul Fruchaud
and Daniele Lorenzini
Paris, France

INTRODUCTION

HENRI-PAUL FRUCHAUD AND DANIELE LORENZINI have presented here—in a manner both rigorous and well documented (their critical bibliographic notes are especially valuable and useful)—two sets of interventions by Michel Foucault bearing on the ancient Greek concept of *parrēsia*. One is a talk given at the University of Grenoble in May 1982, and the other is a series of six lectures given at the University of California at Berkeley from October through November 1983.

As is by now well known, Foucault addresses, analyzes, and problematizes the concept of *parrēsia* in his last three courses taught at the Collège de France; these include *The Hermeneutics of the Subject*, *The Government of Self and Others*, and *The Courage of Truth*. The transcription of these talks offers us the missing links for the elaboration of a theoretical framework that occupied the last years of his life and that indisputably constitutes his final major contribution to philosophy. It is remarkable to note that all of the "texts" by Foucault that treat *parrēsia* find their origins in oral presentations and lectures spoken aloud. Only a sudden death prevented him from giving these analyses the dignity of the written word. Still, the fact remains that the very notion of *parrēsia*, as we will see, contains praise for a spoken word that finds its natural place in orality.

Parrēsia is a Greek term that means to "say everything." "Saying everything" undoubtedly can mean to say anything, without filter, unbridled and unhindered, but it also—and perhaps especially—means daring to say what our cowardice or our shame immediately restrains us from uttering. Or even more simply: to express oneself with sincerity and frankness; to speak without shame or fear. One could thus translate it as "frank speech," "speaking truly," "the courage of the truth," or "freedom of speech." These first determinations could give the impression of a notion overwritten by psychological features above all else, but over the course of the years between 1982 and 1984, Foucault will argue the opposite: that this concept has a core *political* value that allows for a reevaluation of the relation between democracy and truth, an *ethical* value that is decisive for problematizing the relation between subjectivity and truth, and a *philosophical* value for sketching a genealogy of the critical attitude. Finally, one could note that beyond the term's actual substance, Foucault also studies the history and transformation of this concept, from classical antiquity until the Hellenistic and Roman periods, while also offering some glimpses of its Christian inflections.

Before giving an overview of these three dimensions of the concept and its evolution, which are the central contributions of the until recently unpublished texts in this volume, it's worth considering two points: the general form of the concept of *parrēsia* and its contextualization by Foucault in his own research. Effectively, Foucault seeks to understand *parrēsia* more as a kind of *prise de parole* than as a personal virtue or even a rhetorical technique. He construes, initially, the concept in the context of a "pragmatics of discourse." Mounting the rostrum entails a certain danger for the one who speaks a truth that he publicly claims as his own: such words immediately expose the speaker to the anger and rejection of his interlocutor(s). One can quickly see to what extent the relation between subject and truth, as Foucault articulates it through *parrēsia,* becomes irreducible to classic frameworks. Certainly, *parrēsia* always raises questions about whether a subject is *capable* of truth, but of a truth of which one wonders less about its correct formulation than about speaking it before others. At no point does Foucault—and this regularly surprises and disorients his listeners and readers—pose the epistemological question of the transcendental or examine logical criteria of truth. His primary concern is the ethical relation of the subject to truth: the kind of freedom and courage that the subject engages when publicly expressing a personally held truth, one that engenders a tension with his interlocutors. Finally, Foucault affirms that this study of *parrēsia* unfolds in the general framework of his analysis of "obligations to truth." It is one thing to show the different internal necessities to which a subject must conform to speak a *truly true discourse*; it's another thing to classify the types of "obligation" that a culture invents to oblige the subject (or by which the subject freely obliges himself) to speak truly before another.

The political determination of *parrēsia* is perhaps the most immediate; for Foucault it corresponds to the first major uses of the term that he finds in the tragedies of Euripides, and particularly *Ion*. It refers to a prerogative linked to the citizenship status given by birth, to a reserved "right." To be an active subject in a democracy is to be able to exercise free speech. That is to say, a democratic regime must permit or even guarantee its subjects—beyond equality before the law—this capacity to speak *in one's own name* so as to freely utter one's *own* convictions about the common good, even if the majority becomes uncomfortable, even if this use of speaking-truly (*parler-vrai*) risks introducing inequality—for example, when the parrhesiast finishes by gaining an advantage through a display of courage. Democratic frank speech (*franc-parler*) thus distinguishes itself from the fearful and submissive speech of the slave, and risks the introduction of inequality and the breakdown of tacit consensus. It further distinguishes between two other regimes of speech. First, it is opposed to the discourse of flattery. The parrhesiast, such as Isocrates, for example, sketches the portrait of the flatterer in his discourse "On the Peace" as the person who, by contrast to the demagogue who seeks to make the people hear only those opinions that please him, creates *dissensus* and runs the risk of a hostile popular response. But authentic *parrēsia* must also distinguish itself from the unbridled, garbled mode of "saying everything" denounced by Plato in book 8 of *The Republic*, a mode in which it would eventually be the right of all to say everything and anything, which is taken to be proof of a democracy in good working order.

Beyond these critiques of "bad *parrēsia*" often associated with democracy, Plato represents a key moment in the history of the concept, since according to Foucault he decisively inflects its meaning. For example, he conjures up a new *parrēsia* in *The Laws*, this time exercised in an autocratic context: Plato commends Cyrus when he lets his vassals express themselves freely by allowing them to give contrary advice or criticism about his spiritual disposition. With that, a figure with a long history takes shape: the parrhesiast as counselor to the Prince. The very target of *parrēsia* transforms and becomes more individualized. The parrhesiast no longer addresses a citizen assembly so as to unsettle consensus, but instead aims to transform the soul. The Platonic moment is emphatically indicated by Foucault as an ethical turning point for *parrēsia* with Plato's staging of Socrates in his first dialogues. Socrates certainly demands from his interlocutors an absolute frankness in their responses, but he especially practices an uncompromising speaking-truly in his effort to shake off false knowledge and deliver souls—and this in a space (the *agora*) that, all the while remaining public, is no longer political in the sense of the *ekklesia*. Nor will Foucault forget Socrates' provocative attitude at the moment of his trial, as portrayed in the *Apology*.

However, for Foucault the ethical dimension of *parrēsia* is concentrated in the practices of "spiritual direction," as they appear within philosophical circles in the Hellenistic and Roman periods. Directors guide souls toward wisdom and truth, in a context this time outside of formal politics, by speaking bluntly so as to denounce unambiguously the evil passions of those guided. It is in this context that *parrēsia* can take advantage of its "technical" aspect, as a technique at once of persuasion and care that makes it possible to say the right words at the right time to those whose errors need to be corrected (be this in the texts of Philodemus or Galen). *Parrēsia* thus characterizes the regime of speech used by the master. It is therefore opposed to Christian technologies of confession that demand a transparency, an openness, an overcoming of fear or shame, but on the part of those guided when confronted with a silent confessor. The task of speaking-truly will be displaced from the master to the disciple.

Within pagan antiquity, Foucault envisions at least three specific modes of conduct. Epicureanism, all the while praising a masterful *parrēsia,* also proposes a model of *parrēsia* as reciprocal frankness within communities of wisdom; disciples mutually and openly confide in one another their progress or setbacks, their good and bad experiences. Imperial Stoicism, with Seneca, offers the model of a dyadic relationship in which the direction of souls is rather the deliberate modulation of a friendship or social relation, for example through sustained correspondence or regular conversation. Finally, Cynicism valorizes a *parrēsia* composed of coarse speech and verbal provocations in public places, aimed at teeming masses and seeking to wound their certainty and shake their naive confidence in the validity of social conventions.

This diversity, however, should not shield and mask the common ground of these varied practices of frank speech: the "care of the self" as a fundamental ethical attitude. This fundamental attention that each must bear toward himself, so as to conduct himself correctly, to valorize through his life just and rational principles, to establish a firm and constant government of the self, demands something other than mere internal vigilance, for Foucault. Without needing to become perfectly wise, one must be regularly summoned to self-examination by another, summoned by another rather than by oneself, to face questions not about the contents of a hidden self but about what governs one's actual conduct. There are things perhaps even more dangerous than the flattery of demagogues: the flattery that each person speaks to himself, allowing for illusion on his own behalf. If the ethical concern for the self for Foucault is irreducible to a complacent narcissism, and far from either an aestheticizing dandyism or the quest for a singular authenticity, then it is by virtue of this uncompromising speech that another can or must speak about oneself. The *parrēsia* of a friend, a spiritual adviser, or a public provocateur prevents the care of the self from succumbing to the flightiness and expediency of egoism. If, for Foucault, the care of the self is not a practice of withdrawal within the self, but a manner of building a relation to the self that can structure our relations to others, then it owes this opening-up to the emphasis on the frank, uncompromising speech of external others.

The philosophical dimension, the last dimension of *parrēsia,* unfolds in a double direction within Foucault's lectures: that of a reevaluation of wisdom in antiquity, and that of a redefinition of philosophy as the task of critique. Initially, *parrēsia* allows the question of the *bios philosophikos* to be posed, and thus displaces the traditional meaning of truth within philosophical thought. Classically, truth constitutes a driver in the quest for knowledge and finds its natural expression in the unfolding of demonstrative discourse. *Parrēsia* is the speech of truth, certainly, but its principal function is to spark the animating force (*lignes de force*) of lives lived, rather than to sustain the writing of treatises. *Parrēsia* is a test of life itself rather than of discourse. For the parrhesiast is not only the person who speaks courageously and publicly before others. The parrhesiast publicly practices this truth by enacting it through his external conduct, by dramatizing it through his body, and by making it ring out even through silent acts and behavior. The parrhesiast realizes truth through his very life. Socrates, such as he appears in Plato's *Laches,* is that musician who coaxes a perfect harmony into resonance between his words and deeds. Seneca construes parrhesiast's existence as a mirror held up before the face, where can be silently read the rational precepts that should guide life. The Cynics permit themselves to raucously denounce the hypocrisy of customs or mock royal houses because they oblige themselves to live austerely, without compromise, sovereign in their bare lives, transparent and pure in the sense of being encumbered by nothing.

For Foucault, *parrēsia,* this provocative public speech, does not find any natural extension through a writing that would contain the holder of truths within a closed, definitive text. It finds its necessary condition and touchstone through the "true life" that demystifies, mocks, and invalidates abstract discourse and distant writings. The "true life" is something other than a contemplative, theoretical existence, and philosophy is something other than a system of knowledge (*connaissances*). At its extreme, *parrēsia* can be understood as an obligation less to speak what one believes to be true than to make truth visible through one's own life. Truth was, at least for antiquity, the name for that which places a life, in the entirety of its practical aspects, in tension.

Perhaps *parrēsia* can claim another name, one more modern: "critique." After all, in his essay on the Enlightenment, Kant gives no other definition for it: *sapere aude*, have the courage to emerge from your own immaturity. If—in returning to the examples from Kant's essay—you need a book to think, a spiritual director to guide your conduct, a doctor to tend your health, it's because you are unable to govern yourself and prefer, through cowardice or laziness, the comforts of obedience. Thinking for oneself means having the courage of an autonomous critical judgment—that is the lesson of the Enlightenment. Yet the threads of this tight knot joining truth, freedom, courage, and subjectivity already broadly characterized parrhesiastic speech. For Foucault, from the clarity of the Greeks to the "Enlightenment" of the moderns, philosophy finds something like a metahistorical resolve through its critical function, one that refuses to dissociate questions of the government of self, the government of others, and speaking-truly.

One wonders if these three dimensions of *parrēsia* (political, ethical, philosophical) unpacked in these lectures are nothing more than an interpretive grid rather than the definition of essences. These dimensions are de facto indissociable and complementary, and they unavoidably overlap. Beyond this general overview, one could return to another contribution of these lectures. They make it possible to establish points in Foucault's intellectual evolution: one learns that as late as 1982 in Grenoble, Foucault rejected the idea of a Cynic *parrēsia* (invective seemed to him too distant from an individualized speech such as Galen depicts) or a Socratic one (irony, and the double game it presumes, initially seemed to distinguish itself from a speech that clearly reflects the convictions of the speaker). One further discovers in the 1983 lectures at Berkeley the first analyses of Plato's *Laches* and the outline for a study of Cynical *parrēsia* that will be resumed and deepened in Paris in his 1984 seminar at the Collège de France. But more generally, these texts enable the discovery, through this and that reference, of more comprehensive developments (be it the confrontation between Diogenes and Alexander according to Dio of Prusa, the dialogue *On the Tranquility of the Mind*, by Seneca, etc.) or even previously unpublished analyses (think of the very long study of Euripides' *Orestes*).

The lectures presented in this work are definitive. They show to what extent the study of *parrēsia* could represent for Foucault the ultimate point of any recentering within philosophy, but a philosophy itself decentered, entirely rethought as critical vigor, courage of thought, and authoritative transformation of the self, of others, and the world.

Frédéric Gros
Paris, France

Translated by Nancy Luxon

NOTE ON THE ENGLISH EDITION

IN THE LECTURES THAT FOLLOW, none of the endnotes provided are original to Michel Foucault's manuscripts; these were added by Henri-Paul Fruchaud and Daniele Lorenzini in preparing *Discours et Vérité* for its initial publication in French (Vrin, 2016). For the lecture given by Foucault at the University of Grenoble, English-language equivalents were then sought for these sources. When possible, those equivalents were editions used in the Collège de France lectures already translated. This lecture was originally given in French, translated by Graham Burchell, and published in *Critical Inquiry* with an abridged scholarly apparatus.

The Berkeley lectures offered a different challenge. Foucault prepared the lectures he gave at the University of California at Berkeley in English and with Greek and English-language sources. Since new, and now standard, translations of Euripides' plays and other texts have since been published, any translation faces a quandary. Should the sources supplied reflect those English- and Greek-language sources used by Foucault during his time at Berkeley? Or should more modern translations be given? The first option encourages readers to treat the lectures as historical documents and to precisely account for what Foucault read, interpreted, and then said in his lectures. The second option takes seriously that these lectures *continue* to be public addresses to an avowedly contemporary readership, a readership attuned to different issues at the nexus of power and truth-telling. The interpretive differences are significant: for example, "Keen-witted varlet this!" (Arthur Sanders Way, 1916) becomes "He too is a clever slave" (David Kovacs, Loeb Classics, 1999) in Euripides' *Trojan Women*. In addition, Foucault often calls attention to passages that are suspected of being later interpolations.

In preparing this English-language edition, for the Berkeley lectures I have chosen to stay with Foucault's choices for translations of Greek or Latin texts when they were known. When they weren't known, I chose references that were used in the translation of Foucault's lectures at the Collège de France. In those instances in which the translation hinders the comprehension of a substantive point, I have offered an alternate translation from the Loeb Classical Editions, usually considered to be the standard scholarly edition. Interpolated passages are noted in the scholarly notes. Otherwise, the critical apparatus is limited to elucidating obscure points, identifying those passages being referenced, or referring readers to other parts of Foucault's corpus for further discussion of certain points or authors. Quotations have been checked and the references to texts used supplied; for Foucault's works, these references are given to both French- and English-language versions.

When editing Foucault's English, I have sought a light touch, and the principle was to remain as close as possible to the course as actually delivered. Footnotes indicate those moments when Foucault deviated from his prepared text and supply the missing passages. The summaries and repetitions of spoken English have been removed when necessary. Punctuation was introduced to divide up long sentences and to correct faulty constructions. When the meaning of a sentence was obscure, or a phrase was inaudible, there is conjectural addition denoted by square brackets. On a few occasions, I made more decisive changes, such as the decision to render "criticism" as "critique" throughout the manuscript. For the question-and-answer periods that occurred during or after the Berkeley lectures, a few of the questions from audience members were condensed and edited for clarity. Ellipses indicate either that Foucault's voice trailed off or that several voices were speaking at once; bracketed ellipses indicate that the words were inaudible.

Special thanks to Shai Gortler for his unflagging research support on the English edition.

Nancy Luxon
Minneapolis, MN

PARRĒSIA

Lecture at the University of Grenoble
*May 18, 1982**

THANK YOU VERY MUCH FOR inviting me.** I am here, as you know, as a supplicant. What I mean is that until four or five years ago, my field, at any rate the domain of my work, had scarcely anything to do with ancient philosophy; and then, following a number of zigzags, detours, or steps back in time, I began to say to myself

* This lecture was originally translated by Graham Burchell and published in *Critical Inquiry* 41, no. 2 (Winter 2015): 219–53. For the present edition, Nancy Luxon has modified the initial translation in light of the definitive French version, with the editors' supervision.

** Foucault is addressing Henri Joly, who had just introduced him with a few words:

HENRI JOLY: Given that the time available is somewhat accounted for—for personal reasons Michel Foucault has to return to Paris this evening—I will confine myself to stating his subject: he will deal with *parrēsia*. I will leave the task of translating it, I just transliterate, which is a kind of cleverness . . . a clumsiness on my part, for which I apologize. And then, on the other hand, I am anxious to clarify that the texts you have in front of you are not necessarily the texts to which Michel Foucault will refer. They are supporting texts that we have put together a bit here, not that we have not spoken on the telephone . . . We have even telephoned several times . . .

that, after all, it was very interesting. So I come to ancient philosophy as part of the work I am doing. One day, when I was asking him some questions, telling him about my problems, Henri Joly was kind enough to say that you might agree to discuss my work with me, in its present imperfect state. It is some material, some references to texts, some indications; what I am going to sketch out to you is therefore incomplete, and, if you were willing, it would be very good of you, first, to call out if you can't hear me, stop me if you do not understand or if it's not clear, and then anyway, at the end, tell me what you think.

So, to start with, this is how I came to be asking myself this set of questions. What I had been studying for really quite a long time was the question of the obligation to tell the truth: what is this ethical structure internal to truth-telling, this bond that, beyond necessities having to do with the structure or reference of discourse, means that at a given moment someone is obliged to tell the truth? And I tried to pose this question, or rather I encountered this question of the obligation to tell the truth, of, if you like, the ethical foundation of truth-telling, with regard to truth-telling about oneself. In actual fact it seems to me that I encountered it several times. First of all in medical and psychiatric practice because, from a given moment, which is moreover quite precise and can be pinpointed at the beginning of the nineteenth century, we see the obligation to tell the truth about oneself becoming part of the great ritual of psychiatry.[1] Obviously we come across this problem of truth-telling about oneself in judicial practice and more especially in penal practice.[2] And, finally, I came across it for the third time with regard to, let's say, problems of sexuality and more precisely of concupiscence and the flesh in Christianity.[3]

And so, while looking a bit more closely at this question of the

---

MICHEL FOUCAULT: It is not important.

HENRI JOLY: It is inefficient. You have some texts; put them aside, and you will reread them afterwards. And now we are going to the text and words of Michel Foucault, and I am delighted, we are delighted to hear you.

obligation to tell the truth about oneself, the history of Christianity, of early Christianity, seemed curious and interesting to me. You know better than me that the penitential form with which we are familiar and that constitutes the sacrament of penance, or rather the form of confession (*aveu*) linked to the sacrament of penance, is a relatively recent institution, dating roughly from the twelfth century, and that it was developed, defined, and structured in the course of a slow and complex evolution.[4] And if we go back in time, let's say to the fourth and fifth centuries, we see that, of course, the sacrament of penance did not exist, but we find distinct forms of obligation to tell the truth about oneself and more precisely two distinct forms: one is the obligation to manifest the truth about oneself and the other is the obligation to speak the truth about oneself. And these occur in two contexts with two completely different forms and series of effects.

The obligation to manifest the truth about oneself forms part of the penitential ritual. This is *exomologēsis*, a kind of dramatization of oneself as a sinner, which is realized through clothing, fasting, ordeals, exclusion from the community, standing as a supplicant at the door of the church, and so on. A dramatization of oneself as a sinner, a dramatic expression of oneself as a sinner, by which one acknowledges one is a sinner, but without doing this—at any rate, without necessarily, primarily, or fundamentally doing this—through language: this is *exomologēsis*.[5]

On the other hand, if we look at the institutions and practices of monastic spirituality, we see another practice that is completely different from penitential *exomologēsis*. This other practice is imposed on every novice, every monk, until he has finally reached a sufficient degree of holiness, and it may even be imposed on every monk until the end of his life. And this practice does not consist in the monk putting himself into, representing himself in the dramatic state of the sinner—he is, after all, already situated within the penitential ritual—but the monk has to tell someone, his director, in principle everything that is taking place in him, all the movements of his thought, every impulse of his desire or concupiscence, what in Greek spirituality, in Evagrius Ponticus, is called the *logismoi* and that is quite naturally translated into Latin as *cogitationes,* whose etymological meaning, Cassian recalls, is what he calls *co-agitationes,* that is to say the movement, the agitation of the mind.[6] It is this agitation of the mind that must be rendered into a discourse that is in principle continuous and that one has to deliver continuously to the person who is one's director. This is what is called in Greek *exagoreusis.*[7] And so we have here a very strange obligation, which is not found again afterwards because, after all, the confession of sins is not the obligation to say everything (*tout dire*); the confession of sins is, of course, the obligation to say what faults one has committed; it is not the obligation to say everything, to reveal one's thought to someone else. The obligation to say everything is quite unique in the Christian spirituality of the fourth and fifth centuries. It does occur subsequently, in fact; it has a long, parallel, and somewhat subterranean history in relation to the great ritual of penance, but it is found again obviously in the spiritual direction (*direction de conscience*) that develops and flourishes in the sixteenth and seventeenth centuries.

It is this telling-all (*tout-dire*), this obligation to say everything regarding the movement of one's thoughts that captured my attention, and I have tried to study its history or, at any rate, tried to see where it came from. Naturally I was led to take a look at what we may call Greco-Roman philosophy to see if it was possible to find the roots of this obligation to say everything in this practice. So I looked at this philosophy, I studied it as a practice—not exactly as a form of spiritual direction (*direction de conscience*) because I do not think this notion is exactly applicable to the form of philosophy I am thinking about. It seems to me that the forms and concepts of this philosophical practice can be identified and its development understood by considering it as the set of theoretical principles, practical precepts, and technical procedures by which one is led, called upon to ensure the *epimeleia heautou,* the care of oneself; so, if you like, it is philosophy as philosophical foundation, practical rule, and technical instrumentation of the care of self.[8] It is from this perspective that I will consider the philosophy of the Hellenistic and in particular Roman period of the first two centuries of the empire. It is in this framework therefore that I will try to consider the problem of the obligation to tell all.

And, of course, we encounter here an important notion, that of *parrēsia*.[9] Etymologically, the notion of *parrēsia* indeed means telling all (*tout dire*). Now, the first thing that struck me was that the word *parrēsia*, which we find in Christian spirituality with the meaning of the necessity for the disciple to open his heart entirely to his director in order to show him the movement of his thoughts, is actually found in Greco-Roman philosophy of the imperial period, with the crucial difference that this *parrēsia* does not refer to an obligation imposed on the disciple but rather to an obligation imposed on the master. Moreover, it is an absolutely characteristic feature of this philosophy, as I have just defined it, that it is much more concerned with imposing silence on the disciple.[10] The regulation of attitudes of silence, the prescription of silence, is long established, from the Pythagoreans to even much later. It is found in the Pythagoreans, you remember in Plutarch's *De audiendo*,[11] and you recall, in a completely different context, Philo of Alexandria's *On the Contemplative Life*,[12] the whole regime of silent postures imposed on disciples; for the disciple is basically the one who remains silent, whereas in Christianity, in Christian spirituality, it is the disciple who has to speak. On the other hand, *parrēsia*, the obligation to say everything, appears as a precept applied to the master, the guide, the director, let's say the other person who is necessary in the care of self; in fact, one can take care of oneself, one can *epimeleisthai heautou*, only on the condition of being helped by someone, and it is for this person, this other person in the care of self, that *parrēsia* is an obligation.

So this evening I can only present the framework, if you like, in which I posed the question, but, basically, what I would ultimately like to study is this: a kind of reversal of responsibility wherein *parrēsia*, that is to say a certain obligation to speak, which fell on the master in ancient philosophy, now, in Christian spirituality, falls on the disciple, on the person directed, and obviously with all the changes of form and content linked to this reversal of responsibility.

That is the problem then. So first of all, if you like, I would like to look with you at some texts from before the period I have chosen.

The period I have chosen is the first two centuries of the empire; I will take some texts that extend roughly from the famous treatise by Philodemus,[13] which is from right at the start of the empire, to Galen, that is to say the end of the Antonines. This then was the period I chose. But I would also like to take a brief look at some texts from before this period, well, to look at them with you, to tell you what they suggest to me, and to ask you what you think.

Concerning the word *parrēsia,* there is a famous text by Polybius in which he speaks about the Achaeans and says that three things characterize their regime, and these are *dēmokratia, isēgoria,* and *parrēsia:*[14] democracy, that is to say, the participation of everyone, at any rate all those who make up the *demos,* in the exercise of power; *isēgoria,* that is to say, a certain equality in the distribution of offices; and *parrēsia,* that is to say, the possibility, for all, it seems, to have access to speech, the right of everyone to speak, speech being understood as speech that decides in the political field, speech inasmuch as it is an act of asserting oneself and one's opinion in the political field. This text associating *parrēsia, dēmokratia,* and *isēgoria* is clearly important. But I think we can go back even beyond Polybius and identify a number of other interesting uses in the classical period, in Euripides and Plato in particular.

There are four passages in Euripides in which the word *parrēsia* is employed.[15] The first is in *Ion*: "If I do not find the woman who gave birth to me, life is impossible for me. And if I was really allowed to make a wish, may she be Athenian [the woman who gave birth to me and I am looking for—M. F.], let her be Athenian so that from my mother I have the right to speak freely [*hōs moi genētai mētrothen parrēsian*: so that *parrēsia* comes to me from my mother—M. F.]. If a foreigner enters a city where the race is unblemished, even if the law makes him a citizen, his tongue will remain servile, he does not have the right to say everything [he does not have *parrēsia*: *ouk echei parrēsian*—M. F.]."[16] So I think this text is interesting, in the first place, because we see that *parrēsia* is a right; it is a right linked to citizenship. In a city in which the race has remained pure, anyone who is not a citizen cannot speak; only the citizen is authorized to do so, and one has this right of speech by birth. And, [second], the right of speech here is obtained from the maternal line; it comes from the mother. In any case, in a properly organized city it is solely birth, being a citizen, that can permit one to speak. First of all, *parrēsia*.

The second text is *Hippolytus*. This text is interesting because it takes up the theme we found in *Ion*, with a slight, yet noteworthy modulation. In Phaedra's confessions, she confesses her passion for Hippolytus, and she evokes all those women who secretly dishonor their husbands' beds and in doing so dishonor their children as well. Phaedra says: "Ah, may they live and flourish in illustrious Athens [she is speaking about children, her children, those she has—M. F.], with the free-spokenness [*franc-parler*] of free men and with pride in their mother! For although he may have a bold heart, a man is a slave when he knows a mother's or father's misdeeds."[17] So we see that *parrēsia*, which is the citizen's right, is tainted by wrongful acts, even secret ones, committed by the father or mother. When the father or mother has committed wrongful acts, the children are in the situation of the slave, and in that situation they do not have *parrēsia*. The moral stain deprives one of *parrēsia*.

The third text is *The Phoenician Women*. It is a dialogue between Jocasta and Polyneices. The dialogue concerns exile, and Jocasta questions Polyneices about the sorrows and misfortunes of exile. Jocasta says, or asks rather: "Is it a great sorrow to be deprived of your homeland?" And Polyneices replies: "Great indeed. Much worse than it sounds." Jocasta: "What is this evil then? What is so unfortunate about exile?" Polyneices: "The biggest drawback, *ouk echei parrēsian* (he does not have *parrēsia*)." And Jocasta replies: "That's being a serf [a slave: *doulos*—M. F.], to keep silent one's thoughts (*mē legein ha tis phronei*)." Polyneices replies: "One has to be able to put up with the foolishness of the master." Jocasta: "Another suffering, to be mad with the mad!"[18]

This text is interesting because you see that here too the right to speak is linked to being a citizen in one's city. When one lives in one's own city one can speak; when one is not in one's own city, one does not have *parrēsia*. The slave does not have *parrēsia* because he does not have citizenship. But someone who does not have *parrēsia* is at the same time subject to the master's foolishness, to his madness; that is to say, you see the idea appearing not only that *parrēsia* is a right, in its foundation and origin, if you like, but also that its function is to speak something like reason and truth to those who are wrong, who do not possess the truth, and who have the mind of the foolish or mad. *Parrēsia* speaks truthfully; it is therefore the right to speak the truth in front of someone who is mad, someone who does not possess the truth. And [what] greater sorrow than to be in a slave's situation, subject to the madness of others, when one could tell them the truth but may not do so?

Finally, the fourth text is *The Bacchae*. The messenger brings Pentheus news of the excesses of the bacchantes. He arrives with the news but is afraid to tell it to Pentheus. He is afraid to speak and says: "I would like to know whether I should tell you this news in plain language [I am quoting the translation—M. F.], or whether I must watch my words? I fear your angry spirits, O Prince, your swift wrath and the excess of your royal temper." And Pentheus replies: "You may speak: you have nothing to fear from me. One should not be angry with one who does his duty."[19]

Here, then, you have a completely different situation. Here, it is not a citizen who asserts or claims his right to speak, since he is on his land. Rather, it is the messenger, the servant who arrives with bad news to announce; he is afraid to report it and asks if he may, as it were, benefit from *parrēsia*, that is to say, speak freely. To which Pentheus replies, yes, you may speak freely.

So you can see that this situation is, in a way, the opposite of the situation we saw earlier. We have a servant who has something to say; he brings bad news, news that is bad for the person to whom he is going to deliver it. Will he be able to benefit from the right to speak? And Pentheus, as vigilant master, as one who knows his interest and also knows his duty, replies, certainly, you have the right to speak. I will not punish you for telling me bad news. I will take it out on the bacchantes afterwards, and he promises to punish them. I think this text has, if you like, a double interest. On the one hand, it poses the problem that we come across so often in other tragedies, which is what to do with the messenger who brings bad news.

Should the bringer of bad news be punished or not? The right of *parrēsia* granted to the servant promises him impunity for the bad news he brings. And then, at the same time, you see something appear that I think will have considerable importance, which is what could be called the theme of commitment, of the parrhesiastic pact: the stronger person, the master, opens up a space of freedom, a space of the right to speak for the person who is not the master, and he asks him to speak, to tell the truth, a truth that may upset him, the master, but for which he commits himself to not punishing the person who tells it, who utters it, and to leave him free; that is to say he commits himself to separating what is stated from the person who states it.[20] So there are four passages in Euripides that seem to me to set out fairly clearly a certain number of themes of *parrēsia* as the exercise of a political right. There are also a number of texts in Plato, and I will not consider all of them, but only those that seem to me the most significant.

First of all, in book 8 of the *Republic*. As you know, this is concerned with the description of the democratic city, of the motley, diverse, and soon democratic city in which each person may choose the form of life he wishes (*idia kataskeuē tou hautou biou*), each may form his own mode of life.[21] Freedom consists in this, with the possibility of doing as one likes and saying what one likes. So *parrēsia* is one of the characteristics of the democratic city.

Another text, which is more interesting because it will have a much greater historical success, is found in book 3 of the *Laws*.[22] This text is about the monarchical regime, specifically the regime of Cyrus—the good, moderate monarchy, the militaristic and moderate monarchy. And two things should be noted in [Plato's] praise of Cyrus's regime. First of all, the soldiers in Cyrus's kingdom, his monarchy, had a certain share in command; they could converse with the generals, which gave them boldness in combat as well as friendship with the generals. At the same time, the king himself authorized competent individuals in his entourage to exercise, as you might say, their freedom of speech, to practice *parrēsia*. The king gave them this right, which assured him real successes and prosperity and which meant that this monarchy was characterized by, at the same time, *eleutheria* (freedom), *philia* (friendship), and *koinonia* (community).

On this subject I would like to quote a very similar passage found in the oration by Isocrates, "To Nicocles," in which, as you know, there is also a theory, a representation of the good autocratic monarchical power. In "To Nicocles," Isocrates says: "Consider as loyal to you, not the friends who praise everything you may say or do, but those who condemn your faults. Give *parrēsia* to prudent people (*tois euphronousin*) so as to have counsellors for thorny matters. Distinguish clever flatterers from devoted servants so as not to let dishonest people prevail over honest people. Listen to what people say about each other; strive to discern at the same time the character of those who speak and the questions they are talking about."[23] Let us let go of the end of this passage, if you will. We may come back to it shortly. You see that what characterizes, what ensures the quality of a good monarchical government is the monarch allowing around himself a space of freedom in which others are able to speak and give him well-pondered advice.

I would also like to add to the first texts of Plato that I will cite a passage from book 8 of the *Laws*, where, as you know, Plato explains how song, gymnastics, and music should be regulated and governed in the city. He proceeds from this to the control of the passions and the expulsion of bad passions. He begins this new argument by evoking the possibility, the necessity for someone who would be like a sort of master of morality.[24] What would this moral master be? He would be someone who would prevail over everyone by *parrēsia*, who would prescribe to each person what was in accordance with the *politeia*, with the city's constitution. And in so doing he would do nothing other than listen to reason, to reason alone, and in a way he would be the only one in the city who would listen solely to reason. Being the only one listening solely to reason would be the characteristic quality of this person who might thus be called the moral parrhesiast of the city.

To these three texts from Plato I would like to add another from an earlier period, but which I think is also very interesting because it brings us to the problem I would like to raise today. It is a text from the *Gorgias*, and I would like to read it. The passage comes at the moment when Callicles has just made his first shattering entrance, and after summarizing the inadequacies of the interventions of Gorgias and Polus, he says, fine, I shall speak, I shall go the whole way, I am not going to be burdened with the timidity of those who spoke before me. And he explains how and why one can reasonably commit an unjust action. It is after this argument that Socrates intervenes and here too speaks of *parrēsia* in an interesting way: "If my soul were made of gold, Callicles, can you doubt that I would be happy to find one of those stones that are used to test gold? A stone as perfect as possible which I would apply to my soul, so that if it was in agreement with me in establishing that my soul had been well cared for, I might be certain of my soul's good condition without further verification.—What is your question getting at, Socrates?—I will tell you: in reality, I believe I have made this precious find [that is, the stone that will make it possible to test his soul—M. F.] in your person.—How so?—I am certain that, regarding the opinions of my soul, whatever you find yourself in agreement with will, at the same time, be true. I consider, in fact, that to judge correctly whether a soul lives well or badly, one must have three qualities, and [I see indeed—M. F.] that you possess all three: *epistēmē, eunoia,* and *parrēsia* (knowledge, benevolence, and *parrēsia*). I often meet people who are unable to test me, not being learned like you; others are learned" and so on.[25]

So *parrēsia* appears here with a very different meaning from those we saw at work a moment ago, either when it was a right of citizens or when it was the need or criterion of a rational monarchical government that let the truth be spoken to it. Now it is a matter of a *parrēsia* that will serve as a test and touchstone for the soul. When the soul wants a touchstone, that is to say if it wants to know—and then at a certain point the text employs the important word *therapeuein* (the translation does not render it well, but never mind)—that is to say if, in its will to look after itself, to take care of itself, the soul seeks a touchstone that will enable it to know the state of its health, that is to say the truth of its opinions, then it needs someone, another soul characterized by *epistēmē* (knowledge), *eunoia* (benevolence), and *parrēsia*. There are some who lack science, and they cannot serve as good criteria; others lack friendship, they do not have *eunoia*; and as for Polus and Gorgias, who have just spoken, Socrates says in effect that they lacked *parrēsia*, they were timid, they were ashamed to take their thoughts through to the end, namely, that it was reasonable to commit unjust actions. Callicles, Socrates says, obviously ironically—but the irony is not important for the moment—will be the good touchstone of the soul in good health; he has *epistēmē*, or at least he claims to have it. He claims to have friendship, and then he precisely does not lack *parrēsia*; he is not held back by that scruple, that sense of shame, that characterized Polus and Gorgias.[26]

It seems to me that we have here the first formulation in Greek thought of *parrēsia* as a constitutive and indispensable element in the relationship of souls. When a soul wants to take care of itself, when it wants to assure that *epimeleia heautou* which is fundamental, when it wants to *therapeuesthai*, look after itself, it needs another soul, and this other soul must have *parrēsia*.

This is the context in which I would like to situate a little not so much the analysis as the questions to raise this evening. It seems to me that anyway if we were to analyze *parrēsia*, it would certainly not be by trying to embrace the whole notion in its entire field, in its entire range of meanings. Ultimately, the notion of *parrēsia* is, I believe, always linked to a practice. If you take the texts, then, in which I am interested—the first to the second century CE—you see in fact the notion of *parrēsia* in rather different practical contexts.

First, you find it in the context of rhetoric, in Quintilian, in a chapter devoted to figures of thought, *sententiarum figurae*, that is to say, to all the ways in which the expression of thought is made to depart from the *simplici modo indicandi*.[27] So in this chapter on figures of thought, Quintilian gives a place to a figure of thought that is a nonfigure, the zero figure, that which arouses the hearer's emotion, which consequently acts upon the hearer without being *adsimulata* and without being *arte composita*, so without being pretended, simulated, or composed by art and technique; it is *oratio libera*, that is to say, the exclamation and direct expression of thought without any particular figure, that *oratio libera* which Quintilian says the Greeks call *parrēsia* and Cornificius calls *licencia*. That is the first context in which you find the word *parrēsia*.

A second context: well, this is very interesting, very broad; it should be categorized—I have not made this classification, I may try to do so later. It would be the use of the word *parrēsia* in political thought.[28] And here we would need to go back over Plato's description of the kingdom of Cyrus or the text Isocrates addressed to Nicocles, the oration "To Nicocles." Here, then, *parrēsia* obviously emerges as a very important notion when we are dealing with a political structure in which princely rule, monarchy, and autocracy have actually become political reality. In all these historical and political texts, *parrēsia* is clearly no longer linked to *isēgoria* or *dēmokratia* but rather to the exercise of personal power and a strongly inegalitarian structure. Thus understood, *parrēsia* does not have at all the status of a right that is exercised by birth; it is a freedom granted and conceded either by the sovereign or by the rich and powerful individual. But it is a freedom that one has to grant in order to be a good sovereign, in order to be rich and powerful in the proper way. *Parrēsia* is the criterion of the good sovereign, of the illustrious reign. Think of all the historians' portraits of the different emperors of this period; I think that the presence or absence of *parrēsia* is certainly one of the major distinctive features of the good or bad sovereign; moreover, the whole problem of the relations between the emperor and the senate is present in this issue of *parrēsia*.

Parrēsia is therefore a freedom, a freedom the sovereign has to grant. And this freedom thus granted by the prince to others should not be understood as a sort of delegation of power or as a sharing of power. What is the object of this liberty that the prince gives to the parrhesiast of whom he has such need in order to govern? What is its domain of application? It is not politics, it is not the management of the republic, it is not part of his power that he has given to others. He grants others the freedom to exercise, if they can, and if they are able to, a power over his, the sovereign's, own soul; the point of application of political *parrēsia* is not the domain of political action but the prince's soul. And to that extent, you see that this political *par-*

rēsia is really very close to the kind of *parrēsia* we will be looking at in a moment, which is the *parrēsia* exercised in a spiritual direction (*direction de conscience*). You see too that this *parrēsia* understood as freedom to speak in order to act on the prince's soul is linked to a certain type of political structure and also to the political form of the court. And I think there would be a long history of *parrēsia* [. . .]* through various political systems, in all the forms of political systems that have involved a court. In European political thought up to the eighteenth century, the problem of *parrēsia*, of the freedom of royal advisers to speak, is a political problem. Before the problem of universal freedom of expression is raised, a major political problem was that of the right to free speech within the space of the court. It would be interesting to look at how the good counselor has been portrayed in terms of *parrēsia*; to look at the figure of the favorite, a negative character or, more precisely, the flatterer and not the parrhesiast; to look at the court preacher, the person who, protected by his status as priest and by the place from which he speaks, his pulpit, is committed to *parrēsia*. These are the limits of *parrēsia*. I think a whole historico-cultural analysis could be made of *parrēsia* in its relationship with the structure of the court.

Anyway, these are not the problems that I would like to study today; I would like to take another practical context, which is neither that of rhetoric nor [that of] politics but which is spiritual direction.**[29] So, if you like, I would like to indicate two or three questions of method. First, the question of *parrēsia* in spiritual direction has been evoked in a number of studies, but I do not think it has ever been given a direct and clear analysis. You are no doubt familiar with the text that seems to me to contain the most information, the one by Gigante that appeared in the proceedings of the 1968 Guillaume

* Interruption to the recording.

** The manuscript adds: "In fact, one is quite close to political problems: the government of self, the government of others. But I would like to abstract away from this dimension, so as to imagine solely the direction of souls, independently of the role and political function that can be played by the one who is guided."

Budé conference[30] and is a presentation of Philodemus's *Peri parrēsias*.[31] Well, through Gigante's text, and referring to Philippson[32] and other earlier authors, we see more or less what is at stake in this debate: the question of whether *parrēsia* should be considered as a virtue, if it should be considered as a technique, or if one should consider it as a mode of life. To put it very schematically, it seems to me [. . .]* that it may be a mode of life, in the way that, for example, the philosophical mode of life could be. There is absolutely no doubt that the philosophical mode of life entails *parrēsia*; there can be no philosopher who is not a parrhesiast; but the fact of being a parrhesiast does not coincide exactly with the philosophical mode of life.[33] I think—at any rate this is what I would like to suggest—that we should consider *parrēsia* from the point of view of what is now called a pragmatics of discourse, that is to say, that *parrēsia* should be considered as the set of characteristics that grounds and renders effective the discourse of the other in the practice of care of self.[34] In other words, if you like, if philosophical practice really is, as I was telling you a moment ago, the exercise of the care of self, if the care of self has need of the other person and of their discourse, what then is the essential characteristic of this discourse considered as act, as action on myself? I think this discourse has, must have, the character of being the discourse of *parrēsia*. *Parrēsia* characterizes the discourse of the other person in the care of self.

To try to analyze this a little, I will make use of a certain number of sources. Gigante, in his presentation of the text by Philodemus, obviously focused on the Epicurean tradition about which, unfortunately, little is known on this precise point. He takes issue with what I will call the famous "Italian" hypothesis of the lost Aristotle,[35] and he tries to show that Philodemus does not depend upon Aristotle. I will attempt to take—because clearly I am not able to resolve this problem—a slightly broader field of reference, and I will look at, I will try to study *parrēsia* from the point of view of the pragmatics of discourse, a little in the Philodemus text—but this is so mutilated

* Passage partially inaudible. All that can be heard is: "Well, what I would like . . . you [. . .] maybe a bit too broad."

that it is rather difficult to draw much from it—in Seneca, in Epictetus, in Plutarch, of course, and also in a text by Galen.

And I would like to begin by taking two texts that will serve me as something of a guideline for studying this notion of *parrēsia*. One is quite simply the introductory text to the *Discourses* of Epictetus written by Arrian. It is a very interesting short tract on *parrēsia*, [a] reflection on *parrēsia*—a short page. Arrian explains that he was led to publish the *Discourses* of Epictetus because of the existence of some defective versions in circulation. I want, he says, to publish these *Discourses* so as to make known the *dianoia* and *parrēsia* of Epictetus: the *dianoia*, that is to say, the movement of thought, of Epictetus's thought, and then [the] *parrēsia*, which is precisely the specific form of his discourse. *Dianoia* and *parrēsia* are associated and moreover not separated throughout the text; what Arrian wants to make present is the whole formed by the *dianoia* and *parrēsia* of Epictetus. What will he do so as to be able to restore the *dianoia* and *parrēsia* of Epictetus in this way? He will, he says, publish, make available to the public, the notes he has taken, the *hupomnēmata*.[36] Now, *hupomnēmata* is an important technical notion; it means the transcription of notes taken by the listener while the philosopher is talking. It also refers to notebooks of exercises, since, with these *hupomnēmata*, which one must reread regularly, one ceaselessly reactivates what the master has said.[37] You recall Plutarch, for example, who, sending the *Peri epithumias* to Paccius, says to him, I know you are in a hurry and absolutely need a treatise on the tranquility of the soul very urgently. You cannot wait, so I am sending you the *hupomnēmata* I wrote for myself.[38] And there are a number of references to this in Epictetus's text itself. For example, at certain times Epictetus says that there is what I have told you; now you must *meletan*, meditate on it, reactualize it, and constantly think about it again. You must *graphein*, write it, you must read it and *gumnazein*, practice on it. So Arrian gives, makes available to the public, the *hupomnēmata* of the discourses of Epictetus.

These *hupomnēmata* will, of course, meet with objections because it will be said, readers will say that Epictetus cannot write properly, and they will despise the unaffected speech of Epictetus; but this is precisely because the function of the *hupomnēmata* is to deliver the spontaneous conversation of Epictetus himself, what he said himself, *hopote*.[39] As for Arrian, he takes the risk of being reproached for not being a writer of quality, but this does not matter, for what is it that he wants to do? [It is] to see to it that the way in which Epictetus acted on souls when he spoke is retransmitted in transparent fashion through the notes he delivers, in such a way that its action now works on his readers. And just as the speech of Epictetus was such that it made those who were listening to him feel exactly the feelings, the impressions he wanted them to feel, well, in the same way, Arrian hopes that those who read this text will feel what Epictetus wanted them to feel. And if they do not feel it, Arrian says, concluding his introduction, it is because of one of two things: either he, Arrian, has been unable to transcribe them properly and has made a mistake; or, he says, it is because that is how it had to be, that is to say, those reading them are incapable of understanding. So *parrēsia* appears here as breaking with or as disregarding the traditional forms of rhetoric and writing. *Parrēsia* is an action, it is such that it acts, that it allows discourse to act directly on souls; and to the extent that it is this direct action on souls, *parrēsia* conveys the *dianoia* itself by a sort of coupling or transparency between discourse and the movement of thought. This is the first text I wanted to refer to.

I will now take a second text, which is from Galen and is found at the beginning of *On the Passions and Errors of the Soul*.[40] The trouble with this text is that it is the only one of those I will cite today in which the word *parrēsia* does not appear—neither the Greek word *parrēsia* nor the Latin words *libera oratio* or *libertas* by which *parrēsia* is usually translated. The word *parrēsia* does not appear in Galen's text, and yet I think it is absolutely undeniable that it exactly describes *parrēsia* but from a different angle and is extremely interesting technically.

Arrian posed the following problem: Epictetus spoke, and only his speech had an action on the souls of others. How then can this action be conveyed and by what vehicle can this *parrēsia* be conveyed? The problem Galen poses is entirely different and quite strange: how can we search out, find, and be sure that we have really discovered the parrhesiast we need when we want to take care of ourselves? In this text, Galen in fact posits that, on the one hand, we cannot become a good, an accomplished man (*teleios anēr*) if we do not keep watch over ourselves (*sautōi pronooumenos*). We must have passed our life, he says, keeping watch over ourselves. And keeping this close watch on oneself demands exercises, continuous exercises: *deitai gar askēseōn,* he says. We need an exercise, a lifelong practice.[41] Now this practice cannot be controlled by itself; someone else is needed to regulate it. Those, he says, who have called upon others to say what they are are rarely mistaken; however, those who have not done this and believe themselves to be excellent are often mistaken. So we need someone else to monitor the exercise by which one becomes a *teleios anēr,* an accomplished man. How and where is this other person to be found? What is remarkable in this long passage from Galen is that he absolutely does not speak of either the technical competence or the knowledge that this other one needs. He simply says that we need, as it were, to listen for talk about someone who is renowned for not being a flatterer. And if we hear this said of someone, we move on to a number of verifications in order to be quite sure that he is capable of *alētheuein,* of speaking the truth; and it is at that point, when we are quite sure that he is capable of speaking the truth, that we will seek him out and ask for his opinion of ourselves; we ask him for his opinion of ourselves and set out for him what we believe to be our faults and qualities, and we see how he reacts.[42] And it is when we are quite sure that he really does have the requisite severity—I will come back to this—that we can entrust the help we need to his care. And Galen explains that he had himself performed this role of helper and guide for one of his friends who was quick-tempered and had wounded with his sword two of his slaves who had lost his luggage during a journey, and, well, let's skip the details. Anyway, the angry man was cured of his anger.[43]

I think we have here a little picture of spiritual direction and of the constitutive elements of *parrēsia,* all very clearly linked to the care of self. We see it quite clearly linked to *askesis,* to exercise, we see it quite clearly linked to flattery, and we see it contrasted with anger. On the basis of these two texts, and making use of them as among the most dense and, at the same time, most developed expositions on *parrēsia,* I would like now to see a bit how we can study this *parrēsia,* not then as a virtue, or simply as technique, but also not as a mode of life.

What can we say about *parrēsia* in this practice of spiritual direction or, rather, if you like, in the practice of the care of self? First, *parrēsia* is opposed to flattery.[44] As you know, flattery is an extremely important notion in the ethics, and in the political ethics, of the whole of antiquity; there are infinitely more texts on, references to, or considerations of flattery, for example, than on sexual ethics or the pleasures of the flesh, gluttony, or concupiscence. Flattery is at the heart of many problems of the government of self and the government of others. Furthermore, I think that flattery must in turn be coupled with what is complementary to it; I would say that *parrēsia* is the opposite of flattery and [that] flattery is the complement of anger. In ancient ethics, anger is not just the anger vented by someone against someone or something else; anger is always anger vented by someone with more power in a situation where he exercises this extra power beyond reasonable and morally acceptable limits. Anger is always anger vented by the stronger; the analyses of Seneca and Plutarch are absolutely clear on this. So anger is the behavior of someone who loses his temper against someone who is weaker than him. Flattery is exactly the opposite attitude; flattery is the behavior of the weaker person who is intent on attracting the benevolence of the stronger. We could say, if you like, that we have therefore a rather complex set: anger, the opposite of which is clemency; and flattery, the complement of anger, with its opposite, *parrēsia.* Anger and clemency, flattery and *parrēsia. Parrēsia* is opposed to flattery, limits, counters it, just as clemency limits, counters anger. Anger is behavior that begets flattery, while clemency on the part of someone who exercises power is reasonable behavior that leaves open the space of *parrēsia.* I think we should keep in mind this figure of four terms—anger, clemency, flattery, and *parrēsia.*

As antiflattery, *parrēsia* appears in three forms. First, *parrēsia* is directly related to the Delphic precept *gnōthi seauton* [know yourself]. [On] flattery, I refer you to Plutarch, *How to Tell a Flatterer from a Friend,* which is of course the basic text on this question.[45] This text—which I will refer to, if you like, as the treatise on the flatterer—is actually a treatise on the flattery-*parrēsia* opposition. The true friend, who is contrasted with the flatterer, is always the friend inasmuch as he speaks the truth. To that extent, I think Plutarch's text is absolutely central for most of the analyses that we have to make of the problem of *parrēsia* and particularly of its opposition to flattery. Plutarch's text is very clear on this, and he says that the flatterer is someone who interferes with the Delphic precept, who prevents one from knowing oneself. And, consequently, *parrēsia* is the necessary instrument possessed by the other that enables me to know myself. Galen echoes this link between *parrēsia* and the Delphic precept, or between flattery and ignorance of the Delphic precept, at the beginning of the same passage I quoted a moment ago, that is to say, at the beginning of *On the Passions and Errors of the Soul,* where he says that when he was young, he, Galen, did not attach any importance to the precept *gnōthi seauton* and that it was only later, when he had come to understand the danger of loving himself and of allowing flatterers to flatter him, that he understood its importance.[46] So *parrēsia* is, will be, antiflattery and as such the agent of the precept *gnōthi seauton.*

To say that *parrēsia* is the agent of this precept does not mean that *parrēsia* has to speak to the subject about the subject himself; the parrhesiast is not someone who speaks to the subject, the individual, about the subject himself, about his business, telling him exactly what he is, what his character is, and so on. Certainly he has to do this, but the most important part of the parrhesiastic function is rather to point out to the subject his place in the world; the parrhesiast is therefore someone who has to say things about what man is in general, about the order of the world, and about the necessity of things. In particular—and the texts of Epictetus are very clear about this—the parrhesiast is someone who, whenever and every time the other needs it, says what elements do and do not depend upon the subject. And inasmuch as he is the criterion, or possesses the criterion, for distinguishing between what does and does not depend upon ourselves, the parrhesiast can at the same time be the agent of the precept *gnōthi seauton.* See again Epictetus and also Marcus Aurelius.[47] And then I wonder if this is not at least an aspect of the meaning of the text by Epicurus which has kindly been reproduced for you—something I wouldn't have dared to ask for. This is the passage in Epicurus mentioned and translated by François Heidsieck: "I myself," he says, "with the liberty of the physiologist, would prefer to speak obscurely of things which are useful to everyone, even if no one understands, rather than compromise with received opinion in order to gather the praise which falls thick and fast from the mouths of the majority."[48] I do not want to comment on the rest of the text, which is very difficult. Anyway, it is an isolated text that cannot be clarified by any context; but it seems to me that the physiologist's liberty, the *parrēsia* that the *phusiologos* makes use of, refers to this function. The person who knows the nature of things, who knows what *phusis* is, can be the parrhesiast, who dispels illusions, silences fears, dismisses chimeras, and tells man what he truly is.

Anyway, there is that whole axis of *parrēsia* as a function of the precept *gnōthi seauton.* You see that this is, in a sense, the opposite of the Platonic structure. In the Platonic structure, *gnōthi seauton* is carried out by a movement of the subject turning back into himself in the form of memorization. If you want to know who you are, remember what you were; here, [on the contrary, if you want] to know who you are, ask for someone else who possesses *parrēsia,* who makes use of *parrēsia,* and who really tells you what the order of the world is in which you find yourself. This is one of the first aspects of *parrēsia* I wanted to stress.

The second aspect is that *parrēsia*—we saw this quite clearly in Arrian's presentation—is characterized by a freedom of form. The parrhesiast does not have to take account of the rules of rhetoric—that goes without saying—or even of the rules of philosophical demonstration; he is opposed to rhetoric, he is opposed to *elegkhos,** and he is opposed also to demonstration, to the rigor of proofs, to what forces the individual to recognize this is the truth and that is nothing. From this point of view *parrēsia* is therefore a form of dis-

* *Elegkhos* (proof).

course different from both rhetoric and philosophical demonstration, strictly speaking.[49] The question then arises whether *parrēsia* is not that kind of intense and occasional affective modulation of discourse that we find in, for example, the literature of the diatribe. Is *parrēsia* that interpellation by the philosopher, stopping someone in the street, questioning someone in the middle of a crowd, or, like Dio of Prusa,[50] standing up in the theater and telling the crowd what he has to say, persuading it with a forcefully intoned discourse?[51] Well, I think a certain number of texts should be read in these terms, and some of Seneca's texts in particular.* There are several passages in Seneca's letters that are quite clearly concerned with this literature of the diatribe. You find this in letter 29, I think, and in letters 40 and 38.[52] You have there a number of pointers about this impassioned, violent, interpellatory literary genre from which Seneca wants precisely to distinguish himself, saying that it involves, as it were, supplementary effects that go beyond thought and lack the necessary measure for obtaining the desired effect on the soul. Rather than this literature of the tribune, Seneca prefers either individual letters or conversation. I think conversation, the art of conversation, is the form that most immediately coincides, converges with the demands of *parrēsia*; speaking as one needs to, in a form such that one can act directly on the other person's soul, speaking without burdening oneself with rhetorical forms and without exaggerating the effects one wants to obtain, is what conversation realizes. So here, too, we would have to look at how, and to what extent, the literature of conversation, the rules of philosophical conversation suggested in these texts, particularly in Seneca, diverge from what might be involved in a Socratic style of questioning.

Why does *parrēsia* need this form, which is not that of rhetoric, or that of philosophical argument, or that of the diatribe? The point of attachment which *parrēsia* needs if it is to act on souls is essentially the *kairos*, that is to say, the occasion.[53] It is not a matter of an act of memory by which the subject finds again what he was, what

* Foucault is heard to say: "Well, this is where I am sorry for my mistakes: if I have not given the right references, I am the only one responsible for this."

he once could contemplate; nor is it a question of constraining him by the logical force of an argument. What is involved is grasping the *kairos*, the opportunity, when it arises in order to tell him what he has to be told. And this opportunity must take two things into account. First of all, it must take [into] account what the individual is himself. I refer to Seneca's letter 25, which is very interesting and in which he speaks to Lucilius about two friends to whom advice is to be given and who are portrayed differently—one more malleable, the other rather less so.[54] How is one to proceed? How is one to intervene? So, second, you have here a problematic of individual *parrēsia*. You have a problematic of *parrēsia* in terms of the *peristasis*, in terms of circumstances; one cannot say the same thing to the same person in different circumstances.

Plutarch, for example, cites the case of Crates—Crates the Cynic, who was precisely the man of *parrēsia*, stripped of all rhetoric—and [especially] his relationship with Demetrius Poliorcetes.[55] When Demetrius had conquered Athens and was a powerful sovereign, Crates always attacked him with *parrēsia*, which showed him how much his sovereignty was of small account and how he, Crates, found his own kind of life preferable to that of Demetrius. And then, Demetrius, having lost power, sees Crates coming towards him, and, Plutarch says, Demetrius greatly feared his *parrēsia*. Crates, precisely, approached him and facing him expounded the thesis that exile, loss of power, and so on are not really evils, and he offered him words of consolation. Consequently, the true *parrēsia* of Crates does not consist in always wounding the person he is addressing but in seizing the moment and circumstances and speaking accordingly. Plutarch also has a text in which he clearly says, regarding what characterizes the *parrēsia* of the true friend, that this *parrēsia* employs the *metron*, measure, the *kairos*, occasion, and *sugkrasis*, the mixture, the softening, the mixture that makes possible the softening.[56]

To that extent, *parrēsia* appears as an art of the *kairos* and so an art akin to that of medicine. [Think of] all the metaphors of *parrēsia* as assuring the *therapeuein* of the soul; it is an art similar to the art of medicine, to the art of piloting, and similar also to the art of government and political action. Spiritual direction, piloting, medicine, the art of politics, the art of the *kairos*. *Parrēsia* is precisely the way in which the person who gives spiritual guidance to another must seize the right moment to speak to him in the right way by refraining from the necessities of philosophical argument, the obligatory forms of rhetoric, and the bombast of the diatribe.

There is a third characteristic of *parrēsia* (the one I have just spoken about being *parrēsia* in terms of the *kairos* and the first being the opposition of *parrēsia* and flattery). Contrasted with flattery, *parrēsia* appears close to being a virtue. But in the context of the *kairos*, *parrēsia* appears akin to a technique. But I do not think we can leave it at that because *parrēsia* is not just an individual virtue; it is not even just a technique that someone could apply to someone else. *Parrēsia* is always an operation involving two terms; *parrēsia* takes place between two partners. And *parrēsia* issues, in a certain way—even if we can say, and the texts tell us, that one, the director, has *parrēsia*, that the person who guides must have *parrēsia*—*parrēsia* is actually a game of two characters and takes place, unfolds, between one and the other, and, in some way, each must play his specific role.

First, and this is very important, the person seeking a parrhesiast, the person wanting to take care of his own soul and of himself and who therefore needs someone else, someone who has *parrēsia*, cannot just seek out a parrhesiast. He must also give signs that he is able and ready to receive the truth that the parrhesiast will tell him. There is an indication of this in the text from Galen I was speaking to you about, where Galen says that when you think you have found your parrhesiast, that is to say, someone who really has shown, has given signs that he is not capable of flattery, you may be surprised to find that he does not want to be your parrhesiast; he will shy away or compliment you by telling you that you have no defects, only qualities, and that you do not need to take care of yourself. Well, Galen says, if he tells you this, be sure to say to yourself that it is you who has not conducted yourself properly. You have given signs that you are not capable of receiving the other's *parrēsia* or that you are capable of harboring resentment for the truths he might tell you, or the signs you have given are such that he is not interested in you.[57] These are only fleeting indications in Galen. However, I think that

Epictetus, discourse 24 in book 2,[58] corresponds exactly to this type of question. It is a very curious and strange discourse. I do not know if you remember. It is the story of a handsome young man, his hair elaborately dressed, who is all made up, and who has often come to listen to Epictetus. And then, after some time, he addresses Epictetus. This is how the discourse begins: I have often come to listen to you, but you have not responded to me; would you please say something to me, I beg you to say something to me (*parakalō se eipein ti moi*). Certainly, he was there, he had put himself in front of Epictetus; this was in fact his role, since his role was not to speak but to listen. But now the other, the person who should have spoken and who, as master, was committed to *parrēsia*, has said nothing. It is a request for *parrēsia* that the young man addresses; and Epictetus replies that there are two things, two arts. There is the art of speaking (*technē tou legein*), and there is also—he does not say art, he says *empeiria*—the experience of listening.

A problem then: is listening an art or just an experience, or a certain competence? This is open to debate. I think, yes, there is an art of speaking, and there is an ability to listen. Anyway, Epictetus says that there is an ability to listen. At this point we might expect Epictetus to do as Plutarch does in the *De audiendo*, that is, to start explaining what this skill in listening is—what posture to assume, how to open one's ears, how to direct one's gaze, how to take notes afterwards, how to recall what the other said.[59] In actual fact, Epictetus does not expand on this ability to listen, this technique of listening. He expounds something else: what the listener needs to know in order to be able to listen properly. The listener needs to know certain things and show that he knows them, and these things are precisely the fundamental themes of the philosophy of Epictetus, the fact that our good depends simply on the *proairesis*,[60] that it is in ourselves and from ourselves only that we must expect that which will constitute the perfection of our existence, and so on. And Epictetus rapidly summarizes the fundamental themes of his philosophy and says to him, this is what you should know and should have shown for me to speak to you. Because, Epictetus says, the person who speaks is the master, he is like the sheep; if you want the sheep to graze, you must lead it to a pasture where the grass is green, where the lushness of the grass stimulates it to graze. In the same way, when we see small children playing, we are stimulated to play with them; similarly, if you do not stimulate me to speak, then I will not play the role of the one who speaks. At this point the young man replies, but after all I am handsome, I am rich, I am strong. And Epictetus replies, but Achilles too was handsome and even more handsome than you; he was richer and stronger than you. You have not aroused (*erethizein*) me; show me your ability to hear what I want to say, and then you will see how much you will arouse the person you are addressing to speak, the person who has to speak (*kinēseis ton legonta*).

As unfortunately time is passing, I don't want to dwell a lot on these questions. [. . .]* We can see how close we are to, and how distant from, the basic structure. That the person to whom one speaks must arouse the desire in the master was fundamental in Plato.[61] You see that we are in an entirely different world here, where pederastic love is wholly absent, or rather, I think the elements here—the little clues about the young man, hair curled, perfumed, and dressed up—are interesting; they are [a set] of elements that cannot arouse the master. What arouses the master is not the individual's body, beauty, and youth but the fundamental bases on which master and disciple can understand each other. The disciple must show that he really is in agreement on that, and then he will arouse the other to speak. The other will speak, and he will speak in a way to act effectively on the disciple's soul and to improve it; but he will desire nothing other than the improvement of the disciple's soul. Anyway, you can see, there can be no *parrēsia*, no freedom of speech on the part of the master, none of that liveliness of the master's speech acting on the other's soul, if the other has not given certain signs. So signs on the disciple's side, but also signs on the part of the parrhesiast. And the problem arises here, which is also technically very difficult, of how to recognize the true parrhesiast. *Parrēsia* develops therefore through the communication of signs in both directions, from the disciple's side and from the master's side. Plutarch's treatise *How to*

* Indecipherable passage.

Tell a Flatterer from a Friend is precisely the treatise that replies to this question. When looking for a parrhesiast, how should I go about it and how will I recognize him? For, Plutarch says, you think that things would be very simple if flatterers were all the easily recognizable kind, you know, those who compliment you in order to get invited to dine. These flatterers are not dangerous; the dangerous ones are the, so to speak, true flatterers, that is to say, those who most resemble the person you are looking for. And in particular, it is part of the good flatterer's craft, his skill, to resemble a parrhesiast as much as possible. And the true flatterer, like the parrhesiast, is someone who tells you some harsh, disagreeable things, someone who tells you a few home truths, but who actually may very well be a flatterer.[62]

How will we resolve this question and define what the true flatterer is? Plutarch devotes his treatise to this, but there are many other texts that deal with this, and Galen's in particular, which I have talked about. I refer to Galen's answer first of all because it is actually the simplest and, if you like, the most empirical; it does not raise any major theoretical problems. Galen simply asks one to take certain precautions. He says that if one is looking for a parrhesiast, one must first of all address oneself to someone who has a good reputation; one must then keep an eye on him, follow his steps, see if he frequents the powerful and rich. It is a bad sign if he does; he risks not being the good parrhesiast one is looking for. But one must go further, and if he frequents them, one must still see how he conducts himself, if he is a flatterer or not, and so on. And when one has made contact with this man, who has thus guaranteed that he is not a flatterer, when one has asked him to provide the service of being the parrhesiast, one must continue to test him; and one must see if he does not compliment us too easily, whether he has the proper severity. Galen's analysis is quite interesting because it goes relatively far. He says that if the parrhesiast, the person one has chosen as director, compliments you, this is either because he is not really a parrhesiast or because he is not interested in you and because you have not given him the necessary sign of your ability to hear the truth. But if he is severe with you, it may also happen that he will say things to you that you consider too severe; in that case you are still in the wrong, for, like every man, you are someone who loves himself, and you must always postulate that what the other says, in its severity, is true. But suppose even that the parrhesiast says such severe things to you that you are not only sure they are not true but also that you can demonstrate they are not true. Well, tell yourself that, even so, you have found a good parrhesiast, for actually it is a test that, if not indispensable, is at least useful to have pejorative, even dreadful things said in order to get rid of the love of oneself.[63] We have here a [...].*

Let us now return to Plutarch, whose text is more interesting theoretically and is entirely constructed around this question: how does one distinguish the true parrhesiast from someone who is a flatterer? Fine, he says, the true signs of the parrhesiast are these: first, we recognize that we have encountered the parrhesiast we need if he manifests *homoiotēs tēs proaireseōs*, that is to say, if he manifests an analogy,** a similitude due to their *proairesis*. I don't need to tell you that this is untranslatable; you know this better than me. Let's say it is a similitude in the choice of existence, the fundamental will, and so on, so there must be a similitude between that of the subject seeking the parrhesiast and that of the parrhesiast himself. There must be this fundamental agreement of the *proairesis*. And you find the same thing that was pointed out by Epictetus a moment ago with regard to a young man when he said, you have not aroused me because you clearly show that you do not have the same *proairesis* as me. So the first criterion is analogy between the *proairesis* of both.

Second, the parrhesiast must always take pleasure in the same things and approve of the same things. Constancy, consequently, in his own system of aversions and inclinations, in his system of judgment. You see, incidentally, the degree to which the landscape in

* Interruption of the recording.

** Foucault is heard to ask in an aside: "Can one say homology? Will it do for translating *homoiotēs*? We cannot say identity; a resemblance, yes, a similitude, perhaps."

Plutarch's text is completely utopian. So it is necessary that he sticks always to his same choices, in his aversions as well as his inclinations.

Finally, third, he must direct his life towards one and the same *paradeigma*, towards one and the same schema of life. So homology between the two partners in their choices of existence, constancy of aversions and inclination in the parrhesiast, and singleness of paradigm, of schema of life in the parrhesiast. You see that these criteria of the true parrhesiast refer to two very well known conceptions. On the one hand, of course, that of friendship as *homonoia*. This analogy, this similitude founds true friendship, and it is in this sense that the parrhesiast is fundamentally the friend. And, second, you see that this conception of the true parrhesiast as the person who remains constant in his choices and who aims entirely at a single schema of life refers to the Stoic conception of the unity of existence, which is contrasted with the plurality of *stultitia*, of the disordered and morbid soul.[64] Plutarch expands on this here very clearly and visibly. The nonparrhesiast, that is to say the flatterer, is someone, he says, who has no fixed rules for conducting himself. The flatterer models himself now on one, now on another; the flatterer, he says, is neither simple nor one; he is composed of heterogeneous and varied parts; the flatterer is like a fluid that passes from one form to another according to the vase into which it is poured.[65] Thus Alcibiades was not the same as he moved from one place to another; he was not the same in Athens as in Sicily, he was not the same in Sicily as in Sparta, and he was not the same in Sparta as among the Persians, and so on, unlike Epameinondas, who also changed countries but always kept the same *ethos* in his clothing, his regimen (*diaitē*), his *logos*, and his *bios*.[66] There is nothing fixed and solid about the flatterer, he has nothing of his own, he never loves, he never hates, he is never delighted, he is never distressed *oikeiō pathei* (through his [. . .]).[67] The true parrhesiast, on the other hand, will be someone who has an *oikeiov pathos* and who, having always the same *biotē*, the same diet, the same regimen, can serve as a fixed point for the person who, precisely, is looking for one and who seeks in the parrhesiast someone who can help him form the unity of his existence.

And so this leads us to what I think constitutes the very center of *parrēsia*. In fact, if the parrhesiast is someone one recognizes as having one and only one mode of existence, what then is *parrēsia*? I think that *parrēsia* will be the presence, in the person who speaks, of his own form of life rendered manifest, present, perceptible, and active as model in the discourse he delivers. And it is here that I would like to read letter 75 of Seneca (it is one of the other texts in which the word *parrēsia*—well, the words *libera oratio* or *libertas*—does not appear, but which I think is also a commentary on *parrēsia*): "My letters are not to your taste, not polished as they should be, and you complain about it [a reference then to the problem of rhetoric—M. F.]. In truth, who thinks about polishing his style, apart from lovers of pretentious style? If we were idly sitting or strolling together, my conversation would be unaffected and easygoing (*inlaboratus et facilis*). I wish my letters to be like this: there is nothing mannered or artificial about them (*accersitum nec fictum*)." Here we are dealing with those themes I was referring to a short while ago. *Parrēsia* is external to all the artificial methods of rhetoric. You see the reference to conversation, which is, if you like, the initial, the matrix form of *parrēsia*, the letter here being this by reference to conversation; it is a substitute for conversation, since conversation cannot take place. Then parrhesiastic continuity par excellence, if you like, from conversation to letter, avoiding the composed treatise, eloquence, the tribune, and the violence of the diatribe: "If it were possible, I would like to let you see my thoughts rather than translate them into language (*quid sentiam ostendere quam loqui mallem*)." To show thoughts rather than to speak. So I think that in the reduction of speech to what would be simply the indication of thought, in a *parrēsia* that is immediately in contact with the *dianoia* that it is intended simply to show, to indicate, we find again what Arrian mentioned, what he referred to regarding Epictetus: "Even in a regular lecture, I would not stamp my foot, wave my arms about, or raise my voice, leaving that to orators and judging my end achieved if I have conveyed my thought without ornament or platitudes." So much for orators, so much no doubt for the orators of diatribes. I would be *contentus sensus meos ad te pertulisse* ([satisfied] if I have conveyed my opinions directly). You recall what Arrian said regarding Epictetus: he acted directly on souls, doing what he wanted to do. Arrian's problem was one of assisting this direct action by circulating, by publishing *hupomnēmata*. This is also what Seneca wants to do: *sensus meos ad te pertulisse*. "Above all, I would dearly love you to understand that I think everything I say, and not content with thinking it, I love it. The kisses we give to our children are unlike those a mistress receives; and yet this embrace, so chaste and reserved, sufficiently reveals tenderness. Assuredly," and so on—I am skipping—"This is the most important point of our rhetoric [unfortunately, this is a not very happy addition of the translation—*haec sit propositi nostri summa*: this then is the summary of my remarks, the most important point, rather, of my remarks—M. F.]: to say what one thinks, to think what one says, to see to it that language is in harmony with conduct. He who is the same when seen and heard has fulfilled his commitments (*ille promissum suum implevit, qui, et cum videas illum et cum audias, idem est*)."[68]

So I think that here we are a bit closer to the heart of what constitutes *parrēsia*. That is to say, there is *parrēsia* when the master, the person to whom one entrusts the direction of one's soul, [when he] says what he thinks with such great transparency that no form of rhetoric acts as a screen but says what he thinks not in the sense that he expresses his opinions or says what he thinks true but by saying what he loves, that is to say, by showing what his own choice is, his *proairesis*. And what guarantees for us, what manifests with the greatest transparency the profound and fundamental choice one makes, are not the more or less rhetorical embraces in which one enwraps one's mistress but that measured kiss one places on the cheek of a child one loves; this is the seal itself of the truth of the feeling one experiences. I must be myself in what I say; I must myself be implicated in what I say, and what I affirm must show me really true to what I affirm. And it is here that we find again something that could be called the parrhesiastic pact, which is different from the one I referred to earlier. You recall that we saw a parrhesiastic pact appear in Euripides that would be, if you like, close to the political pact of *parrēsia*: I am all-powerful; you come with a truth that may be disagreeable to me and might irritate me—the theme of anger—but, in my clemency, I give you permission to speak and will not punish you for the bad news or disagreeable thing you will say. This is the structure of the political pact of *parrēsia*. And then here we have the structure of what we can call the individual pact, of the tutorial (*directionnel*) pact of *parrēsia* in which what is involved is this: when I myself advise you, you who ask me to speak frankly, I do not content myself with telling you what I judge to be true. I tell this truth only inasmuch as it is in actual fact what I am myself; I am implicated in the truth of what I say. It is this implication of the subject of enunciation in the statement of the master's speech that, it seems to me, is characteristic of this exemplary *parrēsia* of the master developed in this set of texts.[69]

So—but I do not have much time—there is still this to add: this implication of the subject in *parrēsia* may take place in two ways, if you like. Either, in what I would say is a perfect and exemplary fashion, the high philosophers alone may manifest what they are in the truth of what they say. Or there is a reciprocal opening of two partners when the one who speaks of the other implicates himself in what he says, not just in order to affirm that he is exactly true to the truth of what he says, but to strive himself to arrive at it. Well, here you have a series of letters from Seneca, and in particular the preface to book 4 of the *Natural Questions*,[70] in which Seneca, addressing Lucilius, tells him, [shows] him, on the one hand that he is guiding him; he says to him, I am taking you in hand and will try to conduct you towards the better things. But, he tells him, we will give each other advice. And we have here the theme that runs through Seneca's letters of the reciprocal opening of souls that is one of the forms of *parrēsia* and in which, I think, will be found one of the points of anchorage of the *parrēsia* developed in Christianity, which will be precisely the implication of the one who speaks, but on the part of the disciple, that is to say, on the part of the one who is imperfect, who sins, who is trying to make his way and progress; he is the one who will have to speak.[71] So there is a change, a reversal of responsibility, as I said, but you can see, I think, that right within the structure of *parrēsia* as it is developed in some texts—not in Epictetus, who, after all, is a professional teacher, but in someone like Seneca—you see a *parrēsia* [that] begins to switch and that becomes a sort of double obligation in which, in relation to the truth expressed, two souls exchange their own experience, their own imperfections, and open up to each other. A question, for it is just a question: in the text of Philodemus, you may find a very precise passage—I shall be able to find it for you shortly—in which he speaks of *parrēsia* as a means for the disciples to save each other, which would seem to indicate that there was actually a *parrēsia* that was not just the discourse of the master, of the master implicating himself in the truth of what he says, but in which there was this game of individuals opening their souls to each other and helping each other as a result. It may be an Epicurean type of practice that developed in this way. In any case, it is very clear in Seneca where there are constant references to reciprocal openness.

There you are. So I have tried to show you this kind of rather curious figure of *parrēsia* that seems to me very different from the Platonic or Socratic game of questions and answers and relationships between master and disciple and that is also very different from what will be found later in Christian spirituality and monastic institutions.

The lecture was followed by a discussion, some of the passages of which are inaudible or barely audible:

MICHEL FOUCAULT, *right after the last words of the lecture*: I'm sorry, that was a bit . . .

HENRI JOLY: No, it was a masterful survey. There are a huge number of questions that are opened up in terms of what I would call the polysemantic and polyphonic lines of investigation that Michel Foucault has brought to this topic, and there are also some implicit, less obvious, but nevertheless evident questions, questions of method, to use academic language. Unfortunately, as we are strictly limited to an hour's time, we have no more than ten minutes, a quarter of an hour maybe [. . .], let's say a quarter of an hour of questions. We had better not waste any of our short time lamenting that our time is short.

FOUCAULT: Actually, there is a very interesting passage in Aristotle's *Nicomachean Ethics*[72] which causes me great difficulty, and at the same time I feel that there is a structural opposition between *parrēsia* and irony that everything else confirms. Socrates is not the man of *parrēsia,* clearly not.[73] And irony, as a way of showing . . .

JOLY: Excuse me [. . .] I have found this to be a very awkward, isolated, fleeting, and interesting Socratic text. There is another in the *Rhetoric,* II, chapter 5.[74] It is difficult to interpret locally and contextually, but it seems to me to mark a turning point in relation to the Platonic usage, in the sense that, really, *parrēsia* becomes freedom of discourse, whether as an object of praise or criticism. Because praise and blame enter into the two Platonic texts you cited, the texts from the *Republic* and the *Laws,* there is a definition, a completely univocal conception in antiquity of *parrēsia* as political conduct, which is either condemned when it is a matter of democratic conduct or honored when precisely this *parrēsia* is conceded by the prince, by the *basileus,* and when it is conduct that annuls the differences in a political system in which these differences are precisely inscribed, differences between those who command and those who are commanded. You indicated this opposition quite clearly. Then there is a first turning point in Aristotle, but it is difficult to establish, on the one hand because the occurrences are very rare and on the other it is caught up in the analytical context of the *ethei* and *arētai,* and so on, and it is extremely fleeting; it is found in a character trait—I will put it just like that—it is a character trait of the *megalopsuchos.* There you are.

FOUCAULT: [. . .] he says: good, with all the wine we have drunk, fine, we have spoken frankly, and there he employs the word *parrēsia* [. . .]

[. . .] *A listener*: So in the text you quoted, in a popular state [. . .] the freedom of free-spokenness [*franc-parler*] reigns everywhere [. . .]

FOUCAULT: It is in *Republic* book 8 [. . .] of the democratic state; *parrēsia* is classed among the factors of the motley character of the city. So it is negative.

JOLY: Yes, it is even frankly polemical; it forms part of a critique of the political figure of democracy, of the corresponding critique of the *dēmokratikos anēr,* as [Plato] puts it, and he describes him as someone who pushes *eleutheria, parrēsia,* and *exousia* to extremes. *Parrēsia* constitutes a kind of intermediary vice between *eleutheria* and *exousia.* I wonder moreover if there is not here a freedom as freedom of being, a *parrēsia* as freedom of speaking and an *exousia* as a freedom of doing. There are moreover terms, verbal forms that come to cooperate in this: *areskeiv, bouleisthai,* and so on. And what greatly interested me in what you said is the famous *heautou bios,* a life that is completely private, individual. There is moreover . . .

FOUCAULT: . . . *idia kataskeuē.*

JOLY: . . . *idia kataskeuē.* There is also the term *hekastos,* which is very pejorative.[75] One must not be a singularized individual; one must not have a practice of life that corresponds to a *bios oikeios,* a personal life. You ended on that point. The *oikeiotēs* changes meaning when we pass from Plato to the Stoics. Because in the time of Plato—I am just adding a little pedantic parenthesis here—there were three types of life (this is the problem of the *bioi*), so you have *tupoi* or *paradeigmata,* models, and one could not fashion one's own life outside of these models. One could be *philochrēmatos,* that is to say, love wealth and choose the *apolaustic*[76] life ("old" Festugière teaches us this in his *Les trois vies*[77]—which is still very interesting and very much alive). There was the political life, the lover of power, the *philotimos.* And then there was the life of wisdom, the one who loves knowledge (*connaissance*) and who loves himself, who constructs himself.

There was no alternative, no choice outside of these three types of life. In the degenerate democracy criticized in the *Republic,* book 8, one arrives at a totally individual life of frankness and license throughout the city. This is the democratic individualism parodied by Plato in this text. And you have shown very clearly the inversion of the meaning of the famous *parrēsia* evoked by Epictetus. This is absolutely critical and all the more so as it completely reverses the democratic values of the Athenian *politeia,* in which *parrēsia* figured, in the same way as *isēgoria,* as a right, a right to speak; this is *isēgoria,* and a right to say everything was the correlative right. So what I would like to add—and then I will keep quiet, because maybe others would like to speak—is a sketch of meaning that you did not indicate. I have not leafed through the whole corpus of orators, of course, but I know that there are some usages—and Françoise Létoublon has looked a bit at it—some uses of the verbal form "to say the whole truth" in the orators, but there are some verbal expressions that, in the absence of the concept of *parrēsia,* may take its place, certainly. Forms of the type *apanta legein,* to say everything. I refer you to a little text of Lysias, which is moreover absolutely spicy, since it is the text *On the Murder of Eratosthenes;* it concerns a trial for *moicheia* and in which there is a duty, a sort of deontology of *apanta legein,* of telling all, which is formulated from both the master's and the slave's point of view.[78] So it is interesting on more than one score; it confirms what you said. The deontology appears at the level of the free man, who in a way must have an obligatory logographic conduct, which is that of telling the truth as it happens, so of matching his discourse to the events, *ta genomena* or *erga* or *pragmata,* and so on.[79] And then there is another conduct that is demanded quite differently, by constraint and under torture, and the term is present there—one could torture slaves, of course—and the little slave, who will tell who slept with whom, will be tortured and again one will impose a duty of truth on him, a duty to tell all.[80] Moreover a triple characteristic of this discourse must be pragmatic, which must bear on the true facts, as they occurred; it must be epidictic; that is to say, it must show them in a transparent discourse. And the *apanta legein,* the *mēden pseudein,* which are two correlative forms, affirmative and negative, configure, with a veridical function, the truthful discourse. And from the point of view of the translation, I do not know if we could not approach the notion of veracity as the objective object of this discourse of . . .

FOUCAULT: Lysias employs the word *parrēsia* here?

JOLY: No, no, he does not employ the concept *parrēsia.* He employs solely verbal forms. I have searched, I have looked, I do not guarantee it. One should ask someone more knowledgeable than I am.

FOUCAULT: [. . .] notwithstanding the etymology of *parrēsia*, telling all does not seem to me, really or fundamentally, entailed in the notion of *parrēsia*. And precisely, the problem of judicial confession, where what is involved is telling all concerning, and so on, never seems to me to be designated by the word *parrēsia*. You will say that I have quoted texts in which the word *parrēsia* does not enter, but it seems to me that the structure . . .

JOLY: But that doesn't matter. There may be some semantic configurations . . .

FOUCAULT: Yes, I know. For myself, I think that *parrēsia* is not a notion applying to judicial confession.

JOLY: Françoise Létoublon, you have looked a little [. . .]?

FRANÇOISE LÉTOUBLON: [. . .].*

JOLY: So we should indeed distinguish here between a parrhetic, if we can use this expression, a parrhetic and a judicial rhetoric, which have somewhat similar objectives, but in configurations that are completely . . .

FOUCAULT: I think it is a political notion that was transposed, if you like, from the government of others to the government of oneself, that it was never a judicial notion where the obligation to say exactly the truth is a technical problem concerning confession, torture, and so on. But the word *parrēsia* and, I think, the conceptual field associated with it, has a moral profile.

[. . .]

A LISTENER: [. . .] I am no doubt leaving the field of *parrēsia* to which you have wanted to restrict yourself—one cannot do everything—but I wonder what we find if we go back in the direction of the Judeo-Christian source of Christianity. In this domain [. . .] there is what is probably a common foundation,

* Françoise Létoublon's answer is almost inaudible; one understands only that there do not seem to be any occurrences of the word *parrēsia* in the judicial domain but that we find it used in the domain of politics.

namely, the notion that one cannot know oneself; one is constantly, originally mistaken about what one does, what one is, and what one believes. And there is an example that I was thinking about constantly while listening to you, which is that of the prophet Nathan's descent to King David. When David has taken Bathsheba, gotten her pregnant, [. . .] her husband, has dispatched the husband to the front to be slaughtered. And Nathan goes down and proceeds in a way that is neither *parrēsia*, because it is not simple and natural, nor really irony. He takes the detour of a fiction presented [. . .]: in my village . . .[81]

FOUCAULT: I see what you mean.

SAME LISTENER: You are that man, he says, and David is caught. Whereas if Nathan had just come saying, you are a bastard, he would have been locked up because the relation of force is that of . . .

FOUCAULT: Yes, it is the problem of the freedom of speech of the prophet or, in any case, in the person who speaks to power.[82] I do not think that *parrēsia* or the obligation to tell all that we see emerging in Christian spirituality of the fourth to fifth century comes directly from there. Simply because in the monasteries, the monks are seen as philosophers and as the heirs of philosophical practice, of the Greco-Roman *bios philosophicos* and because I think we can practically derive their techniques from those of ancient philosophy. [. . .] This text was in fact cited; the Church Fathers cite it in their texts on penance moreover.

DISCOURSE & TRUTH

Lectures at the University of California–Berkeley
October–November 1983

OCTOBER 24, 1983

The theme of these seminars is the notion of *parrēsia*. The word *parrēsia* is to be found throughout Greek literature from the end of the fifth century BCE, and you find it also in the patristic texts from the end of the fourth century, and from the fifth century CE. The word *parrēsia* appears for the first time in Greek literature in Euripides, and you find it still, dozens and dozens of times, in John Chrysostom, for instance, in the Christian literature at the end of the fourth century.

There are three forms of the word: there is the nominal form, *parrēsia*; there is the verbal form *parrēsiazein*, or better *parrēsiazesthai*; and there is also the word *parrhesiast*, which is not very frequent and cannot be found in the classical texts. You find it only rarely in the Hellenistic texts or in the Greco-Roman period, in Plutarch, in Lucian. In Lucian, for example, you find a character in one of the dialogues with the proper name Parrēsiades.[1]

Parrēsia is ordinarily translated in English by "free speech," and in French by "franc-parler." *Parrēsiazein* or *parrēsiazesthai* means to use *parrēsia,* and the parrhesiast is the one who uses *parrēsia* and who tells the truth.

First point: in the first part of today's seminar, I would like to offer a brief survey of the meaning of the word and the evolution of this meaning through the Greek and the Greco-Roman culture. First, what is the general meaning of the word *parrēsia*?[2] Etymologically, *parrēsiazein* or *parrēsiazesthai* means "to say everything": *pan* which means "everything," and the root you can find in, for instance, rhetor, or rhetoric, *rhēma,* which is "the thing you say." The one who uses *parrēsia,* the parrhesiast, is someone who says everything he has in mind.* He says everything, *pan-rhesia,* he does not hide anything, he opens his heart and his mind to other people. In *parrēsia,* the words, the discourse, are supposed to give an exact account, a complete expression of what the speaker has in mind, so that the audience is able to catch exactly what he says. That's the first characteristic of *parrēsia.* So, as you see, the word *parrēsia,* the notion of *parrēsia,* refers to a kind of relationship between the speaker and what he says. With *parrēsia,* the speaker makes it manifest, clear, and obvious that what he is saying is his own opinion. He makes it manifest and clear by avoiding any kind of rhetorical form which could hide or veil what he thinks. The parrhesiast uses the most direct words, the most direct forms of expression he can find. Of course, that does not mean that the parrhesiast does not worry about the effects of his speech on other people's mind. But whereas rhetoric provides the speaker with technical devices in order to act upon the audience's mind, whatever his own opinion is, in *parrēsia,* the speaker acts on other people's minds by showing them as directly as possible what he thinks.

If we make a distinction between the subject of the enunciation, the speaking subject, [and] the grammatical subject of the sentence, of the enounced, then we could say that there is a third subject, which is the subject of the *enunciandum,* the thing which is

* Foucault uses the Greek word *parrēsiastēs* here, which he translates as "parrhesiast" in his final lectures at the Collège de France. That is the term that we will use here and in the text that follows, instead of *parrēsiastēs.*

enounced as the belief, as the opinion, to which the *énoncé* refers.* I think that in *parrēsia* the speaker emphasizes the fact that he is both the subject of the enunciation and the subject of the *enunciandum*, that is, the subject of the belief, of the opinion to which he refers. "I am the one who thinks this and that": such is the specific speech act you can find in the parrhesiastic *énoncé*. That's the first point.

Second point: *parrēsia* is more than this sincerity or frankness. *Parrēsia* is something more than the openness of mind. The parrhesiast doesn't say everything he has in mind. Well, let's be a little more precise: there are two kinds of *parrēsia*.[3]

The bad kind, and in this case, *parrēsia* consists in saying anything one has in mind, without any distinction, without taking care of what he says. In this usage, using *parrēsia* is not very far from chattering. This pejorative use of the word *parrēsia* is rare in the classical texts. You find it sometimes, for instance, in Plato, in order to characterize the bad democratic constitution, where anybody is able to address himself to the citizens and to tell them anything he wants, even the most stupid and the most dangerous things for the city.[4] This pejorative meaning of *parrēsia* is also to be found more frequently in Christian texts where this *parrēsia*, this bad *parrēsia*, is opposed to silence, to silence as a discipline, or to silence as a condition for contemplating God. *Parrēsia* is then an obstacle to contemplating God. *Parrēsia* here is a verbal activity, one which reflects every movement of the mind and of the heart, and so is obviously an obstacle to contemplation.[5] That's the bad side, or the bad form, of *parrēsia*.

But most of the time in classical texts, *parrēsia* does not have this pejorative meaning. It has a positive one. *Parrēsiazein* or *parrēsiazesthai* is "to tell the truth." But that is not quite clear. Does the parrhesiast say what he *thinks* to be true, or does he say what *is* really *true*? And the answer is that the parrhesiast says what is true because he thinks that it is true, and he thinks that it is true because it is really

* The notion of the subject of the *enunciandum* prompting some reservations from the audience, Foucault adds: "Well, perhaps we will be able to talk more about this afterwards." In the end, nobody raises any questions on that subject.

true. Not only is the parrhesiast sincere, not only does he state his opinion frankly, but his opinion is also the truth. He says what he knows to be true. In *parrēsia,* there is a coincidence, an exact coincidence, between belief and truth. And that is the second great characteristic of *parrēsia*.

And I think it would be interesting to compare the Greek *parrēsia* and the modern notion of Cartesian evidence. For us, since Descartes, the coincidence between belief and truth is to be obtained in a certain mental experience which is that of evidence. For the Greeks, the coincidence between belief and truth takes place, not through a cognitive experience like evidence, but through verbal activity—and this verbal activity is *parrēsia*. Anyway, you can see that *parrēsia* refers to a kind of relation between subject and truth, and that this relation between subject and truth is established through verbal activity. That's the second characteristic of *parrēsia*.

Third point: there is something more in *parrēsia* than this relation, this coincidence between belief and truth, and this relationship between subject and truth. One uses *parrēsia,* of course, when he tells truth because he is certain that it *is* truth. But somebody is said to use *parrēsia,* and deserves to be considered as a parrhesiast, if and only if there is a risk, there is a danger for him in telling the truth. For instance, in the Greek perspective, from the Greek point of view, a teacher who teaches grammar tells the truth to children he teaches, and he has no doubt that what he teaches is true. But, in spite of that, in spite of this coincidence between belief and truth, he is not a parrhesiast. And the Greeks would never say that a teacher is a parrhesiast, at least under normal conditions for teaching.[6] But when a philosopher addresses himself to a king, to a sovereign, to a tyrant, and tells him that tyranny is unable to make him happy because tyranny is not compatible with justice, in this case the philosopher says the truth, in this *énoncé* there is an exact coincidence between belief and truth, and, more than that, the philosopher takes a risk, because the tyrant may become angry, may punish him, may exile him, may kill him. That was exactly the situation of Plato with Dionysius in Syracuse, and there are very interesting references to all that in Plato's *Seventh Letter*,[7] and in the *Life of Dion* by Plutarch;[8] we'll study those texts later on.[9]

So you see, the parrhesiast is somebody who takes a risk. Of course, this risk is not always the risk of his life. When, for example, you see a friend doing something wrong, and when you take the risk of making him angry by telling him he is wrong, you are a parrhesiast. You don't risk your life, but you may hurt him, and your friendship may be hurt as a result. In a political debate, if an orator takes the risk of losing his popularity because his opinion is contrary to the majority's opinion, he uses *parrēsia*. So, as you see, *parrēsia* is linked to danger, it is linked to courage. It is the courage of telling the truth in spite of its danger. In *parrēsia*, telling the truth takes place in a game of life or death. That's the third characteristic of *parrēsia*.

Fourth point: *parrēsia* is not linked to any kind of danger. For instance, if you know an important secret and if you disclose it, at your own risk, you are not a parrhesiast, in spite of the fact that you tell the truth and it is dangerous to tell it. You are not a parrhesiast, at least in the positive meaning of the word, if you say something that can be used against you. For instance in a trial, that [speech] is not necessarily *parrēsia*. In *parrēsia*, the danger comes always from the fact that the truth you say is able to hurt or anger the interlocutor. *Parrēsia* is always a game between the one who speaks and the interlocutor. For instance, *parrēsia* may be the disclosure of a mistake by the interlocutor. It may be the advice that he has to behave in such and such a way. *Parrēsia* may be the opinion that he is wrong in what he thinks or in the way he behaves, and so on and so on. It may be a confession of what you have done, insofar as you make this confession to somebody who exercises a power over you, and who is able to punish you for what you have done.

As you see, the function of *parrēsia* is not to give a demonstration of the truth, and it is not a discussion or a contest about truth with somebody else. *Parrēsia* has always the function of criticism. Criticism of oneself, the speaker himself, or criticism of the interlocutor: "That's what you do and that's what you think, and that's what you shouldn't do or you shouldn't think." "That's the way you behave and that's the way you should behave." "These are all things I have done and these are the mistakes I have made." And so on and so on.* It is this position of criticism which is the specific characteristic of *parrēsia*. *Parrēsia* is a criticism, it is a criticism, a self-criticism or a criticism oriented towards the others, but always in situations where the speaker is in a position of inferiority to the interlocutor. *Parrēsia* comes from "below" and is oriented towards those "above." The parrhesiast is less powerful than his interlocutor. He is weaker than the one to whom he speaks and to whom he addresses his critiques. That is the reason why the Greeks wouldn't say that a teacher or that a father, when he criticizes a child, uses *parrēsia*. In these situations, there is no *parrēsia*. But when a philosopher criticizes the prince, when a citizen criticizes the majority, when the pupil criticizes the teacher, then he uses *parrēsia*. So, you see, *parrēsia* implies sincerity, *parrēsia* implies a relation to truth, a coincidence between belief and truth, *parrēsia* implies a risk, *parrēsia* implies a criticism, a game of critique, in those situations where the speaker is in a position of inferiority towards the other.

—*If parrēsia could be self-criticism, then why isn't the criminal confessing his crime a* parrhesiast?

—In some cases, criminals, when they confess what they have done, use *parrēsia*. When they are obliged to do it (and this was my previous point) by, for instance, torture, it's not *parrēsia*. But when voluntarily, using their own freedom, they decide to tell the truth about what they have done, and when they are in such a situation that the one to whom they confess is able to punish them, or to retaliate, in such cases, there is *parrēsia*. We'll see it in a very specific and interesting case, in Euripides' *Electra*. There are two confessions, one from a position of *parrēsia*, and another which excludes *parrēsia*.[10] So your question was a very good one.

—*My question concerns your fourth point. Is the risk linked to* parrēsia *inherent in the content of the statement, or does the risk come from the relation between the speaker and his interlocutor, one that makes it possible for the statement to be taken as an insult? Differently put, for*

* The manuscript adds: "or here are the limits you should not trespass."

there to be parrēsia, *does critique lie in the content of the claim or in the relation between the one who speaks and the interlocutor?*

—If my answer is not the good one, please tell me, and use *parrēsia*! *Parrēsia* is a question of the status that makes one more powerful than the other. For instance, there is the philosopher and the king. We'll also see the example of Electra and Clytemnestra: Clytemnestra is the queen, and Electra, for various reasons, occupies the position of the slave. Electra uses *parrēsia*, and Clytemnestra does not. It is this question of social status that creates risk, the danger, and the possibility of retaliation . . .

—*But is parrēsia linked to the utterance itself, or if the interlocutor responds and takes it as an insult, does that after the fact make it an instance of* parrēsia?

—Yes, for instance when Dionysius punished Plato and exiled him from Syracuse, he did not conduct himself as a good prince, for certain reasons that I will explain later, because it's the duty of the prince to accept *parrēsia*. But if the prince doesn't play the game, and simply punishes the speaker, the philosopher has still used *parrēsia*.

So I would like only to add one last point about these general characteristics [of *parrēsia*], and then I could answer questions again, if there are more.

The final characteristic of *parrēsia* is this: in *parrēsia*, telling the truth is not only taking a risk or confronting a danger, it is also a duty. The orator, for instance, who tells the truth to people who are not ready to accept it—to people who may punish him, condemn him to death or to exile—this orator is free to keep silent. Nobody forces him to speak; he feels that it is his duty to do so. When somebody has committed a crime, and when the judges force him to confess his crime, it is not *parrēsia*. When he voluntarily confesses his crime to somebody else because of a certain moral duty, then he has used *parrēsia*. Criticizing a friend or the prince is an act of *parrēsia*, insofar [as] it is a duty to help a friend who does not understand that he is doing wrong; it is an act of *parrēsia*, insofar as it is a duty towards the city to help the prince to become better than he is. *Parrēsia* is related to freedom and to duty.[11]

So we could say that *parrēsia* is a certain verbal activity in which the speaker has a specific relation to truth through frankness, a certain relation to himself through danger, a certain relation to law through freedom and duty, and a certain relation to other people through critique (self-critique or critique of other people). More precisely, it is a verbal activity in which the subject expresses his personal relation to truth and risks his life because he recognizes that telling the truth is his own duty, so as to improve or to help other people. In *parrēsia,* the speaker uses his freedom and chooses truth instead of lies, death instead of life and security, criticism instead of flattery, and duty instead of interest and selfishness.

That's the general meaning of the word *parrēsia* in the positive sense of the word in most of the Greek texts from the fifth century BCE to the fifth century CE. Are there any questions about those five characteristics of [*parrēsia*]?

—*Does speaking the truth create a bond?*

—Yes, as you see, all that is something which has to be discussed, because it's very complicated. For instance, when somebody says something, "the sky is blue," of course he is committed in a way. Every affirmation, every kind of assertion is a kind of commitment either to give evidence that what you are saying is true, or it is a commitment in that you are able or ready to repeat the same thing, and so on. So there is always a kind of commitment when the speaker asserts something. But with *parrēsia,* the commitment is much more important, it is different from this normal kind of commitment between somebody and what he says when he asserts something. This commitment is linked to a certain social situation, to certain differences of status, and it is also linked to the fact that the parrhesiast says something which is dangerous, and he risks something.

—*Could this bond be seen as an act of love, could it be seen as commitment to the person you're speaking to?*

—We'll see that in some texts, the relation between *parrēsia* and friendship is very important. The two major social frameworks for *parrēsia* are, first, the democratic constitution and the use of *parrēsia* in the *agora*; as a good citizen, you must use *parrēsia.* And the second great framework is friendship or love, which are very closely related in the Greek culture. Then, towards a friend, you must use *parrēsia*. It's another kind of commitment than the commitment between somebody and what he says when he answers something. That's something else.

—*Yes, I don't mean a promise or an obligation . . .*

—Yes, you see, it's not at all a speech act in the sense, or a performative *énoncé*, in Austin's sense. Not at all. It's something else, which is why I didn't speak about speech acts, but about speech activity.[12] It is an activity with different procedures, with the interlocutors' context, with a social backdrop, and so on.

—*How do we reconcile the criteria that you've given us, which include risk and difference in social status, with the definition that you underlined in the case of* Ion, *which seems to be predicated on one's civil status and [connected] to the safety that [corresponds to] that civil status, that free speech in* Ion. *That status that he aspires to, that would be the result of his citizenship in Athens, seems to give Ion a situation in which there is no risk.*

—If you read all of the speech (*tirade*) you see that before Ion speaks about his own *parrēsia,* his need of *parrēsia,* and that he does not want to come back in Athens without *parrēsia,* before that he gives a very interesting description of democratic life in Athens, with three categories of citizens. Some of them do not speak at all, because they are stupid but jealous. The citizens who do not speak in spite of the fact that they are rich, clever, and so on, are not interested in political life. And the people who use—the Greek expression is *logo te kai polei chromenoi*—who use discourses in order to rule the town, these people are struggling one against the others, and [Ion] does not want to arrive to this struggle without *parrēsia.*[13] So *parrēsia* is part of the risk of political life.

—*But you can't be a slave and have* parrēsia.

—Well, you'll find a text in Euripides where a slave uses *parrēsia,*[14] but most of the time, and in *Ion* and in other texts, there is a sharp opposition, a very clear-cut opposition between being a slave and being a parrhesiast or using *parrēsia.* When you are deprived of *parrēsia,* you are in the same situation as a slave, which means that you cannot be a part of the political life, and so that you cannot play the game. But the game is that a parrhesiast doesn't flatter the Assembly, the *ekklesia,* he does not flatter the city and his fellow citizens, he says the truth even if he takes the risk of being punished, exiled, killed, and so on. And this risk, I think, is something which is part of *parrēsia.*

—*So the criteria that we have to establish before you have* parrēsia *is to know one's own status; before you can fit into the game you must know its genealogy as it were.*

—Yes, we'll see that with *Ion.* You have to be a citizen to use *parrēsia.* But the king does not use *parrēsia,* because he faces no risk.

—*Does* parrēsia *ever make a statement by refusing to speak?*

—No, that's wisdom. No, I am quite serious when I say that. We'll see later on that the difference between the parrhesiast and the wise man is that the wise man is never obliged to speak.[15]

—*I think I'm using the word more strongly than that, like when you're being pressured to make a political statement and you refuse.*

—That's the problem of the silent parrhesiastic attitude, for instance with the Cynics. In the Cynic life, you have some behaviors, some elements of this life, that belong to the parrhesiastic attitude.[16] [The Cynics] do not use words, but rather [their speech] is something like the Japanese *koan*: it means something, and the others have to discover what that means.

—*Like when you refuse to convert, you're being burned at the stake but you refuse to convert, that kind of thing.*

—You're referring to the Christian meaning of the word *parrēsia.*

—*Can one speak of* parrēsia *if you refuse to convert, and if, as a result, you're burned at the stake, or if you are pressured to convert or maybe tortured? Most people would take that as an act of courage.*

—Well, I don't think that the Greeks would call that *parrēsia.* For instance, you'll find that the Cynic attitude is a kind of *parrēsia.* The martyr is also a kind of parrhesiast, since you show your faith when people ask you to abjure your own God. So that may be called *parrēsia,* and you will find some Christian texts where *parrēsia* is used with this meaning.[17] But you see there is something in those attitudes, in those behaviors, quite similar to a kind of affirmation, of assertion.

—*Before you were saying that you established a specific relation to the law, and a specific relation to the self. So that being said, the specific relation that you established to the self is danger. Why not the specific relation you establish toward others? You are endangered vis-à-vis others. Why do you say that that is a relation to the self?*

—I think that when you accept to play a game in which your own life is exposed, it's a relation to yourself. You choose death instead of life, in order to tell the truth. And, of course, death comes from others and, in a way, it's a relation to others. But I think that the way the parrhesiast chooses truth instead of life, and prefers telling the truth rather than living, is something that is a personal choice and a kind of relationship to himself. He prefers to be a truth-teller than simply a living being. That's a relation to yourself.

—*Two points of clarification. How do you define this relationship of friendship? For instance, is Diogenes, who is living in his supposed barrel, is he considered a parrhesiast based on friendship?*

—Yes, sure.

—*Or the minister in the king's court who has hidden everything for a long time and says, "Aha! I have hidden everything"?*

—We'll speak about all that, this evolution of the parrhesiast from democratic institutions to the prince's court. Diogenes is classically a parrhesiast when he says to Alexander that he prefers his own life as a dog to the life of a prince. Or when he says to Alexander, "Please, step out of my sun," that's typically parrhesiastic. It is very different from the Platonic form but very typical for the Cynic school: he uses very short words, always linked to a certain physical and social behavior, and also related to a scandalous attitude.

—*Is he an example, Diogenes?*

—Well, here are thousands of examples.

—*Because I think that answers the earlier question about whether there is something inherent in the utterance. What he said could easily have gotten him killed by Alexander, but Alexander chose not to kill him, and so then there's nothing inherent in the utterance.*

—Yes, you see, the fact that the prince reacts in one way or another means only one thing: that the prince is a good one or a bad one. But anyway *parrēsia* is still the same.

—*Is there a distinction made between moral truths and cognitive truths?*

—Well, that's a problem. I think that most of the time, and fundamentally, *parrēsia* is related to moral truth. For instance, a teacher or a philosopher or a wise man who knows what are the laws of the cosmos and tells people what are those laws does not use *parrēsia*. But if he is in a city where people cannot accept this kind of truth, because it is a scandal, because the belief is something else, and if he takes the risk of saying that, then he is a parrhesiast. And we could say for instance that when Galileo gives a demonstration of these laws, he does not use *parrēsia*, but when in his trial he says, "Well, it turns," and then he uses *parrēsia*.[18]

—*Is there a difference between a duty to a moral truth and a duty to tell the truth in spite of its immorality?*

—I think that this idea that truth could be something immoral is very distant from the Greek attitude. Truth is not only a foundation for morals, but a part of them. That will be a large problem for the Stoics, and the Cynics also: to determine which are the truths, the knowledges we need (for instance, from the outside world) in order to behave as we have to behave. The attitude of Demetrius, for instance, or of Seneca is: we need to know exactly what is necessary for our own ethical and moral attitude, and we don't need to bother with any other kind of truth, or with cognitive truth.[19] So, you see, this problem you raise is something very important, but I think it is something very important after the Medieval Ages, at least in Western societies.

You also raised the question of whether, in the Soviet Lysenko affair, somebody who was Mendelian and who supported Mendel's theory could be said to use *parrēsia*. But in Western countries, when people discussed genetics in the same historical moment, they did not use *parrēsia*. Do you understand the difference? I think that it's not a question of the content, it's not a question of what kind of truth is put to work in *parrēsia*. Instead it speaks to the problem of the personal and social game that is implied by telling the truth about morals, about ethics, or about nature, about the world, about history, and so on.

—*As you explained it further, the concept of friendship operates in this notion of* parrēsia, *doesn't it? I may be a Mendelian biologist in the Soviet Union at the apogee of Lysenko, and I may condemn it on scientific terms, but I don't need to have a very personal relationship, a sort of friendship, with anybody in the party, right?*

—Yes, remember I told you that there were two frameworks, one that is democracy, and the other that is friendship, at least in Greek society. In this case, the framework is not friendship, it is freedom of speech, it is democracy, and so on. When the Mendelian scientist wrote in favor of Mendel's theory in the Soviet Union, he didn't want simply to demonstrate or to prove the truth of this theory, but also he wanted to act against Soviet society: to criticize the social organization of science, of scientific institutions, and so on. That was the parrhesiastic side of his affirmation.

—*You may have something to say about this later, but are friendships always characterized by status differences in Greek society?*

—Well, obviously all that I have said here is a very general outline, and we have to be much more precise on all these points. For instance, in spiritual guidance, there is always a difference between the one who guides and the one who is guided: a difference in age, difference in competence, in wisdom, and so on. So *parrēsia* comes from the one who is older and goes to the one who is younger and so on. But as you'll see, there is a change in the meaning of the word *parrēsia*, and even the one who is guided has to use *parrēsia*. You find also—it's quite clear in Seneca[20]—situations in which both of the partners, the guide and the one who is guided, must use *parrēsia* towards each other because they are useful to one another.

—*But was it then possible for someone to place himself in a position of inferiority simply by criticizing a friend?*

—That's a context in which friendship is important, because of course in such a situation the other person is not in a social position of inferiority. But he risks something, and the risk is that he could lose the friendship of the other. And in the case of the Socratic position with Alcibiades, you will see analyzing the text, that of course Socrates is older, wiser, and so on, but Alcibiades has a much better, much nobler origin. He is young and beautiful, and Socrates loves him, and so if Socrates hurts Alcibiades, he will lose Alcibiades' friendship. So in this situation, he has something to lose when he speaks truthfully.

—*Could you just explain one more time what you meant by the coinciding of belief and truth? Was there a particular epistemological way they approached belief as truth?*

—No, at least not in Plato—in Aristotle it's something different—but there is no epistemological elaboration of this relationship in the Greek texts.

—*What did you mean by coincidence?*

—That the parrhesiast is somebody you can trust because he is the man whose beliefs are true.

—*True to him?*

—They are true, not only to him, but also they are true [in themselves]. That's *parrēsia.* And that's why *parrēsia* cannot take place in our epistemological framework from Descartes onwards. You see, authority, intellectual authority, has something to do with *parrēsia,* since there are still some kinds of verbal activity in our society in which the one who speaks is supposed to tell the truth. [For example], the teacher, the teaching situation. When you are an undergraduate, you trust the teacher because you presume that what he says is true. [Such a] teacher is not a parrhesiast, but we can imagine what the parrhesiast in Greek civilization was like based on the situation of present-day teachers. He is supposed to say the truth. What he believes is true, and what he says he believes, we have to believe it, because it is true. That's the parrhesiast.

—*Is* parrēsia *suspended when the elements that are prerequisites to it are suspended, such as when the herdsman says, "I will tell you the truth, if, given that you could harm me, you won't harm me"?*[21] *Would that then suspend [*parrēsia*] because the danger has been alleviated?*

—That's a very good question, and we have a case like that with Electra. There is something, and you find something in some of the parrhesiastic situations, which imply a kind of pact: I'll tell you the truth, but promise me that I won't be punished. In this case, I think that the parrhesiastic situation is still maintained, because in this pact, there is no real obligation, only a moral commitment. We'll see that is very interesting [in the confrontation] between Electra and Clytemnestra.[22] The good prince, a king who is responsible, who is conscious of his own duty, is someone who accepts that his advisers tell him the truth, and he does not punish them. But he is always able to punish them if he wants. Or even the fact that he no longer takes the advice of the adviser serves as a kind of retaliation.

Are there any more questions?

—*I think you say that in Greek society the king or the princes couldn't, by definition, be a* parrhesiast, *nor could slaves. The dominant economic system of the Greek period was slavery. So it seems to me that being a* parrhesiast *at that time was abnormal, and very few people could be one. So: did being a* parrhesiast *imply that it was a risk that you must pay for that honor?*

—No, not for having that honor, but we'll see that in a much more precise way when we look at Isocrates and the Greek orators, and so on. But we must make a very clear distinction between the monarchic *parrēsia*, where you must speak to the king and give him good advice, and the democratic *parrēsia*, where you have to speak to the *ekklesia*, to the Assembly. Of course as a citizen who speaks in front of the Assembly, you cannot do so without being, first, a citizen, but even that is not enough, you must also be one of the first among citizens, you must have certain personal qualities, certain moral and social qualities, in order to speak and to persuade. So that implies that you cannot be a parrhesiast without having those privileges. That's quite clear. But those privileges, you risk them in saying, in telling a truth which can hurt the majority of people. There is a well-known juridical situation, which is the exile of those Athenian leaders who were exiled only because they proposed things that were opposed to the majority's opinion, or even because they were too influential. The Assembly thought that its own freedom was limited by the influence of those leaders, and they were exiled. And so the Assembly was, in a way, protected against the truth that those orators could tell. That's the institutional background of democratic *parrēsia*.

—But if you play this game and win, do you also raise your own status? So you risk something, but you can also gain from it.

—Yes. There is also a very interesting text—we will try to comment on it—in Thucydides about Pericles. At the beginning of *The Peloponnesian War* there is a very interesting, very beautiful speech by Pericles.[23] The word *parrēsia* is not used in this text, but it is quite clear that it is a parrhesiastic situation, one in which the main figure of Athenian democracy risks his own situation by saying something that maybe is not the majority's opinion.

—What does he gain? More power and authority . . .

—Yes. But he is always exposed to the possibility of being expelled, or exiled, or punished, or put to death, by the Assembly. That's the democratic game in Athens. In a democracy, even the first among the citizens can use *parrēsia*. In a tyranny, or in a monarchy, the monarch doesn't use *parrēsia*.

—How does one know that one has won the game, both in the democratic framework and in the friendship framework?

—Well, in the both situations, when the one who speaks, who tells this dangerous truth has persuaded, convinced the Assembly, the majority, or the prince without being punished.

—So it's in having persuaded somebody that you win, and there's no doubt that you said the truth. How does it work in the friendship framework, if you said, "You're a lousy friend" or "You stole my wife!," what's the test of the truth in that case?

—But there is no test of truth, that is not at all a question of evidence, of proof.

—It's just persuasion.

—No, in *parrēsia*, the one who speaks is supposed to tell the truth. The problem is: will he be able to persuade other people, or will he be punished for saying the truth?

—You also say it's the relation to yourself too. If I have convinced someone that I said the truth, there's no doubt in his mind, but in my relationship to myself, do I say, "Have I said the truth?"

—Well, that's the problem of self-consciousness for the parrhesiast. I have never found any text in which the parrhesiast, in Greek culture, seems to have any kind of doubt about his own possession of truth. That's the difference between the Cartesian problem and the parrhesiastic attitude. Descartes, before he attains evidence, Descartes is not sure that what he knows is true. But in the case of *parrēsia,* because, I think, of the superposition of moral value and access to truth, when somebody has access to truth, that's the proof that he has some moral qualities. And when somebody has those moral qualities, then he possesses the truth. So there is no problem.

—*I can see that it can be a Cartesian problem, but it's also a problem having to do with your sincerity, too. I mean, if I can convince someone that such and such is true, my motivation could be that I want to convince that person, but without having been sincere.*

—Well, no, that's a distortion of the game. The game implies that the parrhesiast is someone who knows the truth and has the moral qualities which are required, first to know the truth, and second to tell the truth, and to be willing to tell the truth to the others. At the beginning of my exposé, I told you that the first characteristic of *parrēsia* was sincerity.

—*But sincerity can never arise if there's no doubt about your motivation for saying something.*

—That's not a Greek problem.

—*You are speaking from a modern epistemological point of view, that's why you cannot understand.**

—*It's not only a modern problem. The first time that I've been able to find the problem of sincerity in this context with any requirement of truth is within a confessional framework, once confession was required in the twelfth century. At that point, there was the institution of an agent. The Church defined itself as in the age of hypocrisy. This whole problem only emerges when truth is mandated, and [Foucault] is talking about when it's not required, and you do it freely . . .*

—Maybe things will become a little clearer when we see the filia-

* The interlocutor here is addressing the previous questioner rather than Foucault.

tion between the wise man and the parrhesiast, because, for instance, the wise man does not need to give any proof of the fact that he is wise. Everybody knows that he is wise, even if there are also some contextual circumstances that indicate he is wise. Solon is wise; nobody doubts that he is wise, and he doesn't doubt that he is wise. The parrhesiast is something different, somebody different from the wise man, but he is in a way the democratic version of the wise man. There is no doubt [of this] either from other people or from [himself], and there is—maybe this could be a kind of answer for you—not exactly a criterion, but there is an experiment. There is a kind of proof of his sincerity, and that is his courage. The fact that he says something dangerous, the fact that he says something different from what the majority thinks, that is the sign that he is a parrhesiast. Now, I see your problem more clearly. When you raise the question of how can we know that somebody is a parrhesiast, you raise two questions. One is: how could we know that somebody is a parrhesiast? And there is another question: how can somebody be sure that he knows the truth? This second question, I think, is a modern one, and I do not remember having ever found any texts addressing this question. But the question, how can I recognize that somebody is a parrhesiast?—which is a very important question, either in the democratic context, or that of spiritual guidance in Greco-Roman society—this question has been very explicitly raised and elaborated by Plutarch in his treatise about flattery.[24] The question is: when I have a friend and I ask him to help me with my moral improvement, how can I be sure that he is a parrhesiast? Galen, also, in a treatise about the cure of passions,[25] gives indications about the way to recognize the real parrhesiast from a hypocrite or from a flatterer. But from an internal point of view, how can I be sure that I tell the truth and that I have no personal interest in saying so . . . that's a question which is not a Greek one.

Let's take a break, and then we'll start again with some things about the evolution of this notion of *parrēsia*.

THE PRECEDING COMMENTS OFFERED ONLY a very general framework, and of course we have to be much more precise in the study of this notion of *parrēsia*. What I would like to do in this seminar is not to study or analyze all of the dimensions and features of this notion of *parrēsia*, but instead to underline some aspects of the evolution of the *parrēsia*, of the rules, the game, the parrhesiastic game in the ancient culture, from the fifth century BCE to Christianity.* I think that there are three great evolutions, or that we can analyze this evolution of *parrēsia* from three different points of view.

One is the relationship between *parrēsia* and rhetoric.[26] It is very clear that in the fourth century, well, even in Euripides, you see clearly that the relation between *parrēsia* and rhetoric is something very problematic. But in Plato, for instance, and in all the Socratic-Platonist tradition, there is a very strong opposition between *parrēsia* and rhetoric.** This opposition between *parrēsia* and rhetoric appears very clearly in, for instance, the *Gorgias* (we can read the text from this point of view).[27] You see clearly that there is an opposition between the sophistic and rhetorical techniques and philosophy. You can see also that the long speech, the continuous long speech, is something that belongs to the techniques of rhetoric and sophistry. By contrast, the dialogue proceeding through questions and answers is typical for *parrēsia*, or rather, in the *Gorgias*, it is the main technique used to play the parrhesiastic game; dialogue becomes a tool, a device for the parrhesiastic game. You can see also the clear-cut opposition between rhetoric and *parrēsia* in the *Phaedrus*, where, as you know, the problem is not at all, as nearly everybody knows, the problem of an opposition between writing and speaking, [but the opposition] between the *logos* which says the truth and the *logos*

* The manuscript adds: "This evolution will be the topic of this seminar since this evolution has been determinant for the relations of subjectivity, truth, ethics and politics in our societies, and also for the genealogy of what we call *critique*."

** On a page of the lecture manuscript that might be a first draft of this passage, Foucault specifies: "In Plato's dialogues, *parrēsia* is opposed to rhetoric. And it is opposed to rhetoric from two points of view:

- Rhetoric is concerned with the effects the speaker is able to obtain through his discourse. *Parrēsia* is concerned with truth.
- Rhetoric needs several techniques which have to be learned. *Parrēsia* needs only the will to find, to discover, to tell, or to show the truth."

which is not able to say the truth.[28] There also you see the difference between *parrēsia* and rhetoric.

This opposition between rhetoric and *parrēsia*—which is so clear-cut in the fourth century, at least in Plato—will last for centuries and centuries in the Platonic tradition, and most of the time in the philosophical tradition. For instance, in Seneca, you can often find this idea that personal lectures or personal conversations are the best way to speak frankly and to tell the truth insofar [as] in those personal lectures or dialogues you don't need to use rhetorical devices.[29] The cultural opposition between rhetoric and philosophy, even in the second century CE, in what we call the "second sophistic," well, this opposition between rhetoric and *parrēsia* is still very clear and very important.

But you can find also in the theoreticians of rhetoric in the beginning of the empire some signs of the integration of *parrēsia* inside the field of rhetoric. Take for instance, Quintilian, *Institutio Oratoria,* book 9, second chapter, the chapter which is devoted to the *sententiarum figurae.* Quintilian explains that some rhetorical figures are specifically used in order to make the emotions of the audience more intense. The rhetorical figures, those technical devices which make the emotions more intense, are called by Quintilian the *exclamationes.* Among those figures, the *exclamationes,* there is a kind of *exclamatio* that is, says Quintilian, not *arte composita,* which is without any technique, or without any art. This natural exclamation is what he calls *licentia,* or *libera oratio,* and he says that it is the Latin translation of the Greek *parrēsia.*[30] So you see that *parrēsia* becomes a figure, it is among the rhetorical figures, but with this characteristic that it is a figure without any figure, because it is completely natural. It is the zero degree of rhetorical figure—the *exclamatio, libera oratio, parrēsia*—through which the orator makes the emotions of the audience more intense through *parrēsia.* So that's a first evolution which, I think, is rather interesting and important: the relation between *parrēsia* and rhetoric.

Second important evolution: this evolution is related to the political field; I think that we spoke about it in the question and answer period we had a few minutes ago. This is the evolution of *parrēsia* in the political field. In the fourth century, *parrēsia,* as it appears in Euripides' texts, was a characteristic of the Athenian democracy. We must, of course, investigate exactly what was *parrēsia* in the political institutions of Athens, but we can see that *parrēsia* was both a general rule for the democracy, and that the Athenian democracy was characterized quite explicitly as a *politeia,* a constitution, in which people enjoyed *demokratia, isonomia, isegoria,* and *parrēsia.*[31] That was an institutional rule, and we have to study, to elaborate a little more all of that. It was a general and institutional rule, and it was also a personal attitude, an ethical attitude, that characterizes the good citizen. So it was both an institutional rule and a personal attitude.

During the Hellenistic period, this political meaning of *parrēsia* as something characteristic of the Athenian constitution, well, this political meaning changes with the Hellenistic monarchies, of course, and *parrēsia* appears as a certain relation between the prince and his advisers or his court men. In this monarchic kind of constitution, of *politeia,* the adviser has to use *parrēsia* in order either to help the prince or to prevent him from abusing of his power. *Parrēsia* is necessary, *parrēsia* is something which is useful either for the prince himself or for the people who are ruled by the prince. Either way, it is the duty on the part of the prince's adviser to tell him the truth.* That's a *parrēsia* that is very different from the democratic *parrēsia* in Athens. In this parrhesiastic game—and that's the beginning of the answer to some of your questions a few minutes ago—the prince in the *parrēsia* game, the prince has to accept the *parrēsia* of the adviser. He is not himself the parrhesiast, but it is the touchstone of a good ruler, of a good prince, to accept (or not) the parrhesiastic game. The good prince is someone who accepts everything that the parrhesiast says, even if it is unpleasant for him to listen to those criticisms. He proves himself to be a tyrant if he does not take into account what the parrhesiast says. He is a tyrant if he punishes him for what he has said. He is a good prince, he is a good king, if he accepts and takes into account what the parrhesiast has said. You'll find that

* The manuscript adds: "It is his duty toward the prince, and his duty toward his fellow citizens."

in all the historical texts, either from Greek writers like Polybius, or Latin like Titus Livius, and much more so in Tacitus and the others. In their depictions of princes, there are always indications about the way they behave towards their advisers: the particularity of *parrēsia* defines them, and something characteristic of the prince can be seen in the way he behaves towards the parrhesiast.

So we can say that this evolution in the political field, the evolution of the notion of *parrēsia*, shows us that in the democratic constitution of Athens, *parrēsia* takes place between the citizens as individuals and the citizens as a totality, as a community, as an assembly. It is this game between the citizen as an individual and the majority or the totality of the citizens which constitutes the framework of the parrhesiastic game. The *agora* is the place where the *parrēsia* appears. *Parrēsia* is a requisite for public speech. In the Hellenistic kingdoms, the parrhesiastic game is something different. It is a game between the adviser and the prince with a third category of players who are what we could call the silent majority, the people, who are not present between the adviser and the king, but to whom the adviser refers when he gives advice to the prince. The place where the *parrēsia* appears is not the *agora*, it is the court. It is inside the court, inside the palace, that *parrēsia* takes place. That's the second evolution in the notion of *parrēsia*.

The third change is the *parrēsia* in the field of philosophy, in the field of philosophy understood as an art or as a *technē* of life.[32] In Plato, Socrates appears as the parrhesiast. The word *parrēsia* is used several times in Plato, never the word parrhesiast, which appears a little later on [in] the Greek vocabulary, but the role of Socrates is typically the role of the parrhesiast, and this role is very well outlined in the *Apology*. In the *Apology*, you see Socrates using his *parrēsia*, and his *parrēsia* consists in calling people in the street, asking them what they know, and inviting them to take care of themselves.[33] You have the example of this *parrēsia* in *Alcibiades*—we will study this text more closely later on.[34] In the *Alcibiades*, you know very well that Alcibiades' lovers flattered him and tried to get his favor. Socrates, in contrast to those flatterers and lovers, takes the risk of making Alcibiades angry by showing him that he is unable to do what he is so eager to do: that is, to become the first among the Athenians, to rule Athens and to be more powerful than the king of Persia. And so the philosopher is typically a parrhesiast.

Later, in the Greco-Latin philosophy and during the first centuries of our era, philosophical *parrēsia* is still associated with the theme of the care of the self. The philosopher has to be a parrhesiast, insofar as he has to invite people to take care of themselves. But it is not only the courage of the philosopher that helps people to discover that they know nothing. *Parrēsia* is not only this kind of provocative attitude that Socrates had towards people and towards the youths like Alcibiades, *parrēsia* is not only a question of questioning, *parrēsia* is now not only an attitude, a provocative attitude, it is also a procedure. It is not only a moral quality of the philosopher, it is a technique, a sophisticated technique, through which the philosopher guides his disciple or his friend. *Parrēsia* is now a *technē* of spiritual guidance. And for instance, Philodemus, who was the main Epicurean figure, the main Epicurean author with Lucretius during the first century BCE, Philodemus has written a book about *parrēsia* and the book was the technical one about teaching and helping each other in Epicurean communities.[35] *Parrēsia* becomes a technique. And it is a technique for *psuchagogē*, for psychagogical technique — it's a technique for conducting souls. Those techniques of *parrēsia* are very well developed, for instance, in Seneca's writings, either in some treatises like the *De tranquillitate*,[36] or in some of the letters to Lucilius. The development of those techniques, through those letters and those treatises by Seneca, is a very significant, very important evolution in those techniques of *parrēsia*.

In the beginning, *parrēsia*, the parrhesiastic attitude, was characteristic of the master's role. The master, the philosopher, had to tell the truth to a youth, with the risk of losing him as a friend. But now, in Seneca's texts, you see very well that *parrēsia* becomes a game where the two players had to speak and to tell the truth to each other. There is the role of the teacher, and of the master, who has to tell the truth to the pupil, or to the disciple, or to the one who is guided. But the disciple, the pupil, the one who is guided, has also to say the truth. But which kind of truth? He has to say the truth about himself. He has to explain without hiding anything what he is, what he feels, and what is the state of his soul. *Parrēsia* is a complete disclosure of the self through a kind of confession. And so you see *parrēsia* with two partners: the parrhesiastic role of the master, who tells the truth to the disciple, and the parrhesiastic attitude of the disciple, who uses *parrēsia* in order to disclose his own soul, his own state of mind, to the master. Of course, things are much more complicated than that, but I think that we can recognize here a very important evolution from the *parrēsia* by which the master shows to the disciple that he knows nothing, to this *parrēsia* by which the disciple tells the master everything he knows about himself.

Those, I think, are the three main evolutions of the word *parrēsia* from the fifth century to the Greco-Roman period and to late antiquity: relations to rhetoric, relations to politics, relations to philosophy and to the care of the self.

In this seminar and the other sessions that follow, I would like to give you a sketch of this evolution, from Euripides and the crisis of relations between truth, to telling the truth and political discourse in the Athenian democracy at the end of the fifth century, to the Greco-Latin philosophy where the master's *parrēsia* is giving place to the disciple's confession. The background of my interest in this notion of *parrēsia* is, of course, the history of the care of the self, and the development of something we could call the culture of the self, which was something very important in the Greco-Roman society, especially during the first centuries of our era.[37] My aim is to analyze the forms and the role of truth, of truth games, in this culture of the self. This verbal activity and this ethical attitude which characterize parrhesiastic activity, the parrhesiastic attitude, is, I think, something which has been very important in the development of the culture of the self. The evolution from the democratic use of *parrēsia* to the spiritual use of the same *parrēsia* is, I think, something important for understanding how this culture of the self was developed from the fourth century, from the Socratic and Platonic philosophy, to late Stoicism. This question of truth games in the culture of the self is the same type of question that I have tried to raise about, for instance, madness, and then about crime. What truth games are implied in our perception of madness and of crime? Where do they come from? How were they built up and developed? What were their institutional and practical conditions? But in the case of madness and crime, those truth games were used in correlation with social exclusion. In the case of the care of the self, the truth games were used in the process of the constitution of the self. That's the first reason why I was interested about *parrēsia* and why I wanted to tell you something about this *parrēsia*.*

In analyzing this notion of *parrēsia*, I would like also to outline the genealogy of what we could call the critical attitude in our society.[38] Most of the time, the historians of ideas are interested in the problem of "ideologies," or in the problem of relationships between society and representation, in order to decipher how far social structures or social processes help or prevent the discovery of truth. I think that there is another problem about the relationships between truth and society. This is not the problem of society's relation to truth through ideologies, it is the problem of what we could call the truth-teller, the *Wahrsager*.[39] The problem of the *Wahrsager*, as you know, is a Nietzschean problem, and you find the elaboration of this problem in Nietzsche.** What is the problem of the *Wahrsager*, of the truth-teller? Well, it is this one: who in a society is qualified, who is considered as able to tell the truth? Who is the one whose words are supposed to be the words of truth and accepted as such?

* The manuscript adds: "Most of the time, historians of ideas raise the question: how did human subjectivity become an object of knowledge? How, and under which conditions, did this objectification take place? How and why has this subjectivity been alienated as a consequence of this integration in the field of objective knowledge?

The question I would like to raise is different from this one, even if it is related to it:

How and in which ways have individuals in western societies become subjects—ethical, political, epistemological, juridical subjects?

How and by what process did the relation to oneself take the shape it did in the domain of ethics, of politics, of science, etc.?"

** The manuscript adds: "This problem has been studied by Nietzsche, by Max Weber."

And I think that we could say that in our society, there are four different roles for the truth-teller.[40]

Three of them are relatively well known:

First, there is the prophetic role. In the prophetic role, somebody speaks, and he speaks as the spokesman, as the mouthpiece — do you say that, mouthpiece? — of someone else, he is the spokesman of a powerful being, who is beyond our present sight. This prophetic role implies a reference to another reality. The prophetic role operates and works as a mediator.

There is also another role for the *Wahrsager*: it is the role of the wise man. The difference between the prophet and the wise is that the first one, the prophet, speaks for somebody else, while the second, the wise, speaks for himself. He says things that other people are not able to know by themselves.

The third role of truth-teller is the role of the teacher. The difference between the wise man and the teacher is that the first one, the wise, says things he is the only one to know, and the second, the teacher, is someone who says things that are already well known, which are accepted and received in the society. The role of the teacher is to teach these truths to people who need to know them in order to be integrated, or better integrated, in the society.

So these are the three roles: the prophet, the wise, the teacher. I think they have been rather often analyzed, that they are rather well known.

But I think that there is a fourth role that for some reasons has never been very well investigated, and that is the parrhesiastic role. And as you can see, the role of the parrhesiast is somehow different from those three main roles. The parrhesiast, first, is different from the prophet, in that the parrhesiast doesn't speak for someone else, he speaks for himself. He says exactly what is his own opinion. He is his own spokesman. That's the difference between the parrhesiast, the main difference between the parrhesiast and the prophet.

The parrhesiast is also different from the sage, since the sage is not obliged to tell other people what he knows. Other people must ask the wise man questions and listen to what he says. But the wise man may keep silent, and often his silence is the best sign of his wisdom. Anyway, the wise says what he wants and he doesn't bother with the effects of his words and of his wisdom. On the contrary, the duty of the parrhesiast is to speak, it is to tell the truth, it is to persuade other people. The parrhesiast has to act upon them and to improve their behavior, to improve the state of mind of the prince, to improve the society, the city, and so on. He has a responsibility, he has a duty, an obligation that the wise man doesn't have.

And I think that finally the parrhesiast is different from the teacher, because the teacher, as you know very well, does not need to be courageous, he doesn't take any risk when he teaches, he says what everybody knows. His role is to integrate people who are not yet integrated [into society], he helps people to come inside, but he is himself inside society. The parrhesiast, on the contrary, is basically in a conflictual situation. He faces power, he opposes the majority, or public opinion, and so on, which the teacher doesn't do. He acts not as an integrating agent but as a disintegrating factor or agent.*

I think that those four roles—the prophetic role, the role of the sage, the teaching role, and the parrhesiastic role—have been always more or less mixed together, or at least there are some combinations of those different figures. The parrhesiastic role, you can find it more or less linked or associated to other roles. For instance, you find the parrhesiastic role more or less linked to the prophetic role in the Judaic tradition, where some prophets are also parrhesiastic figures who criticize society, the way that the Hebrews behave, what they should do, and so on and so on, and they are in a conflictual situation with the Hebrews. You can see also the same combination

* The manuscript adds: "I think that several functions and institutions in our society are rooted in those four major roles:

- For instance the function of religious or political leaders is rooted in the prophetic role. They are the spokesmen of God, or of the people, or of nation, or of proletariat.
- The function of scientists, of experts, of artists is the modern form of the sage.
- The role of teaching has been institutionalized as you know.
- And the role of parrhesiast is to be found in certain specific figures like moralists, or social or political critics."

of the prophetic figure and of the parrhesiastic role in some figures in European history. For instance, you find it very often in the Reformation movements in the sixteenth and in the beginning of the seventeenth centuries, where there were prophetic figures who were also parrhesiastic figures. You can find it also in the Catholic Church: somebody like Savonarola in Italy in the fifteenth century is typically a prophet who plays the role of the parrhesiastic figure in Florence.

The parrhesiastic role can be also linked with the role of the wise man. Socrates from many points of view was in the tradition of the old wise men in the Greek society like Solon and so on. He was a wise man, and he played also the role of the parrhesiastic man. But I think that in the eighteenth century, in the European eighteenth century, you could find the association of those two roles, the role of the wise and the role of the parrhesiast. For instance, Jean-Jacques Rousseau is both a wise man and a parrhesiastic man. And I think that generally, in the *Aufklärung*, you could find this kind of combination.*

The parrhesiastic role is also to be found sometimes in relation or in association with the teaching role. You find this association in Greco-Roman culture, Greco-Latin culture, in this very interesting mixture of the Stoic schools and the Cynic attitude, and the main great example of it is, of course, Epictetus. Epictetus was a teacher, he had a school—a very well-organized school, with hierarchy, progress, and so on, and exams and so on. And he was also the parrhesiastic man who, as a Cynic, played this role, this provocative role, of the parrhesiast. This combination of the teacher and of the par-

* The manuscript adds: "The role of the wise man has also been combined with other roles:

- with the prophetic role (Solon)
- with the role of the teacher ([in] Greece, since Plato and maybe Pythagoras)
- with the role of the parrhesiast:
- Socrates, who changed the definition and characterization of wisdom, and played at the same time the role of parrhesiast
- Rousseau, or maybe more generally the *Aufklärung*, must have been a combination of the sage role and of the parrhesiastic role."

rhesiastic role disappears, I think, over a very long period, because, I think, that parrhesiastic role was more or less confiscated by the preachers in medieval society, and the Renaissance, and [early modern] society. But the combination of the parrhesiastic role and the teacher, I think, this combination appears again in the nineteenth-century university, and especially in the German university, where it became more possible to play both roles, the teaching role and the parrhesiastic role.* And I think that was due to the fact that the *Aufklärung* tradition, the *Aufklärung* themes, the *Aufklärung ideologie* were integrated into the German university at the end of the eighteenth century and in the beginning of the nineteenth century.** We could say that Kant with the *Critiques* has been the first one to combine once more the old parrhesiastic role with the teaching role. In a way, Hegel and the neo-Hegelians in the German university have been both teachers and parrhesiasts. You could find it, I think, the same thing in the French university, not in the philosophy departments, but rather in the history departments. People like Michelet or Renan—it is also very interesting to see, Renan was both a teacher and a parrhesiast, and was parrhesiast at the point when, as you know, he had given his first lecture at the Collège de France, and he was then fired and couldn't give his second lecture because he had said that Jesus was *un homme remarquable*.[41] He was, in a way, a parrhesiast using *parrēsia* in a field of scientific knowledge. Perhaps a figure like Bertrand Russell, in the English university, could be considered as both a teacher and a parrhesiast. I don't know if he would be flattered by this.***

Anyway, I think that in our society, even if we don't have the

* The manuscript says: "once more possible."

** The manuscript adds: "And maybe the importance of the German university in the beginning of the 19th century is due to the fact that people like Fichte, and especially Hegel, tried to play simultaneously those major roles: prophet, sage, teacher, and parrhesiast."

*** The manuscript adds: "Anyway even if a university tried or was tempted to play those four roles at the same time, it is a fact that it did not succeed in this attempt. And throughout the 19th century, it is possible to observe a competition over those different roles in telling the truth, between reli-

word *parrēsia*, the parrhesiastic role, what we could call the "critical role," is something which is very important. There is at least a very sharp, very fierce competition in our society for this function of telling the truth in the parrhesiastic way; there is competition between religious movements, political parties, the university, and the press (the newspapers and the media). Those four kinds of institutions—religious movements, political parties, university, and the press or media—are institutions that pretend to do their own job and to also play the parrhesiastic game. The contest between those four institutions is fierce and sharp.

As you see, the second reason why I am interested in *parrēsia* is this one. I would like in studying this parrhesiastic role both to study the way the culture of the self has been developed in ancient societies through this specific truth game which is the parrhesiastic game, and second point, I would like to analyze through this history of *parrēsia* in ancient culture the beginning, the genealogy of what in our society we call the critical attitude. Since I think that in our society the critical role, the critical attitude—either from the philosophical point of view or the political one, or the religious one—this critical attitude derives from this parrhesiastic role that the Greek philosophy has discovered, invented. At the point of juncture for the genealogy of subjectivity and the genealogy of the critical attitude, the analysis of *parrēsia* is a part of what I could call the historical ontology of ourselves, since we are, as human beings, beings who are able to tell the truth and to transform ourselves, our habits, our *ethos*, our society, to transform ourselves by telling the truth.[42] So that's the general framework of this seminar about *parrēsia*.

Well, thank you.*

---

gious movements, political parties (and above all socialist and revolutionary [parties]), universities, and the press or newspapers."

* After the lecture follows a discussion devoted to the organization of a seminar that Foucault conducts on Fridays during his stay at Berkeley. He hoped to reserve access to those students who were working on the subjects treated in his lectures.

OCTOBER 31, 1983

LAST TIME WE MET, I tried to give you a very rapid and brief view over the problem of *parrēsia,* the general meaning of the word, and what we could call the parrhesiastic game. Today, I'd like to analyze the first occurrences of the word in the Greek literature. Those first occurrences of the word *parrēsia* are to be found in Euripides, more precisely in six different tragedies written by Euripides: *The Phoenician Maidens, Hippolytus, The Bacchanals, Electra, Ion,* and *Orestes.*[1]

In the first four tragedies, in the first four plays—*The Phoenician Maidens, Hippolytus, The Bacchanals, Electra*—the notion of *parrēsia* intervenes in a very precise context which helps to understand the meaning of the notion, but in those four plays *parrēsia* does not itself constitute an important topic, an important motif. On the contrary, *parrēsia* plays, I think, a very important role in the two last plays I just mentioned, in *Ion* and in *Orestes.* In *Ion,* I think we can say that the play in its whole is devoted to the problem of telling the truth, or *parrēsia*—to the problem of who has the right and who has the duty of telling the truth, and to the problem of who is courageous enough to tell the truth. And this parrhesiastic problem is raised in *Ion* in the domain, in the framework of the relations between gods and men. In *Orestes,* which was written ten years afterward, and which is one of the last plays written by Euripides, *parrēsia* is not that important. But there is in *Orestes* a scene which is, I think, a typically parrhesiastic scene. This scene deserves some attention insofar [as] it is directly related to some contemporary problems, issues, in Athens' political life. And there, in this scene, the question of *parrēsia* is raised not in the framework or against the background of relations between gods and men, but against the background, and within the framework, of human relations and institutions.

So today, I'll try first to say very few words about the four occurrences of the word *parrēsia* in other of Euripides' plays, in order to throw some light onto the meaning of the word. Then I'll try to give you a global analysis of *Ion,* as the tragedy of the *parrēsia,* as *the* parrhesiastic play, in which we see human beings take on the role of telling the truth, a role that the gods are not able to play anymore. And then, if I have enough time, I'll analyze the scene in *Orestes* where we can see, I think, a transition to the problem I'd like to consider next week: *parrēsia* as a political and philosophical issue in the times of Plato and Isocrates. Today, the seminar will be devoted to the problem of *parrēsia* between gods and men, and next week to *parrēsia* between politics and philosophy.

So, *parrēsia* between gods and men. First, some of the uses of the word *parrēsia* in several plays by Euripides.

First, in the *Phoenician Maidens*. The theme of the *Phoenician Maidens* is the fight between Oedipus's two sons, Eteocles and Polyneices. Following the story that is implied in the beginning of the play, after Oedipus's fall, his two sons have decided to rule over Thebes in turn, year by year. But after his first year's reign, Eteocles refuses to leave the place and to yield power to Polyneices. In the play, Eteocles represents tyranny, and Polyneices, who lives in exile, represents the democratic regime. So Polyneices, who has been expelled from Thebes, who is not able to come back because his brother Eteocles doesn't want him back in Thebes, Polyneices comes back in order to overthrow Eteocles, and with his allies he besieges the city. During this moment of siege, there is a confrontation between Jocasta—who is not supposed to be dead—and Polyneices. In this confrontation, Jocasta evokes the god's hatred towards Oedipus's family and she asks Polyneices about his own sufferings during the time when he was expelled from Thebes. The first question asked about Polyneices' suffering is about exile: "Is it really hard," asks Jocasta, "to be in exile?" And Polyneices answers: "Worse than anything." "And why that?," asks Jocasta, "why exile is so hard?" "It is because, when you are in exile, you cannot enjoy *parrēsia*." You find that claim on the line 387. I would like somebody to read those lines from 387 to the line ". . . in folly of fools," because my pronunciation is bad. That's the dialogue between Jocasta and Polyneices:

JOCASTA

First, then, I ask thee that I fain would learn.
What meaneth exile? Is it a sore ill?

POLYNEICES

The sorest. In deed sorer than in words.

JOCASTA

In what wise? Where for exiles lies its sting?

POLYNEICES

This most of all—a curb is on the tongue.

JOCASTA

That is the slave's lot, not to speak one's thought!

POLYNEICES

The unwisdom of his rulers must one bear.

JOCASTA

Hard this, that one partake in folly of fools![2]

Thank you. As you see through those few lines, *parrēsia* appears to be linked to the problem of the citizen's status. If you are not a citizen in the city, you don't enjoy *parrēsia*. And, of course, when you are exiled from a city, you no longer enjoy *parrēsia* in this city. That's quite simple, that's quite clear. But there is something else in those few lines. If you don't have this right to speak, you are unable to exercise any kind of power and you are in the same situation as a slave.* In fact, as you know, to be exiled in a city and to be a slave is, from the legal, from the institutional point of view, something very different. But for somebody whose destiny, whose birth was such that he had to rule the city, if he is deprived of those privileges, then he feels himself to be in the same situation as a *doulos*, as a slave. For the leading citizens in the city, being deprived of the right of speaking is to be a slave. And there is something else. If you are not able to use *parrēsia*, then—this is quite clear in the last lines—you cannot oppose the ruler's power, you cannot criticize him, you cannot say anything against him, and then the power exercised by the ruler upon you, this power is without limitation. And you see that this power without limitation is characterized by Polyneices as the power of somebody who is mad. A power without limitation and madness, those

* The manuscript adds: "(of course the word *doulos* is to be taken as having a metaphoric meaning)."

things are directly related. The man who exercises power is *sophos,* is wise, insofar as there is somebody who can confront him, who can use *parrēsia* to criticize him and put some limitations to his power.* So that's the first passage I wanted to quote.

The second one is to be found in *Hippolytus.* You know this play is about Phaedra's love for Hippolytus. The passage about *parrēsia* takes place right after Phaedra's confession: when Phaedra, in the beginning of the play, confesses to her servant her love for Hippolytus. But in this passage, the word *parrēsia* does not refer to this confession. It refers to something quite different. Phaedra, just after having confessed her love, evokes those women, those queens, those noble women, who brought shame upon their own families, their husbands, and children. She says that she does not want to do the same, that she wants her sons to live at home, in Athens, being proud of their mother and using *parrēsia.* She comments: a man is a slave if he is conscious of a stain in his family. What a magnificent tone!

> Me—friends, 'tis even this dooms me to die,
> That never I be found to shame my lord,
> Nor the sons whom I bare; but free, with tongues
> Unfettered, flourish they,** their home yon burg
> Of glorious Athens, blushing ne'er for me.
> For this cows man, how stout of heart soe'er,
> To know a father's or a mother's sin.
> And this alone can breast the shocks of life,
> An honest heart and good, in whomso found.
> But in his hour, Time lifts his mirror,
> And shows the vile, his vileness there,
> As a girl sees her face. With such may I be never found.[3]

* The manuscript specifies: "And then, last consequence, without any limitation, without at least this limitation due to the *parrēsia,* the ruler's government has no regulation; it gets rid of any kind of rationality. It cannot be *sophos.* And people are submitted to his madness."

** At this moment, Foucault can be heard saying: "It's *parrēsia.*"

So in this text you see once more the relation between *parrēsia* and freedom of speech, and the lack of *parrēsia* and slavery. If you don't enjoy *parrēsia,* you are a *doulos,* you are a slave. And you also see that following this text, citizenship by itself is not enough to get and to guarantee freedom of speech. You need something else to address yourself to the people and tell them the truth. You need something more: you need honor, and you need a good reputation for yourself and for your family. *Parrēsia* needs some moral and social qualifications, which come from birth, and from reputation on both sides (on the mother's side and on the father's side).

Third text, in the *Bacchanals,* there it's a very short passage that is not very important in the play, but only a transition. It's at a certain moment when a slave, a servant, comes and he has to tell Pentheus all the disorders the Bacchanals are doing in the country. As you know, it was an old tradition that people who brought good news got a reward and that those who brought bad news were exposed to being punished or to [being] injured because of this bad news. That's the very simple, the very clear reason why the slave is very reluctant to deliver the message he is bringing. Then he asks the king if he may use his *parrēsia* and tell exactly what he knows: "May I use parrēsia?" He fears the king's anger, and the king gives him the promise that he won't get any trouble if he tells the truth.

HERDSMAN

I have seen wild Bacchanals, who from this land
Have darted forth with white feet, frenzy-stung.
I come, King, fain to tell to thee and Thebes
What strange, what passing wondrous deeds they do.
Yet would I hear if freely I may tell
Things there beheld, or reef my story's sail.
For, King, I fear thy spirit's hasty mood,
Thy passion and thine over-royal wrath.

PENTHEUS

Say on: of me shalt thou go unscathed.
For we may not be wroth with honest men.

> The direr sounds thy tale of the Bacchanals,
> The sterner punishment will I inflict
> On him who taught our dames this wickedness.[4]

So, you see, those lines are interesting because they show a case where the parrhesiast, the one who says the truth, is not a free man, he is a servant, he is a slave. But the slave cannot use his *parrēsia* if the master, the king, is not wise enough to accept this *parrēsia*. If the king gets angry, if he is carried away by his passions, if he is not enough master of himself to accept the servant's *parrēsia*, well, he won't be a good ruler for the city. Pentheus, as a good ruler, as a wise prince, offers the servant what we could call a "parrhesiastic pact," which will become something very important in the political life, in the political behavior of the rulers in the Greco-Roman world. The parrhesiastic agreement consists in the following: the prince, the ruler, the man who has the power but does not know the truth, addresses himself to the one who has the truth but does not have power, and tells him: "Tell me the truth. Whatever this truth can be, you won't be punished. People who are responsible for their deeds will be punished, but not those who tell the truth about those deeds." This idea of a parrhesiastic agreement by which a ruler gives freedom to speak to people around him has been very important, and it is the counterpart of *parrēsia* as a privilege for citizens and for the best among these citizens.

A fourth text can be found in *Electra*.[5] It is the great confrontation between Electra and Clytemnestra. I don't need to retell the story. At this moment of the play, Orestes has just killed Aegisthus, but as Clytemnestra is at the point of coming onto the scene, he hides himself and he hides Aegisthus's body. So Clytemnestra makes her entry. She is not aware of what has just taken place, and she does not know that Aegisthus has just been killed. She makes a very beautiful and solemn entrance with a royal entourage. She is on a chariot with captive maids of Troy. Electra, who is on the scene when her mother arrives, behaves like a slave. She behaves like a slave in order to hide the fact that the moment of the revenge is coming; she also behaves like a slave so as to insult Clytemnestra and to make her remember her crime. And it is also a dramatic means to introduce the confrontation between the two women.

The discussion starts, and we have then two speeches, equally long (forty lines). One is given by Clytemnestra, and begins: *Lexo de* (I'll speak). She speaks, she tells the truth, she explains that she has killed Agamemnon and she explains why: she has killed Agamemnon as a punishment for Iphigenia's death.[6] Then, after this speech, Electra answers and she begins her speech with a symmetric formulation. She says: *Legoim' an* (I'll speak). Those two speeches are exactly symmetrical. But in spite of this symmetry, we can see a very clear difference. At the end of her speech, Clytemnestra directly addresses Electra and tells her: "Well, I have said what I have done. And I have said all that very frankly. Now it's your turn." And she says: "Use your *parrēsia* in order to prove that I was wrong when I killed your father." And Electra answers. She answers, and she says: "Well, you gave me *parrēsia,* don't forget your last words, *didousa pros se moi parrhesian,* you gave me *parrēsia* towards you." And Clytemnestra answers: "Yes, I remember, I gave you *parrēsia,* I do not retract what I have just said." But Electra is still distrustful. She says: "Well, maybe you'll listen [to] what I want to say, but you will punish me." And Clytemnestra says: "No, I grant grace of licence to thy mood."[7] And then Electra accepts to speak, and she blames Clytemnestra for what she has done.[8]

So you see, we have two symmetric discourses. But there is a difference in the status of those two discourses. Clytemnestra is the queen, and in order to plead for her own defense, she does not need any *parrēsia.* But Electra, who is in the situation of a slave, who plays the role of a slave, Electra, who does not live anymore in her father's house and under her father's protection, Electra, who addresses her mother like a servant addresses a queen, Electra needs *parrēsia.* There is here another parrhesiastic agreement: I'll tell you the truth if you promise that you won't punish me. And Clytemnestra promises, exactly as Pentheus in the *Bacchanals.* She promises, but there is another difference: it is the fact that in this situation, the agreement, the parrhesiastic agreement, is distorted. It is distorted, not by Clytemnestra, who could as a queen punish Electra, but by Electra herself, since she makes her mother promise that she can speak frankly without any punishment. Clytemnestra gives permission, and she does not know that she, Clytemnestra, will be, in a few minutes, punished for her crimes. The parrhesiastic agreement is reversed, is distorted in a way that the one who has given *parrēsia* does not punish but is punished, and is punished by the one who is in a situation of a slave, and who was asking for *parrēsia*. The parrhesiastic agreement was a trap for Clytemnestra herself.

You can recognize here in these several texts the different features of the parrhesiastic game I have tried to explain to you last time. Are there any questions about these texts?

—*When the queen gives* parrēsia *to the servant and promises not to punish her, then it's actually not* parrēsia *anymore because there's no real courage involved, because this person knows she won't be punished.*

—I think we discussed a little this question, but you're right to raise the question, because in the parrhesiastic game, there is courage on the side of the one who tells the truth, but that does not mean that he cannot be cautious about the consequences of what he has said. It's a game with two partners. One needs to know the truth, and sometimes he is aware of needing the truth, and sometimes he is not aware. Let's take the example of Pentheus. Pentheus needs to know exactly what is going on in his country. So in order to learn the truth from his slave's mouth, he gives the parrhesiastic agreement. But even after that, since he is the master, since he is the king, since the other is a servant, he has the right to kill him or to punish him. It is only a moral agreement, without any legal or institutional regulation. So, regardless, there is always a risk, but I don't mean that the risk is always the same all throughout the game. The risk is great in the beginning, but at the end, it is not. For instance, those two women, Clytemnestra and Electra, hated each other, and they were each decided to kill the other. And Electra won the game. But in the end, Clytemnestra decided to kill Electra.*[9]

* After this response, and in answer to another question about his second example of *parrēsia* in Euripides given earlier, Foucault talks through a few points regarding the English translation of *Hippolytus* with which he

So let's turn to *Ion*, which is, I think, a parrhesiastic play, a parrhesiastic tragedy.[10] The mythological framework of this play is the foundation of Athens, it is the first dynasty of the city, it is Erechtheus and his first successors. As you know, following the myth, Erechtheus was the first king of Athens. He was born from the earth, and he returned to earth when he died.[11] He was really born from this earth, and he was the symbol of what the Athenians were so proud about, that is, their autochthony. They were born on the soil of Athens, and they were born from this earth. The use of those mythical elements at this moment—the play has been written around 418 BCE—at this moment of the history of Athens, these mythical references had an obvious political meaning.[12] Euripides wanted to make people remember that the Athenians were *autochthones*,* that they were born on and from their own earth. Euripides also wanted to recall that through Xuthus (one of the characters of the play, who married Erechtheus's daughter, Creusa), who was a foreigner in Athens, the Athenians were related through this marriage to others people living in Greece, and more precisely in the north of the Peloponnese, in Achaia. Referring to the history of Creusa and Xuthus, he also wants to show that there are very close relations between Athens and Phoebus, between the pan-Hellenic god of the Delphic sanctuaries and Athens. The fact was that at this moment of its history, Athens was trying to build, or to rebuild, a pan-Hellenic coalition against Sparta. Since the Delphic priests were mostly on the side of Sparta, there was a contest or rivalry between Athens and Delphi. But to the extent that Athens wanted to present itself as the leader of the Hellenic world, Euripides wanted to show that between this Delphic sanctuary and Athens, there were links, relations, and a mythical *parenté* (kinship). All of these mythical elements are sup-

---

is working—one that he describes as a flamboyant and "very free one." The interlocutor presses Foucault on the use of "shame" (line 420) and "honest" (line 427); Foucault disputes the rendering of *gnōmēn dikaian kagathēn* as "an honest heart and good." This exchange has been omitted because only fragments are audible.

* Foucault expresses himself here in French.

posed to justify Athens' imperialistic politics towards other Greek cities at a moment when the Athenian rulers still thought that it was possible for Athens to exercise its leadership over the Hellenic world. And through this mythical genealogy, Athens appears to have a pan-Hellenic vocation, alongside Delphi, and, at a certain point, instead of Delphi.

However, that's not the aspect that I'd like to emphasize today. I would like to emphasize another aspect of the play, which is more or less related to this first aspect. By this I mean the praise of Athens as the place where truth comes from, as the birthplace for those who are able, who are entitled, and who are courageous enough to tell the truth. This theme of Athens as the place for telling the truth, as the place for *parrēsia,* also has its political and religious implications, since, as you know, the place in Greece where truth was supposed to be told to human beings by the gods, this place was Delphi. In the play, we'll see a very explicit move from Delphi to Athens as the place where truth is disclosed to human beings and disclosed by human beings. In a way, this play is the play of autochthony of Athenians, it is the affirmation of their blood-affinity with most of the other cities in Greece and in the Hellenic world, and it is also the story of the move of the truth-telling role from Delphi to Athens, from Phoebus to the Athenian citizens. And that's, I think, the reason why this play can be read as the story of *parrēsia,* or as a parrhesiastic play.

I'd like to give you a sort of schema for the play.*

Silence		Truth		Deception
Delphi		Athens		Foreign countries
		Erechtheus		
Phoebus	=	Creusa	=	Xuthus
	Ion		Doros	
		Achaios		

So Xuthus, who is one of the Achaeans. And, not in marriage but through a sexual liaison between Phoebus and Creusa, comes

* This schema was reconstructed from indications given by Foucault as he wrote on the blackboard and from the manuscript of the lecture.

Ion. Then there is a marriage between Creusa and Xuthus, and from this marriage comes Dorus and Achaeus. Ion is supposed to be the founder of the Ionic people; Dorus, the founder of the Doric people; and Achaeus, the founder of the Achaean people. So you have all the Greek ethnicities that derive from Athens, Erechtheus, and Creusa. You thus can see this kind of family genealogy, which was at this moment so important for the Athenians, and for the justification of the imperialist politics. What I would like to show you is the way Ion and Creusa—Ion being the son of Phoebus and Creusa—are the people who tell the truth, who tell the truth against the silence of the gods and in spite of the fact that foreign countries, and their representative Xuthus, have been deceived by Phoebus. Phoebus keeps silent, but more than that, he tells lies. Xuthus as a foreigner is deceived and is also a deceiver—we'll see how—and yet those two are the ones, because they come from Erechtheus and from Athens, who tell the truth.

—*Is it important for Ion to establish the truth of his accession?**

—Yes, certainly. I'll tell you why it is so important for Ion to be the son of Creusa, Erechtheus, and of Athens, to be of the Athenian earth. He must come from there in order to get *parrēsia,* and in order to be the founder of Athens and the author of the Athenian constitution.

Well, so that's the schema, and now I'll try to explain Euripides' play further. I would like first to record briefly the events which are supposed to have taken place before the play begins. After the death of Erechtheus, the founder of Athens, after the death of his other children, Creusa is the only offspring of the dynasty. And one day she is seduced or raped by Phoebus. Is it a rape? Is it a seduction? If some among you are interested by this question, I can try to give an answer, but it would be a side remark, which is very interesting from the point of view of sexual right. You'd like me to explain? Well, I think that most of us think that rape is something which is much more criminal than seduction. But in the Greek texts, you see that

* This partially inaudible question was reconstructed from Foucault's response.

it's often difficult to make a distinction between rape and seduction. Because for [the Greeks] when somebody rapes a man or a boy, he uses violence. When somebody seduces a man or a boy, he does not exactly use violence, but he uses words, he uses his own ability to speak, he uses his superiority, and, in a way, there's no difference from using his physical force and using his psychological, intellectual, or social capacities and abilities. More than that, from the point of view of the law, seduction was something much more criminal than rape, because when somebody is raped, well that's against his will or her will. But when somebody is seduced, that's proof that to some extent she accedes to being unfaithful either to her husband or to her parents or to her family. It is a much more criminal attack against the family's power or the husband's power, to seduce a woman, or a girl, or a boy, than to rape him or her. So this problem, which is for us very important, is not so important for the Greeks. At a certain moment the relations between Phoebus and Creusa are presented and are characterized as a rape, and it's quite standard that when Creusa makes her momentous confession and reproaches Phoebus, she speaks of seduction. It is because in fact seduction is more criminal than rape.

Anyway she has been raped or seduced by Phoebus and she becomes pregnant. And when she is at the point of giving birth, she hides herself in the same secret place where she has been seduced. This place is right under Athens' Acropolis. It is in the center of the Athenian city, of the Athenian country. So the child is born, and she gives the child to a servant, because she is ashamed of what happened and she does not want her father, Erechtheus, to know that, so she gives the child to a servant, and Phoebus then sends his brother, Hermes, to steal the boy and to bring him back to Delphi. The boy is raised as a servant of the god in the sanctuary, but in Delphi, nobody, except Phoebus himself, knows who he is and where he comes from. He is raised as a foundling in Delphi. So you see the reason why Ion is between Phoebus and Creusa on my diagram—he is their child—and he is also between Delphi and Athens. He is born in Athens, but he lives in Delphi without knowing who he is, and with nobody else knowing who he is.

—I understand the status of the relation between truth and deception, but I'm not quite sure of the relation between silence and truth, because you spoke last time of wisdom, which is on the side of truth but also on the side of silence.

—We'll see a little later on the reasons for the silence, and why silence is a reason for deceit to others, and why and how Phoebus deceived people by his silence. So it's not a good silence, it's a bad one. There is no intrinsic value either to silence or to speech, but rather sometimes it is good to speak, sometimes it is good to keep silent, and in this case you see that the god's silence is criminal, or at least can be reproached.

That's one side of the story. The boy is raised in Delphi as a servant and nobody knows his identity, and he does not know himself where he comes [from]. Only a god, only Phoebus knows that. On the other side, in Athens, Creusa, who has given the child to a servant, and who knows through the servant that the child has disappeared, Creusa does not know what happened to the child. She believes that the child is dead, or perhaps she wonders if he is really dead. Then she marries a foreigner, Xuthus, which creates, of course, a great problem of continuity in the Athenian autochthony, and that's the reason why it is very important for Creusa to have a child. But in fact, Xuthus and Creusa, after their marriage, were not able to have any children. The two children, Dorus and Achaeus, are not born at the beginning of the play. Their birth will be the reward of Xuthus and Creusa after the play has finished, but when the play begins, they are not yet born. So Xuthus and Creusa don't have any children. They deeply need children in order to give to Athens its dynastic continuity, and that's the reason why they both come, Creusa and Xuthus, to Delphi, to ask the god if they will have any children. And that's the beginning of the play. Creusa and Xuthus come in order to consult Phoebus about their descendents and their lineage. You see that Creusa and Xuthus don't have exactly the same questions to ask of Phoebus. Xuthus has a very simple question. He says: "I've never had any children, shall I have one with Creusa?" That's a very clear, very simple question. But Creusa has another question to ask.* She must ask if she will have any children with Xuthus, but she must also ask: "With you, Phoebus, I had a child, and I need to know now whether he is still living or not. What have you done with my son, who is your son, what have you done with our son?" And that's the beginning of the play.

They arrive together at Delphi, Xuthus and Creusa. And, of course, the first person they meet in front of the temple—and you must keep in mind the spatial disposition of the place, that is very important. In the background of the scene, there is Phoebus's temple, which is the place where truth is told every day to anyone who comes to consult [the oracle], and truth is given to mortals, to human beings, by the god. Xuthus and Creusa arrive together in front of this door, through which truth comes to mortals, and they meet Ion, who is the servant of the god, and who is the son of Phoebus and Creusa. But nobody knows that he is the son of Creusa and Phoebus. He doesn't know himself, and, of course, his mother cannot recognize him, and they are foreigners to each other. Ion is a foreigner for Creusa and Xuthus, and Xuthus and Creusa are foreigners for him.

And, of course, you recognize the very well-known situation from *Oedipus*, where a child is also, as in this legend, given to a servant who is supposed to kill him.[13] The child is saved in spite of his parents' will, and he disappears, and when they meet again by chance, they do not recognize each other. Oedipus was not able to recognize his father, he was not able to recognize his mother. And the same on the other side. So you see that the family's structure, or the general structure of the plot, is somehow similar in this story and in the *Oedipus* story. But what I think is important are the dynamics. The dynamics of truth are exactly the inverse. In *Oedipus*, the same god, Phoebus, has said the truth, he has said the truth from the beginning, he has said what will happen. And human beings have tried to escape their own destiny, they have tried to hide the truth, or to avoid seeing it, and they are brought to discover the truth through several imperative signs that god has sent to them. They discover the

* The manuscript adds: "(a secret one)."

truth, Jocasta and Oedipus, in spite of themselves. Here, men and women—Ion (who is very anxious to know where he comes from), and Creusa (who would like to know exactly what happened to her son)—try to discover the truth, they are eager to know, they come here in order to know what happened, and it is the god Phoebus who voluntarily hides the truth. The problem of *Oedipus* is: how will men, in spite of their own blindness, be able to discover the truth which has been said once by a god and which they don't want to know? The problem of *Ion* is: how will men, in spite of the god's silence, discover the truth they are so eager to know?

The theme of the god's silence prevails throughout the play. It appears at the very beginning of the play, when Creusa says to Ion, without knowing who he is, that she has come [to consult the gods], but she is still ashamed of what happened, and so she presents the things as if she wanted to consult in her sister's name. She tells a part of her own story as if it was her sister's story. And she says: "Do you think that Phoebus will give me an answer for my sister?" And Ion, as a good servant of the god, says: "No, he won't give you an answer because if he has done what you said, if he has seduced or raped your sister, well, he would be ashamed." Then: "How should the god reveal that he would hide?" The god is a god who would hide in this text. Later, at line 367, "His shame the deed is, question not of him" is the advice given by Ion to Creusa, "question not of him."[14]

> If in the Gods' despite we wrest their will,
> By sacrifice of sheep on altars, or
> By flight of birds, to tell what they would veil,
> Could we of force wring aught from God full loth,
> Profitless blessings, lady, should we grasp;
> But what they give free-willed are boons indeed.[15]

But something else is coming. So you have that, at the very beginning of the play, the god will not tell the truth, because he is ashamed. But what is much more significant and striking is that at the end of the play, when everyone knows everything, when everything has been said by the different characters of the play, when we are waiting for the arrival of Phoebus, [who] couldn't be seen during the entire play, in spite of the fact that he is one of the main actors of the play, we still can't see Phoebus. We are waiting for him because in the tradition of the Greek tragedy, the god who has been the main figure, who has the main role in the tragedy, is supposed to arrive. Everybody waits for him, and who appears? Not Phoebus, but Athena. Athena comes, the doors of the temple are not open, but it is on the roof that Athena appears. And Athena explains why she comes:*

> Fly not: no foe am I that ye should flee;
> But as in Athens, so here, gracious willed.
> I come from thy land—land that bears my name;
> I Pallas from Apollo speed in haste,
> Who deigned not to reveal him to your sight,
> Else must he chide you for things over-past,
> But sendeth me to tell to you his words:
> Thee this queen bare, begotten of Apollo:
> He gives to whom he gave, not that they gat thee,
> But for thy bringing home to a princely house.
> But, when the matter was laid bare and told,
> Fearing lest thou shouldst of her plot be slain,
> And she of thee, saved thee by that device.
> Now the God would have kept the secret hid
> Until in Athens he revealed her thine,
> And thee the son of her and Phoebus born.[16]

So it's quite clear, at the end of the play, even at this moment when everybody knows everything, that Apollo does not dare to come and tell the truth. He hides himself. Of course we have to remember that Apollo, that Phoebus is the prophetic god, the god who

* The manuscript adds: "Athena comes in order to predict the future of Creusa's dynasty and of her city. The reason why this prophecy is done by Athena and not by Phoebus is that Athena is the Athenian goddess. But she gives also another reason."

is in charge of telling the truth to human beings. Well, this god is unable to play this role, and he is unable to play this role because he is guilty. Silence and guilt are there linked together, but on the side of the god. In *Oedipus*, silence and guilt were linked on the human side; now, [they are linked] on the divine side, and human beings have to manage by themselves to discover the truth, to disclose the truth, and to tell the truth. The human fight for truth against a god's silence, that, I think, is the main motif of the play. Phoebus is the antiparrhesiast. He doesn't tell the truth, he doesn't tell what he perfectly knows. He is not courageous enough to tell the truth, and he uses his power and his freedom and his superiority to hide what he has done. In this struggle against the god's silence, the two major characters of the play, Ion and Creusa, will play the role of the parrhesiast. But they won't play the role in the same way. One is a man and he has the right to ask for *parrēsia* as a privilege he has to enjoy in the city. And Creusa will play this role as a woman, as a woman who confesses her fault.* Those two kinds of *parrēsia* are, as you see, the motor of the play. And it is through those two *parrēsiai* that the truth which the god hides, and continues to hide, will be wrenched from the god.

I would now like to show you more about those two parrhesiastic roles in the play: Ion as the parrhesiastic figure, and Creusa's role.

First, Ion. The parrhesiastic role of Ion is to be found in a very long scene between him and Xuthus at the beginning of the play, which starts at line 517. Xuthus and Creusa come to consult the god, and Xuthus, as the husband, as the man, enters first in the sanctuary, asks his question to the god—we don't witness this part of the plot—and when he comes out [of] the temple, he has an answer. As an answer, the god has told Xuthus: "Well, the first one you meet when you leave the temple, this one will be your son." And of course, the first one he meets when he gets out of the temple is Ion, who as

* The manuscript adds: "In this struggle against the god's silence, the two major characters in the play, Ion and Creusa, will play the role of parrhesiast. But not in the same way: Ion will ask explicitly for this role; and Creusa will play this role without using the word *parrēsia*."

a servant is always there, at the door of the temple. But we must pay attention to the Greek words, which are not very well translated, neither here nor in the French translation. The god says: "The first one you'll meet will be your son." The word, the Greek word is *paida pephukenai*, "will be your son by nature."[17] *Pephukenai*—you recognize the same root as in *phusis*—*phusis*, by nature. So you see, the god didn't give the kind of obscure and ambiguous prophecy that Phoebus often gives to indiscreet people who ask questions. The god's answer is a pure lie. Ion is not *paida pephukenai* for Xuthus. The god is not an ambiguous truth-teller, he is a cheater. And Xuthus, deceived by the god, candidly believes that Ion, this youth he meets when he gets out of the sanctuary, is really by nature his son. And then begins the first significant parrhesiastic scene,* which, I think, can be divided in three parts: one which is devoted to the misunderstanding (from line 517 to line 527); then, the part which is devoted to mistrust;[18] and the third one, which is devoted to political misfortune.[19]

First part, the misunderstanding. Xuthus leaves the temple, sees Ion, and based on the god's response believes that Ion is his son. Full of good cheer, Xuthus approaches him and wants to kiss Ion. And of course Ion, who does not know who he is, and does not know the reason why Xuthus wants to kiss him, Ion does not understand and misinterprets Xuthus's behavior. As any young Greek boy who a man tries to kiss, Ion thinks that Xuthus wants to have sex with him. The Greek words that are used in this passage are very clear: this is the interpretation that Ion takes from Xuthus's behavior. And most commentators, when they are willing to acknowledge this interpretation, say that it is a "comic scene," which sometimes occur in Euripides' tragedies, it is true. But I think that we have to recognize that there is exactly the same type of situation that we saw in the Oedipus myth. You remember that in the story of Oedipus, Oedi-

* The manuscript adds: "Then starts a rather strange discussion between Xuthus who tries in good faith to persuade Ion that he is his son, and Ion who, for some reason, does not feel very comfortable with this alleged filiation (or paternity)."

pus kills Laius who wanted to have sex with him.[20] Here we find the same relation, the same attitude. However, in *Oedipus,* Laius does not know that the youth he desires is his son, and it is by denying what the god has said and through ignorance that this misunderstanding happens and Laius is killed by Oedipus. In *Ion,* you see the same situation, you see that Ion says: "If you go on harassing me, I'll dig my shaft in your chest." His is exactly the same as Oedipus's gesture, but in *Ion* the king, Xuthus, does not know that the youth is not his son, and the boy does not know that the king believes that he is his son. So we are in a world of deception, as a consequence of the god's lies. And you see that the same situation is exactly to the contrary of the Oedipal situation. The reference to Oedipus, I think, is implicit, but very easy to recognize. So that's the first part of this scene, the misunderstanding.

There is a second part of this scene: after the misunderstanding comes mistrust and suspicion. Xuthus tells Ion: "Well, take it easy, if I want to kiss you it is because I am your father." And then Ion, who is so eager to know who is his father, who are his parents, Ion could have been very happy for recovering his family, his father and so on. But in fact he is not, and his first question when Xuthus tells him, "I am your father," his first question is: "Well, who is my mother?"[21] For some obscure reason, his mother is for him a major concern. And he asks: "How could I be your son?" Xuthus answers: "Well, I don't know how you can be my son, I have forgotten to ask the god who is your mother. Well, anyway, you are my son, *anapherō eis ton theon* (I refer to the god, I refer to what the god has said)." Then a very interesting line comes from Ion, one that is, I think, very important and that has been completely mistranslated at least in the French version. When Xuthus said, *anapherō eis ton theon* (I refer to the god), Ion responds, *logōn hapsometh' allōn,* and the French translation reads: "Let's speak about something else," which doesn't mean anything. And the English translation is "to other reasonings rather turn we."[22] It's much closer to the real meaning: *logōn hapsometh' allōn* means "let's now use another kind of *logoi,* of discourses." Xuthus says, "*anapherō eis ton theon,* I refer to the god, I tell you that you are my son because the god has told me that you were," and Ion answers, "Well, it doesn't satisfy me, *logōn hapsometh' allōn*, let's use another kind of words, of *logoi*, which might better be able to tell the truth."

And thus starts another kind of *logoi* which is not the oracular formulation, but which is really an inquiry by questions and answers. Ion as an inquirer asks Xuthus, his alleged father, when and how it was really possible for him to have a child: with whom, when, at which place, how? And this other kind of discourse which is so deeply opposed to the oracular formulation, this method of inquiry is developed by Ion, and Xuthus tries to answer Ion's questions, tries to explain how Ion could be his son, and he explains: "Well, I think that I had sex with a girl.—When?—Well, one day, before I was married with Creusa.—Where?—Maybe it was in Delphi.—But how did it come to pass?—Well, one day I was drunk during a religious feast in honor of Bacchus," and so on. And all that of course is pure baloney, pure hypothesis, but they take very seriously, as best they can, this inquiry, led as they are by the god's lies. All of that is in error, but they move towards truth, they try to get to truth by their own means. If they don't succeed, it's not their own fault, they very seriously try, and they seriously try through the inquisitive method of Ion. And you have the same in *Oedipus*, where you have also this kind of inquiry.[23] So that after this inquiry, Ion accepts rather reluctantly, but accepts the hypothesis, and he accepts to consider himself as Xuthus's son. But he is not very enthusiastic.

Then the third part of this important scene between Xuthus and Ion. In this scene, after the misunderstanding and the mistrust and the inquiry, emerges the problem of the political destiny and misfortune for Ion if he returns to Athens. This problem emerges in lines 563 to 675. Xuthus, having persuaded Ion that he is his son, promises to bring him back to Athens where Ion will be rich and powerful.[24] But Ion is really not very enthusiastic with this prospect, or at least he feels a little uncomfortable, and he is still worried about his mother. Or more precisely, by the fact that he does not know who is his mother. Of course we have to remember here that, following Athenian law at this time, nobody could be a regular citizen without being the son of a father and a mother both born in Athens.* So Ion feels uncomfortable at the idea of returning home as the son of Xuthus who, as you know, is a foreigner in Athens, and as the son of an unknown mother. In this kind of situation, he will be considered as a foreigner himself, as a bastard, and so as being nobody. He will be nobody. He says that in the beginning of his speech.[25] This fear, this anxiety gives way to a long development which at first glance seems to be a digression, or at least something which does not seem directly related to the mother's problem. This digression paints a picture. It is a picture of, first, the political life in a democracy and, then, a picture of life in a monarchy.

First, the picture of the democratic life. In this rather long digression, Ion explains that in a democracy there are three categories of citizens. Some of them are what he calls—following the quite normal political vocabulary of the classic Greek—the *adunatoi*, those who don't have power. They are citizens. They are citizens, but they are *adunatoi*: they don't have power, they are not rich, they are not competent, they are not powerful, they do not exercise power, and they hate anyone who is better than them or who is superior to them. There is another category of citizens, those who are *chrēstoi kai dunamenoi*. That means people who are good by themselves and also who have the aptitude, or the capacity, by birth, of exercising power. But those who are *chrēstoi* and *dunamenoi*, good and powerful, are wise, *sophoi*. And since they are *sophoi*, *sigōsi*. *Sigōsi*, they keep silent. That's the second category. They keep silent and *ou speudousin eis ta pragmata*, and they do not take care, they do not worry about *ta pragmata*, the affairs, that means the political affairs, the affairs of the city. So they keep apart from political life. That's the second category of citizens. And there is another, a third category of citizens, those who are powerful and *logō te kai polei chrōmenoi*. It's rather difficult to translate [the qualities of] those people, because the verb *chrēs-*

* The manuscript adds: "There were discussions in Euripides' time about this legislation which had led to a dangerous decrease in the number of citizens."

thai is so rich in its meaning.[26] Literally, it means the people who use both *logos* and the *polis,* who use reason and the city—well, who take care of the city, take part in the affairs of the city by using *logos* (which means discourse and reason, *logō te kai polei chrōmenoi*). Those are the three categories of citizens, the *adunatoi,* those who are wise enough to keep silent and don't worry about the affairs of the city, and those who rule the city by using *logos.* And then Ion explains that if he arrives in Athens as a foreigner and as a bastard, how will those three categories of citizens react? The first group will hate him. The second group, the wise citizens, will laugh at this young man who would like to become one of the first citizens and take care of the city. And the third group will be jealous of this competitor and will try to get rid of him. So, for these reasons, a return to Athens (characterized as a democracy) does not offer a very bright perspective.[27] After a few lines about family life and life with a stepmother who would not accept his presence, Ion then returns to the political picture, but now that of the monarchy and the life of a monarch. Well, many people imagine that kings have a very pleasant life, but that is not the case; they have a miserable existence, with a lot of enemies, and bad advisers around them.[28]

This digression is rather strange since Ion's dilemma was to learn exactly who was his mother. He had very good reason to be ashamed or to feel uncomfortable returning to Athens without knowing [the identity of] his mother, but this digression and this picture of democratic life and of the king's life, all of that seems a little strange at this moment, in this scene. But I think that there are very good reasons [for it]. The scene continues and Xuthus says: "Well, don't worry about that, you'll come with me as a visitor and not as my son, we won't say anything to Creusa, and we'll manage later on to make of you my heir." So then the scene becomes completely crazy and makes no sense. Ion's dilemma was to return as the real inheritor of a first family in Athens, and what Xuthus proposes to him—to come as a visitor—does not fit with the real wants and needs of Ion. Nonetheless, Ion accepts, and says: "Well, I'll come with you, I'll come with you," and he offers only one more reflection on his status and his problem. He says, "Well, I'll come with you, but in fact life will be impossible for me." He says, "I go: yet to my fortune one thing lacks. For, save I find her who gave life to me, my life is naught." And the Greek word is *abiōton*: "I cannot live, it is impossible for me to live in those conditions, if I don't know who is my mother." And why is it impossible for him to live if he does not know who is his mother? It is that

> If one prayer be vouchsafed,
> Of Athens' daughters may my mother be,
> That by my mother may free speech* be mine.
> The alien who entereth the burg of pure blood,
> Burgher though he be in name,
> Hath not free speech: he bears a bondsman's tongue.[29]

So, you see, Ion needs to know who is his mother in order to gain *parrēsia,* and he explains that someone who comes to the city as a foreigner, even if he is legally considered as a citizen, cannot enjoy *parrēsia.* And what does this digression and this final reference to *parrēsia* mean, exactly at the moment where Ion accepts to come back in Athens under these rather obscure conditions? Well, I think that within this digression—first what Ion has said about democracy and then about tyranny or monarchy—these two pictures and two developments are very easy to recognize. This critique of both democracy and monarchy is typically that of a "parrhesiastic discourse." You could find exactly this same type of discourse in Socrates' mouth a little later on, according either to Xenophon or to Plato. Later on you can find it in Isocrates. This kind of picture of democratic and monarchic life is typically the mark of the parrhesiastic man in the Athenian political scene at the end of the fifth century [and] the beginning of the fourth. Ion is a parrhesiast, he is this kind of man who is so important, who is so valuable in a democracy and in a monarchy, and who explains either to the people or to the king what their life really is. Ion shows that he is the parrhesiastic man in this long digression, and when, after this digression, he says, "Well, I want to

* Foucault can be heard saying, "That's the word *parrēsia,* free speech."

know who is my mother because I need *parrēsia*," he shows that if he is by nature, by his own character, and by his unknown birth a man who is able to be a parrhesiast, he cannot legally or institutionally use this *parrēsia* since he does not know who his mother is. It appears that *parrēsia* is not a right equally given to any citizen, but only to some, who are specially prestigious through their family and through their birth.* And Ion appears as a man who is a parrhesiast, but who is at the same time deprived of the right to *parrēsia*. And why is this parrhesiastic figure deprived of the parrhesiastic right? It is because the prophetic god, the god who must tell the truth to mortals, was not courageous enough to disclose his own faults and to act as a parrhesiast. Ion has the personal quality of a parrhesiastic man, but he does not enjoy the status of the parrhesiastic man and he cannot play this role in Athens. Something more is needed now that we know that Ion is the parrhesiastic man, something more is needed to allow him to use his parrhesiastic nature or quality, and this thing will be brought by the other parrhesiastic figure in the play, that is, Creusa. It is Creusa who will, telling the truth, permit her parrhesiastic son to use his *parrēsia*.**

So now let's turn to the second parrhesiastic character in the play, Creusa. And of course the parrhesiastic role she plays is quite different from Ion's *parrēsia*. Ion is a man, he is someone who must become one of the first citizens in the city, and he must enjoy *parrēsia* as a right, as a privilege, and also as a duty. Creusa is a woman, and she has been the victim of Phoebus, because she has been seduced and then deprived of her son. As a woman and as a victim, she will

* The manuscript adds: "So, throughout the scene, we glimpse the grounds of *parrēsia* as a political right. It is not only legal citizenship; it is something more. It is a kind of personal, familial and social excellence. And we have also an example of what *parrēsia* is, what *parrēsia* must be in the political field."

** The manuscript adds: "Something more is needed for him to play this role: this native relationship to Athens, not only his legal citizenship, but a genealogy which links his existence to the city and to the ground of the city. And this relationship will appear through another parrhesiastic act. But a parrhesiastic act of another kind: the confession of Creusa, confession which is at the same time an accusation against the god."

use *parrēsia* in a different way. She won't use *parrēsia* in order to tell the truth about the political life, she won't use *parrēsia* like Ion in the political framework of institutions, be they monarchic or democratic, she will use *parrēsia* towards the god. [She does so] not in order to give good advice to the Assembly and to rule the city, but in order to complain and to blame Phoebus.

So, how does Creusa's parrhesiastic scene go? Creusa is told by the chorus that Xuthus has found a son. And since Xuthus has found a son, of course that means that Creusa won't find the son she is looking for. It also means that when she returns to Athens, she will have in her home, in her own city, a stepson who comes from elsewhere and who will be the successor or the heir to the kingdom. For those two reasons, she is infuriated. She is infuriated against her husband, not because he might have been unfaithful in sexual matters, but because, as a foreigner, he will have more power inside the city since he has an heir. But she is also infuriated with the god, because the god has seduced her, he has raped her, he has let his son disappear, and now he doesn't offer her any answers. So she has an outburst of anger against the god.

I think that's very interesting because we can compare that [response] with Sophocles' *Oedipus*. In Sophocles, people are led to truth by what? By the god's words, by the fact that the god seems to send them several signs in order to lead them, in spite of themselves, towards the truth, and until they find the truth. In Euripides, people are led to truth by the god's silence or lie, by the fact that they are deceived; when Creusa thinks that Ion is Xuthus's Ion, it's the consequence of the god's lie, and, of course, it's completely false. She is misguided by the god's lies, and in spite of those deceptions, she then goes on and at least a part of the truth will come through her own manner. In Sophocles, the god tells a truth that human beings are not able to perceive. In Euripides, the god lies, and human beings disclose the truth in their emotional reaction to what they think to be true.

When Creusa learns from the choir that Xuthus has been given a son by the god, her bitterness, her anger, and her despair burst forth. After having been raped, after having been deprived of her child, that's really too much for her, and she decides to tell the truth. The truth will be said and will come to light in an emotional reaction to the god's injustice and to the god's lies. Creusa's parrhesiastic scene has two parts, which are completely different from one another in their poetic structure and also in their parrhesiastic form. First there is a long and incredibly beautiful speech. And [second], the other part is what was called the *stichomythia,* a kind of dialogue in which each of the actors says a line, and only one line, one after the other.

First, the speech. At this moment, Creusa is accompanied by an old servant, but who says nothing during this speech. The speech is this kind of *parrēsia* in which somebody publicly blames another for a crime or a deed or an injustice he has committed. This blame is *parrēsia* insofar as the one who is blamed is more powerful than the one who blames him and so may then retaliate and punish him for his accusation. This *parrēsia* is a public reproach, a public critique of someone with whom you have a relation of dependence.*[30] That's this kind of *parrēsia* that Creusa makes in this speech, which is, as you see, given under the sign of keeping silent or telling the truth. Until this moment, Creusa has kept silent about what happened with Phoebus, but since she knows that Phoebus has given Xuthus a son, she then decides to speak:[31]

> My heart, how shall I keep silent?
> But how shall I reveal the secret
> union and lose my sense of shame?
>
> What stands in my way to halt me? With whom am I
> contending for the prize of goodness? Has not my
> husband betrayed me? I am being robbed of my house,
> robbed of children, my hopes are gone. Though I wished
> to achieve these hopes by saying nothing of the rape or
> of my tearful childbirth, I could not. No, by the starry
> seat of Zeus, by the goddess who dwells on my high hill,

* The manuscript adds: "(You can later find the definition of *parrēsia* in the *Rhetorica ad Herennium*)."

and by the lordly shore of Lake Triton's deep waters, I shall no more conceal this union! Lifting this load from my breast I shall feel relief! My eyes run with tears, and my soul is pained by the evil machinations of men and gods. I shall reveal that they are ungrateful betrayers of my bed!

O you that cause the voice
of the seven-stringed lyre to resound, which on the
rustic
lifeless horn echoes forth
the Muses' lovely hymns,
to you, O son of Leto,
by the light of day I utter my reproach!
You came to me with your hair
gold-gleaming as into the folds of my gown
I was plucking flowers of saffron hue
reflecting the golden light.
Seizing me by my pale white wrists
as I cried out "Mother!"
into the cave that was your bed
you took me, divine ravisher,
without pity,
doing what gladdens Cypris' heart.
I, the unblest, bore to you
a son whom, in fear of my mother,
I cast upon your couch
where in sorrow upon a bed of sorrow
you yoked my wretched self.
Ah me! And now he is gone, seized
by creatures of the air for their feast, my son—and
yours, hard-hearted one! Yet you forever with
your lyre
go on playing "O Paian"!
You there, I mean the son of Leto,
who allot your oracles

> to those who come to your golden seat
> and to the earth's midmost resting place!
> To the light of day I make this proclamation:
> Oh, ungrateful lover!
> Though you had no previous favor
> from my husband,
> you gave him a child for his house;
> yet my son
> and yours, unfeeling god, has vanished,
> taken as prey for birds, leaving
> his own mother's swaddling bands behind.
> You are hated by Delos and the shoots
> of laurel that stand beside the palm tree's delicate
> fronds,
> there where in holy childbed
> Leto bore you in the bower sent by Zeus.[32]

I don't know if the translation is good, but anyway the text is incredibly beautiful. That's quite a confession!

Well, I don't want to comment very long on this text. I would like to underline a few points. First, as you see, [the speech] is a kind of public accusation and of public malediction. It's quite clear from the first and last lines, the references to Latona [Leto, in Greek mythology] and so on, all of that is a kind of malediction which is put on the god's head, since, as you know, Phoebus also was a bastard from Latona and Zeus. I would also like to point out that there is a constant and very clear contrast in this speech, in those lines, between Phoebus as the god of light with his golden hair, he is the god of the sun, and he is the god of brightness, [and] he is also—this is the other part of the contrast—the god who has seduced a girl and brought her to the gloom of a cave, where he then seduced and raped her. That's the second point. The third point is that there is an opposition, a constant opposition, between the god who is supposed to tell the truth to human beings and Creusa, who reminds him several times that he is an oracular god. She reminds him also that he has a "seven-voiced lyre"—a lyre with seven chords—she reminds him that he is the god of song, of music, of sound, and of beauty. And, in front of him, what does she do? She cries, and she shouts. There are several places where she indicates very clearly this opposition between the music of the god who is not able to say the truth and Creusa herself who through her cries says the truth and is obliged to say the truth. We have to imagine that those cries, those shouts take place before the temple, at the sanctuary's doors, where it is silent: the doors are closed, nobody speaks, and this voice which is supposed to tell the truth to the world through the Pythia, this voice keeps silent. All the while, Creusa is shouting at the door and tells the truth. And that's the first part of Creusa's parrhesiastic scene.

The second [part of Creusa's parrhesiastic scene] starts when, after this very long speech, the old servant who has heard what Creusa has said begins something which is exactly symmetric to the interrogation we had between Xuthus and Ion.[33] You remember when Ion asked: "How could I be your son, how was it possible, when did this took place?" In the same way, the old servant now asks Creusa to tell her story exactly. In fact, the story was told for the first time in this speech, but in order to have this economy of symmetry in the production of truth, we need an inquiry, which is a typically human way to get the truth. There is an inquiry and the old servant asks questions: how did it happen, when, and so on. As you see, this way of telling the truth by inquiry is the reverse of the oracular way of telling the truth. The oracle is ambiguous, it is obscure, the god never answers a set of precise questions, and the oracle never proceeds in the form of an inquiry. Here, we have an inquiry with questions and answers, and everything becomes quite clear.

The second point that is worthwhile to note is that we have here a self-accusation. In the first part of Creusa's parrhesiastic scene, we had the accusation of the woman against the seducer, against the rapist, an accusation from a human being towards god. Now, it's the self-accusation of Creusa herself: it is a confession, which has exactly the same form as Phaedra's confession in *Hippolytus*, with the same type of need and of reluctance to speak, the same game of questions and answers, and also the same form of indirect avowal. Everybody knows, at least through Racine, that Phaedra in Euripides doesn't herself say: "I love Hippolytus."[34] She manages things in order to let the servant pronounce the name of Hippolytus. In the same way here, Creusa speaks in such a way that the old servant says things, and she doesn't confess completely.

I think that we have here what we could call "personal *parrēsia*" as opposed to political *parrēsia*. Political *parrēsia* was Ion's *parrēsia*, where he shows that he is able, either in a democratic city or in a monarchic or tyrannical regime, to make the useful criticism of the way things were ruled. He shows that he is able to do it, he shows that he has the courage to critique. But something is lacking, he needs still something: he needs a sign which could guarantee that he really has the status of someone who may use *parrēsia*. On the other side, you have the personal parrhesiastic scene, and this personal parrhesiastic scene is Creusa's scene, where she tells the truth not as the political critique of institutions, political life and so on. Instead, she uses *parrēsia* in two ways. First, as the blame, as the reproach of somebody who is weak, who is a woman, who has been raped—somebody who is weak against somebody who is much more powerful than she but who has committed a crime and committed errors. That's the first type of personal *parrēsia*. The other type of personal *parrēsia* is the confession, when somebody tells the truth about himself and discloses the crimes, the faults, the weaknesses and so on, which are her own personal faults or weaknesses. It is the combination of the parrhesiastic figure with Ion and the parrhesiastic discourse of Creusa that makes possible the disclosure of the total truth at the end of the play. Of course, there are a lot of other episodes that I do not have time to explain to you, so at this moment of the play, Creusa has said the truth, but nobody yet knows that this son she had with Phoebus is Ion. In order to put together the parrhesiastic need of Ion and the parrhesiastic discourse of Creusa, there must be a number of other episodes—including a very interesting scene where Creusa, still believing that Ion is Xuthus's son, tries to kill Ion and does not succeed.[35] Again you have a very clear reference to the Oedipus situation. But there it's not the son who wants to kill the father, it is the mother who wants [to kill the son].

In the end, we have the truth, and the truth is guaranteed and authenticated not by Apollo — as I told you in the beginning — but by Athena. This series of truths — from Athens, Erechtheus, Creusa, and Ion — is completed at the end of the play. On the other hand, we have Xuthus, who until the end of the play is not supposed to know the truth, such that when he comes back to Athens, he still believes that Ion is his son. So until the end of the play, he is deceived. And until the end of the play, Phoebus kept silent. So the three series are, I think, quite coherent: silence on the side of Delphi and Phoebus; truth on the side of Athena, Athens, Erechtheus, Creusa, Ion; and deception on the side of the foreigners.

That's what I wanted tell you about *Ion*. Next time, I'll try to turn to some more serious things about *parrēsia* between politics and philosophy, with Plato and Isocrates.

Are there any questions?*

NOVEMBER 7, 1983

LAST TIME I QUOTED SOME of the occurrences of the word *parrēsia* in Euripides.** There is still one other occurrence of the word *parrēsia* in *Orestes,* a play that was written or at least performed in 408 BCE, just a few years before Euripides died, and at a certain moment of political crisis, when there were a lot of debates in Athens

* Amidst the hubbub of people leaving the classroom, Foucault can be heard continuing to talk with a few audience members. Then he announces his subject for the next lecture: Euripides' *Orestes,* Thucydides, Plato's *Seventh Letter,* and Isocrates' "On the Peace." He also asks if people are interested in participating in a research group (*groupe de travail*) on the theme "Subjectivity and Truth," one that would be organized around oral presentations.

** Before beginning the lecture, Foucault comments, "In the first hour, [I'll] read with you the text I just distributed and I'll offer you some interpretations of it. I asked Jim Porter, who is a classicist, who has some very interesting things to say about Euripides and about *Ion*—he has written a very interesting paper about *Ion* from a completely different perspective—to say something about Euripides and about *Ion,* at the end of this first hour. Then we will move on to the political problem [of *parrēsia*]. This text [just distributed] serves as a transition to the political problem of *parrēsia*."

about its institutions and about democratic regimes. This text is interesting, first, because it is the only one where the word *parrēsia* is used by Euripides with an epithet, or pejorative meaning. Before analyzing the political and ideological background of the play and this scene, maybe it's best to read it together.

MESSENGER

When now the Argive gathering was full,
A herald rose and cried: "Who fain would speak
Whether Orestes ought to live or die
For matricide?" Talthybius thereupon
Rose, helper of thy sire when Troy was sacked.
He spake — subservient ever to the strong —
Half-heartedly, extolling thy sire,
But praising not thy brother; intertwined
Fair words and foul — that he laid down a law
Right ill for parents: so was glancing still
With flattering eye upon Aegisthus' friends.
Such is the herald tribe; lightly they skip
To fortune's minion's side: their friend is he
Who in a state hate power and beareth rule.
Next after him prince Diomedes spake,
Thee nor thy brother would he have them slay,
But exile you, of reverence to the Gods.
Then murmured some that good his counsel was;
Some praised it not. Thereafter rose up one
Of tongue unbridled, stout in impudence,
An Argive, yet not Argive, thrust on us:
In bluster and coarse-grained fluency confident,
Still plausible to trap the folk in mischief:
For when an evil heart with winning tongue
Persuades the crowd, ill is it for the state . . .[1]
Thee and Orestes he bade stone to death.
But Tyndareus still prompted him the words
That best told, as he laboured for your death.
To plead against him then another rose,

No dainty presence, but a manful man,
In town and market-circle seldom found,
A yeoman—such as are the land's one stay,—
Yet shrewd in grapple of words, when this he would;
A stainless man, who lived a blameless life.
He moved that they should crown Agamemnon's son
Orestes, since he dared avenge his sire,
Slaying the wicked and the godless wife
Who sapped our strength:—none would take shield on arm,
Or would forsake his home to march to war,
If men's house-warders be seduced the while
By stayers at home, and couches be defiled.
To honest men he seemed to speak right well.[2]

You find the word *parrēsia* in line 905. It is translated by the strange words "coarse-grained fluency." Can somebody give me a translation?

—*Crude speech: to speak well, but crudely.*

—*Facile vulgarity.*

—Okay. This text is the narrative from a messenger about Orestes' trial, since Orestes was put on trial because he killed his mother. The messenger gives a narrative of this trial that starts with a rather precise reference to the Athenian procedure for criminal trials. When everybody is present, the herald rises and cries: *Tis chrēzei legein* (who wants to speak)?[3] That's the Athenian right. Then you will have two orators stand up, and those two people are borrowed from the mythological background of the play, both of them belong to the Homeric world. The first one is Talthybius, who was one of Agamemnon's companions during the war against the Trojans, and more precisely was Agamemnon's herald. And the other is Diomedes, one of the most famous Greek heroes.

The way Talthybius's speech is reported is, I think, very interesting. As you see, Talthybius is characterized as someone who is not completely free. Of course, he is not a slave, but he is not independent, he is dependent on people more powerful than he is. The Greek text says he is *hupo tois dunamenois ōn* (under the power of powerful people).[4] He is a servant, and it's interesting to note that there are two other plays in which Euripides criticized this type of person, that is, the heralds.

In *The Daughters of Troy*[5] you see the same Talthybius who plays a role in this play just after the capture of Troy. Talthybius, as Agamemnon's herald, walks onto the scene and announces to Cassandra that she will become the wife of Agamemnon. Cassandra answers this announcement with some predictions, and, as you know, Cassandra's predictions are always true. Of course, Talthybius does not believe those predictions because Talthybius, as a herald, must say what his master tells him to say, but he does not know the truth, he is not even able to recognize what is true, and so he thinks and says that Cassandra is mad: *Ouk artias echeis phrenas* (your mind is not in the right place).[6] Cassandra answers: "Keen-witted varlet this! Why such fair name have heralds, common loathing of mankind, who are but menials of kings and cities." And she goes on to explain: "Well, you have said that my mother will become Odysseus' slave, but in fact the gods have said that she will die here."[7] You see, the herald is one who cannot know the truth, who is unable to tell the truth, or to recognize the truth, insofar as he is dependent on someone else, that is, on his master.

And in another of Euripides' plays, *The Suppliants,* there is a very interesting discussion between a herald—who has no name, and who comes from Thebes—and Theseus, who is not exactly the king of Athens but the first citizen in Athens.[8] When the herald walks in, he asks, "Who is the king in Athens?" Theseus replies, "Well, you will not be able to find any king, because there is no *turannos* in this city, this city is free, that means that in this city, wealthy and poor people are equal."[9] A discussion then starts, one which is of course a digression, but which is very important, about whether monarchy or democracy, or tyranny or democracy, is the best form of government. The herald praises the tyrannical regime, or at least he makes a very sharp and precise critique of the democratic regime, and Theseus's answer is in praise of the Athenian democracy, in which Theseus explains that, first, laws are written, and second, wealthy and poor people have equal rights and, in the Assembly, in the *ekklesia,* everyone is free to speak. Those who speak can win a good reputation and become the first among the citizens, and the others keep silent. Theseus concludes: "Is there anything more egalitarian than that? Can equality go any further?"[10] That's the English translation. As you see, this democracy is characterized by equality and by the fact that everyone is able to speak. That's the objection that Theseus brings against the herald as a representative of the tyrannical power.

In *Orestes,* Talthybius is one of those heralds who represent the power of somebody else, of those people who are dependent on someone else, and so are not able to tell the truth. Freedom, complete freedom, and the aptitude for telling the truth are synonymous. Because of his dependence on Agamemnon and other people more powerful than him, Talthybius won't speak frankly and clearly. He won't speak clearly, he speaks what the text calls *dichomutha*.[11] *Dichomutha* means those kinds of words that mean two things at the same time—"double-talk." And so you see that in one moment Talthybius praises Agamemnon because he has been the herald of Agamemnon, and he does not want any trouble with those who are on the side of Agamemnon and Orestes. He praises Agamemnon but at the same time he doesn't approve of Orestes either, and since he wants to please everyone in the Assembly, since he is afraid of the hostility of both factions, he speaks those *dichomutha*. Since the most powerful people are those who now rule the city (meaning the supporters of Aegisthus),* in the end, Talthybius proposes the condemnation of Orestes and Electra, and he proposes that Electra and Orestes should be killed. He's the first speaker.

Then comes the second [speaker]. After the one with the negative character comes the positive one, Diomedes, who is also a character in Homeric mythology. In this Homeric mythology, Diomedes was famous among Greek warriors, first because of his courage and then also because of his eloquence—which means both because of his skill in speaking and because of his wisdom. He is the opposite of Talthybius. Diomedes is independent, he says what he thinks, and he proposes a moderate solution: a mild punishment on religious grounds that has no political implication, and is neither a retalia-

* Foucault says "Aegisthus," but Aegisthus has already been killed by Orestes.

tion nor revenge. Orestes must be exiled, according to his opinion, since the country must be purified of the crime by this exile, which is the traditional religious punishment for a murder. It's worth noting, first, that [this act] is not a political retaliation, but rather it has a religious motivation. It's also worth noting that whereas Talthybius was doing his best to please everyone, Diomedes, in spite of the fact that he proposes a very moderate and reasonable verdict, was applauded only by some people, while others disagreed. Extreme opinion gives way to unanimity, and the moderate opinion divides the Assembly. Those are the two first speakers.

After those two mythological figures, we have two other speakers who present themselves. They have no name, they don't belong to the world of legend, and they are not heroes. The messenger who reports the trial gives a very precise description of who they are, and they are what we could call two "social types." The first one, who is symmetric to Talthybius the bad orator and a negative character, is this kind of speaker who is so harmful for democracy. I think that we have to read his traits carefully. The first: "Thereafter rose up one of tongue unbridled, stout in impudence."[12] The English translates as "tongue unbridled" the Greek word *athuroglōssos*. This word is a rather interesting word. *Athuroglōssos* comes from *glōssa, glōtta,* which is the tongue, and *thur[a],* which is the door. *Athuroglōssos* is somebody who has a tongue but not a door. That means that his mouth is always open, and that he is not able to close his mouth.

The metaphor of mouth and lips as a door which is closed when one keeps silent and which is open when one speaks, this metaphor is very frequent in Greek literature. You find this idea of some people who are not able to close their mouth, you find it, for instance, in the poetry of the fifth century, in Theognis, book 1, line 421, where he says that there are a lot of people whose doors for the mouth are not tightly closed.[13] Later on, at the beginning of the second century CE, in a text about chatter (*De garrulitate*), Plutarch says that the teeth are a kind of fence or gate, and when the tongue just passes this limit, the teeth are able to bite the tongue.[14] That's a sign that nature has made things as they should be. In the domain of this metaphor—with tongue and door, lips and tongue, and teeth as doors—the notion of being *athuroglōssos* means having a tongue but not a door, of having also an *athuron stoma,* that means a mouth without a door (this image is also found in Aristophanes), the fact of being characterized by *athurostōmia,* is always a pejorative characteristic. That means that someone does not have a door for his mouth, that he is not able to keep silent, that he is prone to say whatever comes to mind. Plutarch, in the same text, compares this kind of person with the Black Sea, which has neither doors nor gate to separate its water from the Mediterranean [Sea]. All the water from the Black Sea flows to the Mediterranean [Sea] without being retained.[15]

And, as you see, this notion of being *athuroglōssos,* this notion of *athurostōmia,* is very close to the notion of *parrēsia,* but it is the negative version of *parrēsia.*[16] This negative notion of *parrēsia* is, I think, characterized by two things. First, when you are *athuroglōssos,* you cannot make any difference between what must be said and what must be kept in mind without being said. You are not able to make a distinction between the circumstances in which you should speak and the circumstances in which you should keep silent; the *athuroglōssos* is somebody who makes no distinction. You can see, for instance in Theognis, that people who are *athuroglōssos* are not able to make any distinction between good thoughts and bad thoughts, and that they indiscreetly intervene in other people's lives. They make no distinction between their own affairs and other people's affairs. The second important reproach that people put to being *athuroglōssos* is found in Plutarch, and it is of course a much more important reproach. Plutarch says that when you are *athuroglōssos,* it's a sign that you consider that *logos* is *atimotatos,* that is, has no value at all. The people who are *athuroglōssos* don't give any value to *logos,* that is, to discourse, to reason, or to the reasonable discourse through which you can get access to truth.

So as you see, *athurostōmia* is both very close to *parrēsia* and also the exact opposite. It is a sign of wisdom to be able to use *parrēsia* without falling in *athurostōmia.* One of the great challenges for this parrhesiastic personage is to distinguish between what must be said and what must be kept silent, and not everyone, even among the philosophers, is able to make this distinction, and to be parrhesiast without being *athuroglōssos.* We have an example in Plutarch, in the treatise *About the Education of Children*; he retells the anecdote of the philosopher Theocritus, who was a sophist, and he gives him as an example of the wrong *parrēsia*, that is, an example of *athurostōmia*. Theocritus was a philosopher, and the king, Antigonus, sent him a messenger to ask him to come to his court. It so happened that this messenger was the king's cook. And Theocritus was of course a little angry about that. And I don't know if you know Antigonus has lost an eye in a battle, he was one-eyed, and when the cook comes and asks Theocritus to come and to visit Antigonus, Theocritus answers: "Well, I know very well what you want, I know very well that you want to serve me raw to your Cyclops." The "Cyclops" refers to the fact that he, Antigonus, was one-eyed, and "to serve me raw" refers to the fact that the messenger was a cook. And the cook says: "You shall pay the penalty for this reckless talk and madness of yours. You shall pay for this, *dōseis dikēn*, you will pay for this *athurostōmia kai mania*."[17] That is *athurostōmia* and not *parrēsia*; the truly good philosopher is able to use *parrēsia* even towards a king, but in this case it was only *athurostōmia*, because making a joke about the king having only one eye and his messenger being a cook had no philosophical meaning. Without philosophical meaning, then, frankness is not *parrēsia*, it is *athurostōmia*.

Well, that is the meaning of the word *athuroglōssos*. It is also the first characteristic of the third orator in Orestes' trial, who is *athuroglōssos*. Three or four other characteristics also explain the fact that he is *athuroglōssos*.

The translation describes him as: "stout in impudence"; that's the first characteristic after the general state of being *athuroglōssos*. He is *ischuōn thrasei*, which means: *ischuein* denotes someone's strength, *ischuein* is to be strong and, most of the time, to have a kind of physical strength which makes you able to overcome other people in a fight or in a competition. Here you see that this orator is strong, but he is strong *thrasei*, that means not by reason, not by his aptitude for speaking, not by the fact that he is able to tell the truth, but only because he is *thrasus*. That means "bold," "boldness," "arrogance." He is strong only through his boldness.

Second characteristic, which is very important: being "an Argive, yet not an Argive." He is not a regular citizen, he is "Argive, yet not an

Argive." That is, he was not born an Argive, he comes from elsewhere and he has been integrated in the city, he is *ēnagkasmenos,* which means someone who has been by force, violence, or fraud imposed as a member of the city.

The third one is *thorubō pisunos,* "in bluster confident": that means that he is confident in *thorubos.* The word *thorubos* is interesting. *Thorubos* means the sound of the voice, the noise made by a strong voice, by a scream, by a clamor, or by an uproar. When, for instance, soldiers scream in a battle in order to reinforce their own courage or to frighten the enemies, the Greeks use the word *thorubos.* Or when people shout in an assembly, they call it *thorubos.* And you see that this orator is confident not in the articulate language that he could formulate, he is confident only in his ability to produce an emotional reaction in the audience by the fact that his voice is strong, loud, and that he is able to shout. This direct emotional relation between the voice and its effect on the Assembly, that is what is characterized by *thorubos. Thorubos* is opposed to the reasonable meaning of an articulate discourse. It is an inarticulate noise which has some emotional effects on the Assembly.

Finally, the last characteristic of this bad orator. He is in "coarse-grained fluency confident," that is, he is confident in *amathei parrēsia;* and we find again the word *parrēsia.* In a way, this *amathēs parrēsia* is a repetition of the expression *athuroglōssos,* but, I think, with its political implications. That means that this orator, as a citizen—even if he has been imposed by fraud or violence in the city—as a citizen, this orator has *parrēsia,* but he does not use *parrēsia* as he is supposed to. His *parrēsia* is only a formal civic right, and in this case, his *parrēsia* lacks what is necessary to make a good *parrēsia,* a useful *parrēsia,* or a politically positive *parrēsia.* This skill that his *parrēsia* lacks is what is called in the text *mathēsis,* which means learning and knowledge. *Parrēsia,* you see, appears here as something which cannot only be the pure freedom of speech given to anyone who is a citizen. *Parrēsia,* in order to be a good *parrēsia,* in order to have positive effects in the city, must be linked to good education, to intellectual and moral formation, and to a *paideia* or a *mathēsis.* Only in this case will *parrēsia* be something other than pure noise, than *thorubos,* and have some positive effects on the city. When people use *parrēsia* without *mathēsis,* when they use an *amathēs parrēsia,* that leads the city to the worst situations.

You can see in this passage, first, the characterization of a social type of orator: violent, passionate, one who is not born in the city and who is dangerous. You can see also the split between two kinds of *parrēsia.* [There is] the bad one, which is a consequence of the Athenian constitution insofar as *parrēsia* is a right which is given to everybody, at least to everybody who is registered as a citizen. And there is the good *parrēsia* that needs something other than pure legality: the *parrēsia* that needs *mathēsis,* which needs instruction and knowledge. You can see that if the bad *parrēsia* is associated with violence and passion, then the good one is linked with *mathēsis. Mathēsis* prevents *parrēsia* from being pure noise, and when *parrēsia* is linked to this *mathēsis,* then the activity, the verbal activity is something other than simple noise coming from a mouth that is always open,* and with *mathēsis, parrēsia* is something that is able to give to the city the good advice it needs. For instance, remember that in Plato's *Seventh Letter,* Plato explains what Dion intended to accomplish in Syracuse, in Sicily, and how he has been prevented from doing what he wanted to do. Plato gives the reason why Dion was not able to succeed in his enterprise in Sicily. There are two reasons: first, perhaps a god was jealous of him; and second, in Sicily there was *amathia,* and about *amathia* Plato says that it is "the soil in which all ills are rooted and grow to produce in the end a bitter fruit for those who have planted them."**[18]

Well, those are the characteristics of the bad *parrēsia* in *Orestes.* Then we can jump to line 914 that begins with: "Thee and Orestes he bade stone to death." That was the punishment that the bad orator proposed. Those seven preceding lines are an obvious interpolation, even if those lines come from Euripides, but from another play.***

* The manuscript adds: "and which, instead of persuading people through reason, exercises violence upon them."

** The manuscript adds: "(Cf. also about the disastrous effects of *amathia* in politics, *The Laws,* III, 688c)."

*** The manuscript adds: "(But we'll turn back to them afterwards because

We now come to the fourth orator, who is symmetric to Diomedes in the political world. What Diomedes was in the Homeric and heroic world, this last orator is in the political world in the city of Athens—or rather in Argos, but regardless, the scene is clearly in Athens. This orator is opposed to the previous one in the same way as Diomedes was opposed to Talthybius. He is the good parrhesiast. What are his characteristics? The first one is that *morphē ouk euōpos*. That means that he has no physical presence. Second characteristic: he is an *andreios anēr*. That means that he is a courageous man. Of course, we have to recall the etymology of *andreios*: *andreios*, which means "courageous," comes from *anēr*, which means "man"; and to be courageous, as everybody knows, is to have a virile quality; women do not enjoy this quality. This characteristic is important; you'll see why afterwards. Third characteristic: he does not come very often to the city or the *agora*, which is the place where the people assemble, the place for political discussions. This is very important because it means that this good orator, the parrhesiast, is neither that kind of professional politician who spent his life in the *agora*, nor is he the kind of poor person who, having nothing else to live on, comes to the *ekklesia* in order to receive the money given to people taking part in the Assembly. He is somebody who takes part in the Assembly only in important moments and for important decisions. He does not live on politics, for politics, or in the political sites of the city. Fourth characteristic, he is *autourgos*, and this word is translated in English by "he is a yeoman," which is not a bad translation, but not exactly accurate because *autourgos* means that he is somebody who works by himself. He is not only a landowner, but also a landowner who works. The word does not denote the poorest among the peasants, but rather is a special category of landowners who live and work on their own estates with some servants or slaves. It is a social category different from the great landowners and different also from the poorest among the peasants. It is this kind of landowner—those spending most of the time working in the fields

---

they are interesting). Let's also put aside the lines where we see Tyndareus supporting this bad parrhesiast's opinion." Tyndareus, king of Sparta, was the father of Clytemnestra.

and watching over servants—who were depicted and highly praised a little later on by Xenophon in the *Economics*.[19] What's most interesting in this text is that Euripides underlines the political competence and the political ability of this kind of person. As you see from the text, he gives two characteristics of this political ability of those *autourgoi*, of those people who work, and so of those who work by themselves with their servants on their estate. Those two aspects are, first, they are always willing to fight for the city, and they do it better than anyone else. Euripides, of course, does not give any explanation for why those people are better soldiers than any others in the city. But if we refer to Xenophon and to the *Economics* where this category of *autourgoi* is described, then you see the reason: the shopkeepers and people living in the city don't care about what's going on in the country, and if the enemy comes and pillages the country, they do not worry because it is not their own property. On the contrary, the landowners are, of course, very much interested in the defense, in the protection of the land, of the country, and that's the reason why they are good fighters. People who work as farmers cannot tolerate that their enemies pillage the farms, burn the crops, kill the flocks and so on, and that's the reason why they are good soldiers. You find this explanation in Xenophon. But you can also see in this text that those *autourgoi* are able to use words and to propose good advice to the city. And I think also that you can find in Xenophon, in the same text, at the end of the *Economics*, the reason for that.[20] Xenophon explains that landowners are used to talking to their servants, to talking to people, to giving orders, to making decisions about what is to be done in different circumstances of life, and so on. They are good soldiers, but they are also good leaders,* and that's the reason why they, following Xenophon, should get the major responsibilities in the city. Anyway, you see very well that those people, when they speak in the *ekklesia*—where they rarely go, and only in important circumstances—when they speak in this Assembly, they don't make noise, they don't use *thorubos*. What they say is impor-

* The manuscript adds: "And that's the reason why they do not trust the *thorubos*, the noise they make with their mouths. They are able to use *logoi*."

tant, is reasonable, and they are able to propose good initiatives and good advice for the city. The last characteristic of this good orator is that he has moral qualities and that his life is without any fault. You find that: "A stainless man, who lived a blameless life."[21]

The last point about this last orator is this one. I think that we have to pay attention to the reason this yeoman, this landowner gives for his opinion. Whereas the previous orator wanted Orestes to be put to death, this orator asks for Orestes not only an acquittal, but also a reward. And I think that request has two aspects. First, in this scene, it is quite clear that the problem of Orestes' trial is the problem of peace and war: shall the decision be an aggressive decision which will initiate the continuation of war or shall we have the peace? And of course the proposal for an acquittal is something that symbolized the will for the peace. But more precisely, he says that Orestes deserves a reward because he has killed Clytemnestra, Clytemnestra who, during the war, infamously took a lover and betrayed her husband. It is quite clear that the dilemma here is the war between Athens and Sparta, the problem of the soldiers who couldn't stay away from their homes during [the length of combat], a problem which is clearly referenced in this intervention by this orator.*

WE CAN NOW SEE OR explain the context for this scene. The historical and political references are, I think, very precise. We are in 408 BCE. There is a competition between Athens and Sparta [that] was at this moment still very pointed and hard. The two cities have been fighting for long years with very short periods of truce, and in 408, Athens, after several defeats, has recovered a part of its power, at least on the sea, but on the continent the situation was not good and Sparta was able to threaten Athens. Sparta had made several peace offers to Athens, and there were at this moment very pointed discussions in Athens about making peace or going on with the war.

* The manuscript adds: "This argumentation may seem a little too prosaic and matter of fact. But it is a very [good] indication of the political context of this parrhesiastic scene."

The fact was that the democratic faction in Athens was, and had always been, in favor of war, and the aristocratic faction was in favor of peace. The democratic faction favored war for economic reasons which are quite clear: the democratic faction was supported by shopkeepers and people who were interested in the imperialistic expansion of Athens.* On the contrary, the conservative faction was supported by landowners who were much more interested in a peaceful situation with Sparta, and who also wanted to give Athens a kind of constitution rather close to the Spartan constitution. The leader of the democratic faction was Cleophon. Cleophon was not born as an Athenian, was said to have been fraudulently registered as a citizen, and was a very skillful orator, very influential, one who was always portrayed by his contemporaries as infamous in his own life. Cleophon was not courageous enough to become a soldier and played a passive role in sexual relations with other men. You can recognize this exact portrait of Cleophon in this text by Euripides. All the characteristics of Cleophon are present here. On the other side, the conservative faction favored peace with Sparta, and Sparta had for a leader someone named Theramenes. Theramenes wanted a change in the constitution of Athens, and following his proposition the primary civil and political rights would have been reserved to some landowners. That is precisely the good orator in this text. You see that this discussion between Cleophon and Theramenes, between the democratic and the conservative factions, about peace and war and about the Athenian constitution, is clearly present [in the background of this text].

But from the point of view of the history of *parrēsia,* I think that

* The manuscript adds: "The democratic party was in favor of war for political and economical reasons: in Athens, democracy and imperialism were linked because people in the town (shopkeepers and so on) were much more interested in broad trade activity than in farming, and because imperialism meant money, money which was given by the city to citizens to take part in the Assembly.

So the war faction in Athens was also the democratic faction; and this faction favored a constitution where every citizen could vote, could take part in decisions, could give his opinion and so on."

this text is very interesting. As you remember maybe, in *Ion,* which was written ten years before, in 418, *parrēsia* was presented as a positive value; it was a kind of freedom and of privilege that someone like Ion, one who could be among the first and the best citizens in the city, wanted to enjoy. The problem was that in order to give Ion his parrhesiastic role, the truth about his birth had to be disclosed. And since the god didn't want to reveal this truth, Creusa had to say what happened, in a parrhesiastic scene with an accusation against the god and with a self-accusation, or confession. *Parrēsia* has to be established, it has to be grounded in the game between gods and men.

Here you see very clearly that the problem lies within the schema of *parrēsia,* within the schema of the human parrhesiastic roles, and that there is a split between the good one and the bad *parrēsia.* We can see that this crisis in the parrhesiastic function has two major aspects. One is the problem of who is entitled to use *parrēsia*: is it enough to accept *parrēsia* as a civil right, and to accept that any citizen can use this *parrēsia* if he wants and when he wants? Or shall we ask for other criteria, shall we say that *parrēsia* should be exclusively granted to some citizens, according to their status or their personal qualities? That's the first question. It is this discrepancy between the egalitarian system which gives *parrēsia* to everybody and the necessity of choosing among the citizens the ones who are able, through their personal qualities or their economic status or social status, to use *parrēsia* for the interest of the city. That's the first problem of this crisis of *parrēsia.* The second problem is this one: [We] can see that the concern about *parrēsia* has to do with the problem of *mathēsis,* of knowledge and education. *Parrēsia* is no longer considered as an activity which by itself is able to disclose the truth. *Parrēsia,* or people who pretend to use *parrēsia* have a certain relation with truth, one that is different from pure frankness or pure courage. This relation to truth has to be established in education, or more generally through personal formation.

Now I think that you can see what is this crisis in *parrēsia.*[22] I think that in few words we could say that it is the problem of truth, the problem of who is able to tell the truth in the field of democracy, in the field of an institutional system where everybody is equally entitled to exercise power and to give his opinion. Truth, democracy, and education, these are the main features of this crisis. We could say that Athens, at the end of the fifth century, experienced this *parrēsia*-crisis at the intersection between an interrogation about democracy and an interrogation about truth. On the one hand, democracy as an institutional system of equality is not able by itself to determine who should have the right and the aptitude for telling the truth. [On the other hand], *parrēsia* as a verbal activity through which one says frankly and courageously what he has in mind, this *parrēsia* as pure frankness is not sufficient to disclose truth. That is, I think, the new problematization of the *parrēsia*: it's not only the need to get access, in spite of the silence of the gods, to *parrēsia*, it's now the problematization of *parrēsia* as a problematic relation between freedom, power, and truth in Athens at the end of the fifth century. I don't mean that the notion of *parrēsia* appears at this moment, I don't mean that people didn't have any idea of freedom of speech before then. What I mean is that at this moment you find a new kind of problematization of the relation between truth, verbal activity, freedom, power, and political institutions.*

I insist on this point for at least one methodological reason. I would like to make a distinction between what we could call the history of ideas and the history of thought. Most of the time, historians of ideas try to determine when an idea appears, and they often identify this moment through the new appearance of a word. But what I am trying to do with the history of thought is something different. It is to analyze the way things, practices, habits, behaviors, become a problem for people who behave precisely this way, who have these kinds of habits, who use these kinds of practices, and put

* The manuscript adds: "And this problematization has been the cradle of some of the major questions of western philosophy.

Tangential remark which may be of some methodological interest:

What I am trying to do is not a history (or even the sketch of a history) of the concept of *parrēsia*. I am trying to show you that the concept of *parrēsia* (and supporting concepts of liberty, equality, truth, frankness, courage) were problematized at a certain moment."

to work these kinds of institutions. That's the difference between the history of ideas and the history of thought. The history of ideas is the analysis of a notion from its birth through its development, and in the context of other notions which constitute its context.[23] The history of thought has to be, I think, something else. It is the analysis of the way a field of experience and a set of practices—which were accepted without any problem, which were familiar and silent, or at least beyond discussion—become an issue and raise discussions, debates, and incite new reactions, and so induce a crisis in habits, in practices, and in institutions. The history of thought—understood in this way and clearly distinct from the history of ideas—is the history of the way people take care of something, the way they worry about this or that, maybe madness, crime, sex, or about themselves, or about truth. And I think that when the word *parrēsia* appears at the end of the fifth century, and through the texts I have just read today, all that is not a sign that freedom of speech was discovered as an idea or as a value at this moment. It is a sign of a new form of problematization of this freedom of speech in Athens, it is a new way for taking care and asking questions about the relations between truth, freedom, political power, and verbal activity.

That's it for this text. Are there any questions?

—*How does one stabilize the history of thought in relation to the history of institutions? Within these institutions, is there a change corresponding to this crisis of parrēsia?*

—Well, I don't think that there is any evolution in the institutions at this moment. There have been [such changes] of course, but it's not to those changes that these texts refer. You see, the Cleisthenian constitution of Athens was still in force at this moment. There had been a sort of antidemocratic constitution for some years during the tyranny of the Thirty, but Athens came back to the old democratic constitution.[24] The problem here is not a problem of institutions, but one of the *use* of these institutions. Is it possible in the framework of the old Cleisthenian constitution to determine and to make a good use of *parrēsia*, or shall we have to change the laws, change the constitution, change the *politeia* in order to determine institutionally the people who deserve to be listened to by the Assembly? So, you see, it is a new problematization, it's not a change in the institutions. Anyway, it happens sometimes that a change in the institutions is the consequence of a new problematization. It happens sometimes that there is a change in the institutions before a clearer and more explicit problematization. But I think that the history of a problematization is neither the history of an institution nor the history of the ideas. For instance, this is quite clear in the case of the penal system at the end of the eighteenth century: you have a dramatic change in the problematization of the penal system twenty to thirty years before the change in the institutions. If you take the nineteenth century, you find that the new penal system was put in place and after that there was a new problematization of those institutions without any change. Institutional change took place before and after two types of problematization. That was the reason why, I think, that there is a place in my historical field for what I call history of thought understood as the history of problematizations, distinct from institutions and ideas.[25]

—*Simply put, why does the text of Euripides exemplify the problematization of thought in Greece? Why choose this text?*

—There is a very simple and clear answer which is that for the ancient world we work on a finite corpus of texts . . . But that's not exactly the answer [I would like give].* What I would like to answer is that nobody, even if he is *athuroglossōs*, nobody speaks to say nothing. Verbal activity is always in answer to a certain situation. I think that the idea that literary, philosophical, theoretical texts are nothing other than the expression or the translation of a context is deeply wrong. If you speak about something, the reason is that you want to play a certain game in this context. And I think that if you read this text, of course there are several possible readings, but there is one reading that is unavoidable: it is the reading from the point of view of its then-contemporary references. You cannot read this description of the trial [of Orestes] without recognizing on one side Cleophon, and on the other side Theramenes. So the problem is: what did Euripides have in mind, what game did he want to play when

* Conjecture: this passage was inaudible.

he superimposes on Orestes' legend and play those very clear references to Euripides' contemporary situation? And, I think, it's not a question of choice; I didn't choose to exemplify what I wanted to say by this text, I cannot read this text without having the possibility of referring it clearly to a certain context. No? I'm afraid you are not satisfied by my answer.

—*You've obviously given a great, excellent explication of* parrēsia, *but recently, in your last remarks, you've also tied* parrēsia *to a whole sequence of other concepts, and I'm wondering how you're using those words, and namely power: are you using it in the Greek sense of* kratos, *or do you mean something else?*

—I am referring to the problem that, I think, has been a permanent problem, and very clearly formulated in Xenophon, in Plato, in Aristotle, when they define the political problem as the problem of the relations between people who govern and people who are governed. This relation between governing and governed people is, I think, a main feature of political interrogations in Greece.

—*What do you mean to say when you speak about education in the text of Euripides that you've selected? To what extent do you mean* paideia?

—Well, I think that the appearance of the word *amathēs* there [is important], that is, the reference to *mathēsis* as something which is necessary for *parrēsia* because *parrēsia* by itself is not sufficient. I think that, with that [reference], you see that the problem is the very contemporary problem of sophistry, Socrates and so on, it is this problem of *mathēsis*. How can the parrhesiastic mode of language be related to *mathēsis*, and by which kind of formation, or education? If you refer to this text, it seems more likely that it means this kind of experience a landowner can get through his own life. I don't think it refers to the Socratic or Platonic conception of *mathēsis*. But he is somebody whose *parrēsia* is not only a *thorubos* but a thing which has *mathēsis*.

—*A question about the history of thought. Do these crises of thoughts and* parrēsia *only take place or should one only look for them among intellectuals, high culture, artists, and experts, or do they come from a broader cross-section within society?*

—Well, that's a good question, but I think that we can't give a uniform answer. In some times, for some questions, you find this problematization in very small elitist circles, and in some other cases, you find it more widespread, and so on. So the problem is to determine in which circle, in which social field arises this problematization; it happens very rarely that it is a general problematization recognized as such by everybody. But sometimes that happens.

—*I would like to understand more clearly the relationship between* parrēsia *and truth. When you first introduced it, it seemed to me that you thought that truth was part of the notion of* parrēsia, *and that what the person says has to be true. Now it is beginning to look like sometimes a person can engage in* parrēsia *and say something that isn't true. Is that right?*

—Yes but with only one small qualification. For instance in *Ion,* when Ion speaks about *parrēsia,* and when he needs *parrēsia,* it is a kind of right that the first rank of citizens can use. When they use this *parrēsia,* they both say what they think and it is true because they are good people, because they are well-born, because they have a certain kind of relation to the city, to the law, and to truth. So there is no problematization of the relation to truth inside this first description of *parrēsia.* But here, you see very clearly that this problematization now bears on two points: first, the problem of equality, and then the problem of the relation to truth. *Parrēsia* by itself is not sufficient, and, of course, it is related to the problem of equality, since if any citizens, even the worst, are able to use *parrēsia,* you cannot expect them to tell the truth. So you have to ask those two questions: Who, socially, politically, institutionally, will be entitled to use *parrēsia*? And under which conditions can we be sure that somebody will tell the truth when he uses *parrēsia*? Those are the two points.

—*I see, so it sounds as though there is some connection between the degree to which a person is likely to be telling the truth and his situation in the society.*

—That's it. You can see it very clearly here when Euripides gives the different criteria that characterize somebody who uses the good *parrēsia.* First, it is a social status, it's a way of life; and it's also a personal virtue.

—*What about last week, Phoebus said some things which were not entirely true but were also not false. And as I recall, the oracle told the husband that he had a natural son . . .*

—That was a pure lie! He uses the word *pephukenai*.[26]

—*But this person who told this lie was of moderately good heritage . . .*[27]

—He was a god! In *Ion*, the god, the god who is entitled to tell the truth to humans, to human beings, didn't tell the truth.

—*And how would you explain this in terms of your view that a person's position in a society has an effect on . . . ?*

—My point of view? It is the fact that in this play, *Ion*, Athens appears to be the place, the city, which has institutions and which is protected by a goddess, Athena, who tells the truth. There you can find it. But in Delphi, which for some political reasons was in a kind of contest with Athens (there were a lot of political problems between Athens and Delphi and the priests in Delphi), Phoebus was represented as someone who didn't tell the truth in this story which was the story of the foundation of Athens. You cannot, of course, put that in the form of a systematic philosophy. We are in the political world, and at a certain moment Euripides gives us a representation of *parrēsia* in which Phoebus is not able to use *parrēsia*, and the Athenians can. Here the opposition is not between Phoebus and Athena, it is not between Delphi and Athens, it is between two people in the city of Athens.

—*In your first lecture, you described the etymology of the word* parrēsia *and said that it meant originally to say everything . . .*

—That's right. That's the etymological structure. It never really meant "to say everything."

—*I would be interested in a further explication of that etymology . . .*

—Sometimes you find the word *parrēsia* used with a pejorative meaning, and also, in the early Christian literature, *parrēsia* has the meaning of "to say everything you have in mind."

—*But specifically, given the pejorative function of a word which seems to mean exactly "to say everything," the definition for* parrēsia *now seems to be that we should say something which is good for the state, that is, there's an element of intentionality as well as a functionality in the con-*

cept. Is that idea of intentionality and functionality implicit in the term as you originally described it? Or is that now a function of the crisis that you're describing?

—You are quite right to raise this question. In the Athenian constitution, since Cleisthenes, there was the problem of *isonomia,* which is the fact that everybody was equal before the law; the problem of *isēgoria,* which was the legal right given to everybody to give his own opinion; and there was the *parrēsia.* The difference between the first two characteristics [of political life] and this third one is that the two first characteristics can be rather clearly defined in terms of institutions. *Parrēsia*—as the freedom to speak and to be sure that you won't be punished or that there will be no retaliation against you whatever you say—that had no clear and definite correlation in the Athenian constitution. There was no law protecting the parrhesiast speaking the truth, and I would like to insist on this point a little later on, the problem of the relation between *nomos* and truth, and *alētheia*: how is it possible to give a legal form to something which has to relate to truth? There is no law for the truth, or no law in the legal meaning of the word. There are formal laws of truth, but there are no social, political, institutional laws. So that that was a problem.

—*Can you tell us where* amathēs *appears in the text?*

—*Amathēs*? It can be found at line 905, in the form *kamathei,* which is a crasis for *kai amathēs: pisunos thorubō te kai amathei parrēsia.*

—*I'm a little confused in a way about the distinction that's being drawn between the way* parrēsia *was used earlier and the way it was later. It seems as though the earlier characterization was that the act of speaking with* parrēsia *couldn't be dissociated from truth because there was this guarantee based on the social status or other sorts of qualifications of the person who's speaking. And it seems that the same thing is still true, except that a tension arises because now there's this notion of speaking which includes both the people who have those guarantees and other people who don't. So there's almost a redefinition of* parrēsia. *It sounds to me as though what you're saying is that what you have is that the substantive notion of* parrēsia *from earlier that is tied up with that back-*

ground and also with the formal demands of Athenian democracy, that everyone has an equal right to speak, there's a tension between the formal equality and the substantive notion. And I wanted to ask, (1) is that a reasonable characterization of how you see the tension?, and (2) why at that particular point in this history does that tension arise?

—Yes, I think that the way you characterize the tension—between formal equality and the problem of truth and of who is able to tell the truth—is good. The reason why at this moment? I think that we should look at the political background for this. This Cleisthenian constitution in Athens worked for several years, and with Pericles I think that they found a kind of equilibrium in which everybody had the feeling that all citizens were entitled to speak, to give their advice, and so on. In fact, Pericles, as the first among citizens, ruled Athens like, not exactly a monarchy, but maybe an aristocracy or something like that. If you read the discourses in Thucydides, and the second discourse of Pericles on the war of Peloponnese, well, Pericles is attacked by some people.[28] He is criticized for the way [that the war had been decided],* and he says: "Well, everybody has spoken now, you have said everything you want, but now I come, as the first citizen, and I will tell you what I have to say. And you and I face the same danger, we have taken some risks, we were right to take those risks," and so on. But I think that you have there an image of good *parrēsia*, well, of this tension between the good one and between people, the citizens who wanted to give their opinion; they recognize in Pericles someone who could tell them the truth and help them to make good decisions. After several defeats, after the disaster of Sicily, and so on, there were a lot of critics in Athens coming from the aristocratic faction and they blamed the democratic system for the defeat. There were a lot of political struggles, but from the end of the fifth century to Alexander, to the end of the democratic freedom in Greece, I think that the principal political struggle was always between aristocratic and democratic factions. The problem of who is entitled to tell the truth and to make a deci-

* Foucault doesn't finish this clause, so this phrase is conjectural.

sion in the city,* you can find it from this text, from Xenophon, Plato, Isocrates, Demosthenes, and so on.[29]

—There's something that strikes me about the notion of the space where one speaks and the space in the city: that the person who "speaks with an open gate" lives only in the city, while the one who is able to speak with a closed gate, basically, has to live outside the city. This suggests then that it's impossible to acquire privacy in the city because you have to be outside the city to both believe in the city and also to have the right distance from it so that you don't have to speak all the time. So there's a stigma, or danger, to the city.

—Yes, the danger of the city. And Greek culture has very often been pictured as a culture in which *logos* was very highly praised. Yes, sure. But silence too, and if I have time, I would like to show you how it was important from this point of view of *parrēsia*—from the distinction between *athurostōmia* and *parrēsia*—to teach children to keep silent, and to decide when was the good *kairos,* the good occasion, the good opportunity to speak and when it was the *kairos,* the opportunity to keep silent. This distrust against *agora* is very clear in this text. The *agora,* which is always pictured as the symbolic place of Greek civilization, is pictured here with negative characteristics: "We have to go to the *agora* sometimes, but please don't live in the *agora,* don't spend your time speaking, discussing, and so on." This distrust of the *agora* is something very, very interesting, and is constant, at least for a certain trend of opinion.

—I think this is the first time that the suburbs are enjoined to be an important aspect of the city. You can't really have the city without the suburbs.

—That's because the city was nothing at the beginning other than the landowners, the community of the landowners. They met sometimes in the city, but of course with the development of the city, the shopkeepers and so on, it was much easier for the shopkeepers to close their shops and run to the *agora* than the landowners. Of course in the democratic institutions it was very important to know who had time to go to the *agora* and who had no time to do that.

* Some words here are inaudible.

—*In any democratic polity there always exists the potential tension between truth and free or frank speech. The evil hearts can always potentially have winning tongues in a democratic society. So isn't the transformation of* parrēsia *that you're talking about somewhat a rephrasing of the tension between, say, speaking well in a democracy and speaking the truth? That there is that inherent tension, and that* parrēsia *originally has a notion of aristocratic virtue around speaking well, whereas now, in a democracy, it's more about speaking frankly.*

—Yes, you are right to raise the question of speaking well, because I think that, for instance in the Homeric text, as far as I remember, when there are references to Diomedes as somebody who was eloquent and spoke well, it meant that he tells the truth. The difference between speaking well and telling the truth is something which becomes very clear with the appearance of rhetoric. Thus, my intention was to speak about that, but not now. So there are two problems of *parrēsia*, the problem of *nomos* and equality and the problem of rhetoric and the formal rules for speaking.*

NOVEMBER 14, 1983

TODAY I WOULD LIKE, FIRST, to complete very briefly what we said last time about *parrēsia* and the crisis of democratic institutions, and then move to the analysis of another form of *parrēsia*, to another context of the parrhesiastic attitude. By this I mean the field of personal relations to oneself and to others, *parrēsia* in the care of the self.**

First and very shortly, a few words about some aspects of the parrhesiastic crisis in the political institutions in the fourth century,

* At the end of the first lecture hour, classicist James Porter gives a presentation on *Ion*.

** Before beginning his lecture, Foucault asks audience members if they know the book by Giuseppe Scarpat, *Parrhesia greca, parrhesia cristiana* (Brescia: Paideia, 2001 [1964]). He comments that it is "a rather good book, with a lot of references, but very few things about the political background and nearly nothing about the role of *parrēsia* in spiritual guidance, but a lot of good references about early Christianity, *parrēsia* in the New Testament."

only in order to complete what I said last time. The representation of bad *parrēsia* we encountered, for instance, in Euripides' *Orestes*, this representation of bad *parrēsia* and the critique of people who make bad use of *parrēsia*, all that was a commonplace in the Greek political thought following the Peloponnesian War. More precisely, the debate was about the relation between *parrēsia* and democratic institutions.* And the problem was the following, very roughly put. On the one side, democracy is a *politeia*, a constitution, where the *demos*, the people exercise power, and where everybody is equal before the law. But isn't it a fact that such a constitution is condemned to give place to any kind of *parrēsia*, even to the worst? And, on the other side, since *parrēsia* is given even to the worst citizens, isn't it a fact that this *parrēsia* becomes a danger for the city and for the democracy itself, since the overwhelming influence of bad orators leads necessarily to tyranny? You may notice that the problem is very simple and it sounds to us rather familiar, but I think that the discovery of this problem—this kind of necessary antinomy between *parrēsia*, freedom of speech, the relation to truth and democratic institutions—I think that the discovery of this problem, the dangerous relations between democracy, *logos*, freedom, and truth, was the point of departure for a very long and impassioned debate and discussion.

Of course we must take into account the fact that we know one side of the discussion much better than the other for the very simple reason that most of the texts which have been preserved from this period come from writers more or less directly acquainted with the aristocratic faction, or the texts come from writers at least distrustful of radically democratic institutions. I would like only to quote three of those texts as examples of this problem of *parrēsia* in the field of democratic institutions.

The first text I would like to quote is borrowed from an ultra-conservative, ultra-aristocratic lampoon that was written during the second half of the fifth century. For a very long time, this text,

* The manuscript specifies: "between democracy and *parrēsia*."

this lampoon has been attributed to Xenophon, but everybody now agrees that this attribution was not correct, and the Anglo-Saxon or Anglo-American scholars have a very nice nickname for the unnamed author of this lampoon: they called him the "Old Oligarch."* And the text must come from one of those aristocratic circles or clubs which were so active in Athens at the end of the fifth century, and which were very influential in the antidemocratic revolution that follows the defeat in the Peloponnesian War. Anyway, the lampoon takes the form of a paradoxical eulogy which was a genre very familiar to the Greeks. It is a paradoxical praise of the Athenian constitution. The speaker is supposed to be an Athenian democrat, and this Athenian democrat picks up some of the most obvious imperfections, shortcomings, failures, blemishes, and so on, of Athenian institutions and political life, and he presents them as if they had the most positive consequences. The text is without any literary value, but it is much more aggressive than really witty. But the main thesis that is at the root of all the critiques found in this text is interesting and, I think, significant for this kind of radically aristocratic attitude. The thesis is this: It is that the *demos*, the people, are the most numerous; since they are the most numerous, they can't be the best among the citizens; and so there is necessarily a contradiction between the *demos* and the *polis*. What is good for the *demos* cannot be good for the city, for the *polis*, because the *demos* is constituted of the most numerous people in the city, and that means that it is constituted of the worst people in the city. With this general principle as background, the author of this lampoon gives paradoxical praise of Athenian institutions, and there is a rather long passage—the lampoon by itself is rather short—about *parrēsia*. It is a kind of caricature of the parrhesiastic game in Athenian institutions:

> Someone might say that they ought not to let everyone speak on equal terms and serve on the council, but rather just the cleverest and finest. Yet their policy is also excellent in this very point of

* Foucault mistakenly refers to the "Old Aristocrat."

> allowing even the worst people to speak. For if the good men were to speak and make policy, it would be splendid for the likes of themselves but not so for the men of the people. But, as things are, any wretch who wants to can stand up and obtain what is good for him and the likes of himself.
>
> Someone might say, 'What good would such a man propose for himself and the people?' But they know that this man's ignorance, baseness, and favor are more profitable than the good man's virtue, wisdom, and ill will. A city would not be the best on the basis of such a way of life, but the democracy would be best preserved that way. For the people do not want a good government under which they themselves are slaves; they want to be free and to rule. Bad government is of little concern to them. What you consider bad government is the very source of the people's strength and freedom.
>
> If it is good government you seek, you will first observe the cleverest men establishing the laws in their own interest. Then the good men will punish the bad; they will make policy for the city and not allow madmen to participate or to speak their minds or to meet in assembly. As a result of these excellent measures the people would swiftly fall into slavery.[1]

Are there any questions about this text? Now I would like to switch to another text which represents a much more moderate position. It's the position of a semi-aristocrat or a semi-democrat. It's a text written by Isocrates in the middle of the fourth century, and Isocrates refers several times to the notion of *parrēsia* and to the parrhesiastic problem, and that's the case, for instance, in the beginning of his great speech "About the Peace," this great speech which he wrote in the middle of the fourth century, in 355 BCE. At the beginning of this text, Isocrates first contrasts very clearly the Athenian people's attitude in private business, in private life, and [their attitude] in public life and in political activity. In their private life, says Isocrates, the Athenian people show themselves very eager to take advice from some people whom they know to be reasonable, clever, well educated, and able to tell them the truth. For instance, they would never choose as a personal adviser a drunkard. But they do exactly the contrary, says Isocrates, when they deal with public affairs. They welcome as speakers or leaders the worst people they can find and they agree with whatever those people say.[2] That's the first point.

The second is this one. There is something which is much more dangerous than that. Not only do Athenians listen to those bad leaders, they are not even willing to listen to others, to the good ones. They even deny the good orator the possibility of speaking and the right to speak. And Isocrates writes: "I observe that you do not hear with equal favor the speakers who address you, but that, while you give your attention to some, in the case of the others, you do not suffer their voice to be heard. . . . you have formed the habit of driving all the orators from the platform except those who support your desires."[3] And I think that's important. You see that the difference between the good and the bad speaker is not or at least is not primarily the fact that one gives good advice and the other bad advice, but the difference lies in this: that the bad ones, the bad orators, who are accepted by people, the bad orators say only what people are willing to hear. They do nothing else than to formulate, to speak aloud and make an articulated case about what the people desire. They are what Isocrates called the "flatterers." But the good orator is, on the contrary, the orator who is able and who is courageous enough to oppose the *dēmos*' desires. So you see, the first criterion that distinguishes the bad and the good orator is not the fact that one gives good advice and the other bad advice, it is the fact that one conforms with the *dēmos*' desires and the other has a critical role, a pedagogical role. He is in contradiction, he is essentially in contradiction with the *dēmos*' desire, his role is to transform the city's will or the citizens' will, since he targets the city's interest.

This contradiction between the citizens' will, the *dēmos*' will, and the interest of the city is something that is, I think, basic in this critique of *parrēsia* and Athenian institutions. Hence Isocrates draws the conclusion that in contemporary Athens, since it is not possible to be heard, to be listened to by the people if you don't repeat back to them their desires, well, in such a situation there is democracy, which is a good thing, but there is no *parrēsia* since *parrēsia* consists in the attitude which confronts the *dēmos'* will or desire. In this text he says that only some people are able to use *parrēsia* and are accepted as parrhesiast, and they are the authors of comedies or playwrights. As you see, Isocrates gives the word *parrēsia* a positive meaning, a meaning of courageous and free speech, which is able to tell the truth and to criticize, correct, and reform the people's opinion, the people's desires, and the people's will. So you see, you have a positive definition of democracy, a positive definition of *parrēsia,* but you also have the affirmation that democracy exists but that *parrēsia* cannot exist.[4]

In another text that can be compared with this one, Isocrates makes another distinction, he presents the things in a way which is rather different, but which, I think, is compatible with this general idea of the incompatibility of a real democracy and a real *parrēsia.* This other text is to be found in the *Areopagiticus,* where Isocrates compares the old Solonic and Cleisthenian constitution to contemporary political life. He praises the old Athenian constitution on the ground that this old constitution has given to Athens *demokratia* (democracy), *eleutheria* (freedom), *isonomia* (equality before the law), and *eudaimonia* (that is, happiness of the city and of the people in the city). But in the present time all of these primary features of the old Athenian institutions have been perverted, and he explains that *demokratia,* democracy has now become what he calls *akolasia.* And *akolasia* is an ethical word, a moral word, a word borrowed from moral vocabulary and which means "debauchery" or the *relâchement des mœurs, mœurs relâchées* (loose moral values); *akolasia* is regularly opposed to *sōphrosynē,* it is the contrary of *sōphrosynē.**

That does not mean that someone is not punished, that he does not punish himself, that he does not control himself, [that there is a] lack of self-control in the moral field. He is not repressed and he

* Foucault speaks these phrases in French. A brief exchange about the best way to translate *akolasia* has been omitted here.

does not use any self-repression. And so *demokratia* now becomes the lack of repression. *Eleutheria,* the old Athenian *eleutheria* now becomes *paranomia,* that is, the transgression of the laws. *Eudaimonia,* the general happiness, has become *exousia tou panta poiein,* or the liberty to do anything you want. And *isonomia,* that is, the equality of everybody in the front of the law, has become *parrēsia.*[5] You see that *parrēsia* has in this text a negative meaning. With the pretext of being equal before the law, anybody is able to stand up and to start speaking, to try to convince other citizens and to suggest to them whatever the speaker wants. And as you see, in Isocrates, there is a permanent positive evaluation of democracy in general. There is the assertion that it is impossible to enjoy both the actual present form of democracy and *parrēsia,* and that in the Athenian institutions in the fourth century, either you have democracy without good *parrēsia,* or if you have a kind of *parrēsia* in those democratic institutions, it must be the bad form of *parrēsia.* You find also in Isocrates this idea that we saw in a much more radical form in the Old Oligarch's lampooning pamphlet, this clear distrust of the *demos*'s will, the *demos*'s feelings, and the *demos*'s opinion or desire. The parrhesiast is the one who has to oppose and to confront the *demos*'s desire.*

The third text I would like to quote is in Plato, in book 8 of the *Republic,* where Plato explains how democracy arises and develops, and

* The manuscript specifies: "As you see, you can find in Isocrates:

- A permanently positive evaluation of democracy in general—as a constitutional form.
- An ambiguous evaluation of *parrēsia* which [is] sometimes good, sometimes bad.
- An implicit characterization of *parrēsia* as a situation in which speakers are able to oppose, in complete freedom, the people's will, and in which the people are willing to accept this opposition.
- A clear distrust towards the *dēmos'* will, and the *dēmos'* feelings and opinion (this distrust being the aristocratic counterweight for endorsing the democracy).
- And finally a tension between *isonomia* as equality of everybody before the law [and] the use of free speech by anyone whoever he is."

he explains that "democracy comes into being when the poor, willing the victory, put to death some of the other party, drive out others, and grant the rest of the citizens an equal share in both citizenship and offices, and for the most part these offices are assigned by lot." "And then, what is the quality of such a constitution?" asks the interlocutor. And the answer is: "To begin with, are they not free? Is not the city chock-full of liberty and of freedom of speech, and has not every man licence to do what he likes?" And the word for "liberty" is *eleutheria,* the word for "freedom of speech" is, of course, *parrēsia,* and the words for "licence to do what he likes" are *exousia poiein ho ti tis bouletai.* You see that you find nearly the same words as in Isocrates. And, says Plato, "when there is such a licence, it is obvious that everyone would arrange a plan for leading his own life in the way that pleases him."[6]

What is interesting, I think, in this text is that Plato, as you see, does not blame *parrēsia* for giving everybody the possibility of becoming influential on the city, and he does not blame *parrēsia* for creating the possibility of inducing people to make the worst decisions. For Plato, the primary danger of *parrēsia* is not exactly the opportunity given to some ignorant leaders to become tyrants. The main danger, at least the first one, is that there is no common truth for everyone in the city, there cannot be any common *logos,* no possible unity, and this lack of common *logos* has as its consequence that everyone has his own way of life, his own type of existence, his own style of existence, his own what he calls *kataskeuē tou biou,* or constitution of life. And of course, following the Platonic principle of a direct, complete correspondence between human life and the city's life, following the principle of a direct, complete correspondence between the hierarchy of the faculties in the human being and the constitution of the city, following the principle that there is an analogy between the way a man behaves and the way the city is ruled, you understand easily that if everyone in the city behaves as he wants and follows his own opinion, will, or desire, then that means that there is no possible unity for the city. There are in the city as many constitutions, says Plato, as many *politeiai,* as many small autonomous cities, as there are citizens doing what they want.[7] That's, I think, the first thing that is worthwhile to note in this text. There is also another thing which is important, I think. It is that, as you see, Plato defines *parrēsia* not only by the fact that everyone is free to say what he wants, but also to *do* what he wants. *Parrēsia* here means saying what one thinks and doing what one wants. And it is this second aspect, doing what one wants, that is criticized the most sharply by Plato. *Parrēsia* is not only freedom of speech, it's a choice of life, it is a kind of anarchy in the freedom, in the choices of everyone; it is the freedom of choosing one's own style of life without limit to it.*

Of course there are a lot more things to say about the political problematization of *parrēsia* in Greek culture. But I think that we can observe two main aspects of this problematization during the fourth century and at the end of the fourth century. First, that the problem—and it is quite clear in the Platonic text—of freedom of speech becomes more and more related to the problem of the choice of existence, or of the way of living. The problem of freedom in the use of *logos* becomes more and more the problem of freedom in the choice of the way you live, and freedom in the choice of the *bios*. The problem of *parrēsia* is to be seen more and more as a personal attitude, a personal quality, a kind of virtue which is useful in the city's political life if it is good *parrēsia*, or which is dangerous for the city if it is bad *parrēsia*. For instance, you very often find in Demosthenes the notion of *parrēsia*. Demosthenes refers several times to *parrēsia*, but it is, I think, very significant to see that it is not as an institution but always as a personal quality. Demosthenes does not make an

* The manuscript adds: "The second point which is important is the way Plato correlates this *parrēsia* to *eleutheria*. He says, in the beginning of the text, that the democratic cities are praised because they are 'full of freedom and *parrēsia*,' and because people are able to do and to say what they want.

But in this text and in a lot of other texts referring to the same problem, Plato shows that *eleutheria* cannot consist in doing what one wants. On the contrary, when someone does what he wants, he is a slave; a slave to himself, to his desires, appetites, and so on. In the same way, a city where everybody does what he wants becomes a slave to the worst people. So that *parrēsia* which seemed to be linked to freedom is in fact at the root of tyranny.

Lack of truth, of unity, of freedom."

issue of the institutions which could reinforce or guarantee *parrēsia*; he insists on the fact that he, as a man, as a citizen, uses *parrēsia*, he insists on the fact that he uses *parrēsia* because he has to blame the city for the bad politics it has chosen, and he insists on the fact that doing so, he takes a great risk, it is dangerous for him to use *parrēsia* if Athenians are so reluctant in accepting criticism.[8]

You can also observe another transformation. It is the fact that the *parrēsia* is more and more linked to another kind of political institution; this *parrēsia* is more and more related to the problem of monarchic institutions and of monarchic power and authority. Freedom of speech must be used towards the king, and the king must accept *parrēsia*,* but it is quite obvious that in such a situation *parrēsia* is much more dependent on the personal qualities of both the king and the adviser,** and it is not as in the city, in the democratic city a question of institutions.

You see that the problem of *parrēsia* appears more and more clearly linked to the problem of personal qualities, personal attitude, the choice of existence, and the problem of *bios*. As a confirmation, you can observe for instance that the word, the notion of *parrēsia* scarcely occurs in Aristotle; you can't find any political analysis of *parrēsia* in Aristotle. You find the word *parrēsia* on two or three occasions, one in book 16 of the *Constitution of Athens*, where Aristotle analyzes Pisistratus's tyranny. As you know, Pisistratus was considered, at least by certain people and even by Aristotle, as a type of good tyrant, whose reign had been very favorable to Athens, and Aristotle gives [him as] an example of good *parrēsia* in the tyrannical situation. According to the story he tells, Pisistratus was walking in the country near Athens and there he met a countryman, a small landowner, who complains very sharply about taxes without recognizing Pisistratus. Pisistratus asks him why he felt so bitterly about

* The manuscript specifies, "References to this kind of *parrēsia* can be found in Plato, and in Isocrates ("To Nicocles")." See Isocrates, "To Nicocles," trans. Norlin, 1: 55–57 (28).

** The manuscript adds: "(Courage on one side, generosity, mastery of oneself on the other side)."

the government, and the peasant answered that he earned such and such, and that he was obliged to give ten percent of what he [earned] to Pisistratus. Pisistratus accepted this *parrēsia* and exempted him from the tax.[9] As you see, this *parrēsia* is typically the *parrēsia* used in the context of monarchy, of tyranny.

You also find in Aristotle another text in which the word *parrēsia* is used and where the parrhesiastic character is analyzed or at least evoked. It is in the *Nicomachean Ethics,* where he describes the *megalopsuchia,* the people who are *megalopsuchos.*[10] *Parrēsia* is not at all a political institution or a political practice, it is a character, an aspect, a feature of this magnanimity. Among other features of this magnanimity, you find some qualities that are more or less directly related to the parrhesiastic character or attitude. You find that Aristotle describes the *megalopsuchos* as someone who is courageous and who has a real and a reasonable courage. He is not what Aristotle calls *philokindunos.* This kind of person so likes danger that they run toward it. He is courageous, but reasonably courageous.[11] The *megalopsuchos* doesn't hide anything; the *megalopsuchos* prefers *alētheia* to *doxa,* truth to opinion; the *megalopsuchos* doesn't like flatterers, and what is interesting is also that the *megalopsuchos* is able to *kataphronein,* to look down on them (*regarder de haut en bas*). That is one of the features of *parrēsia,* the man who is able to tell the truth, who is able to recognize the failures and the faults of the others, and who is conscious of his own superiority.[12] All of [those features], with *parrēsia* and the frankness of speech, are elements of the moral portrait of the *megalopsuchos.* As you see, it's quite clear that for Aristotle *parrēsia* exists either in a monarchical context or as an ethical-moral character, but it does not exist as a political institution.

Well, you see that more and more the personal, the ethical, and the moral features of *parrēsia* are appearing everywhere. But in fact—and much before Plato, much before Aristotle, much before Isocrates—we have evidence that a new kind of parrhesiastic practice was emerging and developing. And it is this other kind of parrhesiastic practice that I would now like to analyze. Of course, between this other kind of parrhesiastic practice and the political *parrēsia* that I was speaking about during this seminar and the previous one, between those two kinds of *parrēsia*, there is not a clear distinction or split. Between them are several important analogies and also some relations of dependence. But in spite of those analogies and relations, I think that this other kind of *parrēsia* has several specific features. In order to define the specific features of this other kind of *parrēsia*, which is directly related to the figure of Socrates, I think it best to read together a text from the beginning of the *Laches* by Plato. I have chosen this text as a testimony about Socrates as a parrhesiastic figure for several reasons. The first is that this dialogue, *Laches*, which is rather short, uses the word *parrēsia* three times, which is rather a lot since the word *parrēsia* is not frequently found in Plato.[13]

In the beginning of the text, it is very interesting to note that the different interlocutors are characterized by their *parrēsia*. Two of them, Lysimachus and Melesias, say that they use *parrēsia*, and that they will use *parrēsia* in order to confess that they have done nothing very special, nothing very important, nothing very glorious their whole lives. They turn towards two other old citizens, very famous, Laches and Nicias, and they say that they turn towards them because they hope that they will speak very frankly—they are old enough, glorious enough, influential enough to be frank and not to try to hide what they think. That is what you will find at the beginning of the *Laches*. This is not the passage that I would like to read with you because it does not deal directly with the Socratic *parrēsia*—it is the ordinary, the everyday *parrēsia*—but it's interesting to see that this passage is right at the beginning of the text. At the end of the text, you find an idea that I like a lot (as maybe some of you know), and that is the idea of *epimeleia heautou*, or the care of the self. After this dialogue—which is from a theoretical point of view a failure, since nobody was able in the dialogue to give a real definition, a true definition, a satisfactory definition of courage, the topic of the dialogue—those four people I mentioned (Nicias, Laches, Melesias and Lysimachus) agree that they have to entrust their sons to Socrates as he is the best teacher. Although Socrates himself was not able to give a definition of courage, in spite of that, they decide to give Socrates as a teacher to their sons. Socrates accepts and he says:

"Well, it's true I don't know anything, I am not able to define courage, but we'll try now to take care of ourselves and of others."[14] So you have, I think, a move from the parrhesiastic figure to the problem of the care of the self, which is visible through this dialogue.

Before we read the text, I would like to recall briefly the situation at the beginning of the dialogue. I'll do it very briefly and schematically because in fact it's very complicated and interwoven. Two old men, Lysimachus and Melesias, feel anxious about the kind of education they should give to their sons. Both of them are aware that they belong to the most eminent families in Athens (one of them, Lysimachus, I think, was the son of Aristides, and Melesias was . . . I don't remember whose son he was, but he also belongs to an eminent family in Athens).[15] But—and this is interesting, this is one of the reasons why they speak about *parrēsia*—if their own fathers became illustrious in their time, Lysimachus himself and Melesias himself didn't do anything very special, very glorious in their lives; [they engaged in] no military exploits, no important political roles. And they are conscious of that, they confess that, and they use their own *parrēsia* in order to confess that publicly. From this experience, they draw this conclusion or question: how is it possible that from such a good *genos*, with such a good family, with such illustrious origins, they were not able to do anything special? Isn't it obvious, then, that birth, that belonging to a famous family, is not enough to enable an aptitude for playing a leading role in the city? [Since something more is necessary, what is this "something more"? Isn't this education?]* And if so, what kind of education?

You recognize very easily the problematic that is common to a lot of Platonic dialogues. Anyway, this dialogue is supposed to take place at the end of the fifth century, at a moment where a lot of people, most of them presenting themselves as sophists, pretended to provide young people with a good education, since it was clear to everybody that birth couldn't afford by itself good moral and political aptitudes. Those new educational techniques, and the debate

* This partially missing passage was reconstituted on the basis of the lecture manuscript.

about them, dealt with several aspects of education; they dealt with rhetoric and learning how to address the political Assembly or a jury, but the sophistic education also dealt with technical skills and occasionally with military education. And in Athens, one of the main problems was the education of infantry soldiers, who were largely inferior to the Spartan hoplites. That's the general context of the dialogue: an educational problem, a political, social, and institutional problem that is obviously related to the problem of *parrēsia*. Who is able to play a leading role in the city? Who is able to govern? But you see that this question, in its general form, is applied to the problem of education.

In order to provide their sons with a good military education, Lysimachus and Melesias led their sons to a teacher who claims to be a teacher for this military formation.* This teacher is a kind of technician, an artist, both an athlete and an actor, which means that he is very skillful in weapons handling. He uses his skill not to fight enemies, but to make money by giving public performances and teaching the young men. This man is a kind of sophist in military techniques. And after having attended this performance, neither Lysimachus nor Melesias is able to know if this kind of training is really useful and effective for [acquiring] a good education. Even after having seen the exploits of this "military sophist" with their own eyes, they don't know what to think about this teaching. Here we encounter the problem of the education's criteria. If one is not well-educated, how could one decide what counts as a good education? You can recognize here, in the field of education, of technical education, of military education, exactly the same problem as the parrhesiastic problem in the field of political institutions. We need someone to tell the truth in the political field, but how is it possible to recognize the one who is able to tell the truth? You find this same problem now in the field of education and, as you see, this problem of education is related to the first one. In order to get people who

* The manuscript adds: "This teacher (and that is important for the story and for the problematic) is not a soldier."

are able to tell the truth to the other citizens, you need people who are well-educated. People who are to be educated have to receive the truth, they have to receive the truth from someone, from a teacher, but who is the teacher who is able to tell the truth? And this parrhesiastic problem becomes *mise en abyme* (one of infinite regress).* It still belongs to the problem of politics, of political *parrēsia,* but it is the reproduction of this problem in the field of the education that is necessary for constituting a political parrhesiast.

After this rather disappointing experience, Lysimachus and Melesias, after having seen the exploits of this military technician, turn to two very well known figures of their time, Nicias and Laches. The first one was a very important political leader who won several victories on the battlefield, and the other one, Laches, played no special political role in Athens, but he was a rather famous and respected general. Lysimachus and Melesias turn to those two, Nicias and Laches, and ask what they think about the sophist's teaching and about the military training they could observe being performed by this technical expert. And then Nicias and Laches each give their opinion in turn, and it turns out that their opinions about this teaching are completely contradictory. Nicias, who is a great general and who has military experience, thinks that the sophist, this technician in military arts, has done a good job and that his teaching may be able to provide the youth with a good military education. Laches, who is also a good general, disagrees completely. He argues that the Spartans, who are the best soldiers in Greece, never have recourse to such teachers, and he also argues that this technician in military arts is not a soldier and has never won any victories.** Through this discussion we see two features of this problematic. Not only are ordi-

* Foucault uses the French phrase *mise en abyme.*

** The manuscript adds: "He refers also to another of those 'technicians,' who had invented a new weapon but has made a fool of himself in a fight at sea." In reality, Laches is speaking about the same person, named Stesilaos, who made himself look foolish in the course of a naval combat when he used a weapon of his own invention (a combination spear-scythe). See *Laches* 183c–184a.

nary citizens without any specific qualities unable to decide on the best education, but even those, like Laches and Nicias, who have shown that they are competent through their own lives led and their own deeds, even they are unable to decide who is the good teacher and who in the field of education is able to tell the truth.* So they now turn to Socrates and ask Socrates what he thinks. And here is the text that I propose you read. It is a text where Nicias and Laches agree—in spite of the fact that they are old, that they are very well known citizens, and that they have played a very important role in the Athenian army—to turn to Socrates and to ask him what he thinks about courage. The reason that Nicias and Laches give to explain why they accept the Socratic game is, I think, a portrait of Socrates as a parrhesiast. The word *parrēsia* is used in the text.**

First, [let's consider] the reason Nicias gives in order to explain why he will accept the Socratic game:

> You strike me as not being aware that, whoever comes into close contact with Socrates and has any talk with him face to face, is bound to be drawn round and round by him in the course of the

* The manuscript adds: "On the other hand, it is impossible to trust the kind of person who claims to be in possession of a certain technique and who pretends to teach it, and at the same time is not able to put this technique to work for himself in real life.

This is the kind of query that is very frequent in the early Platonic dialogues. You can see the relation between this problem and the problem of the political *parrēsia*:

1) In order to determine who can be the best citizens, who can exercise leadership in the city, Lysimachus and [Melesias] turn to the question of education.
2) And in the field of education the same problem appears: who is able to tell the truth—and to tell the truth in the form of an educative activity?

In order to solve this problem, they agree to turn to Socrates and ask him his opinion about the best way to teach military technique."

** Foucault says "the word parrhesiast," but in fact he refers to the word *parrēsia*, which can be found a little later in the response from Laches (188e).

> argument—though it may have started at first on a quite different theme—and cannot stop until he is led into giving an account of himself, of the manner in which he now spends his days, and of the kind of life he has lived hitherto; and when once he has been led into that, Socrates will never let him go until he has thoroughly and properly put all his ways to the test. Now I am accustomed to him, and so I know that one is bound to be thus treated by him, and further, that I myself shall certainly get the same treatment also. For I delight, Lysimachus, in conversing with the man, and see no harm in our being reminded of any past or present misdoing: nay, one must needs take more careful thought for the rest of one's life, if one does not fly from his words but is willing, as Solon said, and zealous to learn as long as one lives, and does not expect to get good sense by the mere arrival of old age. So to me there is nothing unusual, or unpleasant either, in being tried and tested by Socrates; in fact, I knew pretty well all the time that our argument would not be about the boys if Socrates were present, but about ourselves. Let me therefore repeat that there is no objection on my part to holding a debate with Socrates after the fashion that he likes; but you must see how Laches here feels on the matter.[16]

I think that in this speech by Nicias about Socrates, you have the analysis of the parrhesiastic game, that is, you have an analysis of the parrhesiastic game from the point of view of the listener or, more precisely, of the interlocutor. This parrhesiastic game is, as you see, something very different from the parrhesiastic game we have in the political field, or on the political scene where an orator was supposed to know the truth, to be willing to say the truth, be courageous enough to say the truth, and tried to persuade the Assembly of the truth of what he was saying. Here, first point, we have a parrhesiastic game which implies a person-to-person relation. You see that at the very beginning of the text: "You strike me as not being aware that, whoever comes into close contact with Socrates and has any talk with him face to face . . ." There is a problem here because the manuscript tradition is not quite clear; [*logō hōsper genei* is sometimes considered to be an interpolation] and there is another possibility: *hos an eggutata Sōkratous ē logō hōsper genei kai plēsiazē dialegomenos*.* The French Budé edition preserves *logō hōsper genei*, and gives a translation that is a little *tirée par les cheveux* [far-fetched], as they say.** If we translate *mot à mot* (word for word), it reads: "the one who is *eggutata Sōkratous*, very close to Socrates, as close as possible to Socrates," and then the French translation reads: "as close as possible to Socrates *logō hōsper genei*, by *logos*, just as close to him as by *genos*." It's a little far-fetched, but if we continue, we have: "*kai plēsiazē dialegomenos*, and who approaches him *dialegomenos*, through dialogue." Anyway, even if we put aside *logō hōsper genei*, you see that this game implies that there is proximity between Socrates and his interlocutor, and that each must be in touch with the other. *Plēsiazesthai* has sometimes the meaning of the sexual intercourse, which is obviously not in this meaning, but it is the fact of two people who get in contact, or, in another example, *plēsiazesthai* is "to become member of the circle, to follow somebody, a follower of somebody." When you must play the Socratic game, you must get in contact with him, get close to him, and get in touch with him. That's the first point.

The second point is that in this relation, in this Socratic parrhesiastic game, the listener, the interlocutor is, as you see, led by *logos*: *mē pauesthai hupo toutou periagōmenon tō logō*. He is led by the discourse of Socrates. From this point of view, the interlocutor plays the passive role, and he is in a passive position; but there is, I think, a difference between the passivity of the listener in a political assembly and the passivity of the Socratic interlocutor. Whereas in the political game, the passivity leads the listener to be persuaded by what he is listening to, here the interlocutor is led by Socratic *logos*. He is led to what? *Prin an empesē eis to didonai peri hautou logon*: he is led to give an account, *logon didonai*, of his own life. So that *logos*, which leads the hearer, leads him to give an account, to give a *logos*,

* The English edition used by Foucault doesn't retain the interpolation, contrary to the French translation by Alfred Croiset. The text has been adapted to reflect this difference.

** In this sentence and the next one, Foucault expresses himself in French.

and a *logos* about his own life. And how does he give the *logos* about his own life? The text says, as you see: "[he] cannot stop until he is led into giving an account of himself, of the manner in which he now spends his days, and of the kind of life he has lived hitherto." And then, a little further, you see: "For I delight, Lysimachus, in conversing with the man, and see no harm in our being reminded of any past or present misdoing."

When we read this text, or those elements of this text, of course we are inclined to read them through the lens of our Christian culture. We may interpret this description of the Socratic game as a practice in which the disciple, the one who is under Socrates' direction, has to give the story of his previous life and has to confess to his wrongdoings. But I think that it is not the real meaning of this text. In fact, if we compare this text to other descriptions of the Socratic game in other Platonic dialogues, like the *Apology*, the *Alcibiades*, or the *Gorgias*, we very often find this idea that when someone is led by Socratic discourse—the Socratic *logos*—he has to give an account of himself. But we see very clearly that it is not a question of "autobiography," it's not at all a question of confessing sins or faults. We never see in Plato's dialogues about Socrates, we do not see in the portrayal Xenophon has given of Socrates, anything like an autobiographical account of a life, and nothing like the avowal or the confession of sins or faults, or things like that. Giving an account, *didonai logon*, has a precise meaning, I think. When Socrates asks questions about life, or *bios*, he doesn't require a narrative; he asks questions about the *logos*, the reasonable discourse that organizes, that gives form to life and by which one is able to justify what he is doing or what he has done. To give an account, *didonai logon*, about his own life is not to give a narrative of his life, it is to show that there is a harmonic relation between *logos* (reason, and the reasonable discourse you are able to use) and the way that you live. The Socratic inquiry does not deal with the events of a life, it deals with the relations between *bios* as life, as the style of life, and *logos*. It is an inquiry about the way that *logos* gives form—gives, as the text says, a *tropos* to the life. This is, I think, very clearly demonstrated later on in this same dialogue. Socrates does not want Laches to give, for instance, a narrative of his exploits during the war, he does not want Laches to give an account of his weaknesses; he wants him to give reasons for his own courage: "You are courageous," says Socrates to Laches, "everybody knows that, you have shown that you were really courageous. Are you able to *didonai logon,* to give the reason for this courage, to give the *logos,* to make appear the *logos* which gives form, rational, intelligible form to this courage?" And that's the characteristic role of Socrates, to ask people to give the reason, to give an account of their life; it is this role that is characterized in the text as the role of a *basanos*. You find the word *basanos* or *basanizein*: *prin an basanisē tauta,* that is translated by "until he has thoroughly and properly put all his ways to the test." The Greek word *basanos* means touchstone. It is with this stone that you can authenticate gold and determine if it is real gold or not. Socrates is the *basanos,* since he is the one through whom you can accurately see the relations between a *bios* and a *logos*. A *bios* [that] seems to be reasonable, virtuous, or a *logos* that seems to be reasonable and virtuous, are they really what they are? It is through the Socratic "basanic" role, the role of touchstone, that one can determine this experience.[17]

After this definition of the parrhesiastic role of Socrates—first, the personal face-to-face relation, the giving an account of oneself, that is, to examine the relations between the *bios* and the *logos,* and then the role of Socrates as a *basanos*—in the second part of this speech, Nicias explains that having been examined by Socrates, one becomes willing to take care of the way one will live in the future. In order to live in the best possible way, one becomes eager to learn, and to learn not only when one is young, but throughout one's whole life. You see that with this Socratic experience by which one sees the relation between *logos* and *bios,* between his own life and rational principle, one becomes able to learn something. This relation between *mathēsis* and *parrēsia* now takes the form of a permanent attitude, or a permanent willingness to learn something from youth until old age.* That's all for the speech by Nicias.

* The manuscript adds: "What is important in this text is that the rhetorical game that is used in the field of political institutions and life is reversed:

And now [let's turn to] Laches' speech which gives another point of view on the parrhesiastic Socratic game. It is the point of view, not of the listener, but of Socrates himself, since the problem arises: how can we be sure that Socrates is this good *basanos*, this good touchstone that may be able to reveal the relations between *bios* and *logos* to someone?

> I have but a single mind, Nicias, in regard to discussions, or if you like, a double rather than a single one. For you might think me a lover, and yet also a hater, of discussions: for when I hear a man discussing virtue or any kind of wisdom, one who is truly a man and worthy of his argument, I am exceedingly delighted; I take the speaker and his speech together, and observe how they sort and harmonize with each other. Such a man is exactly what I understand by "musical,"—he has tuned himself with the fairest harmony, not that of a lyre or other entertaining instrument, but has made a true concord of his own life between his words and his deeds, not in the Ionian, no, nor in the Phrygian nor in the Lydian, but simply in the Dorian mode, which is the sole Hellenic harmony. Such a man makes me rejoice with his utterance, and anyone would judge me then a lover of discussion, so eagerly do I take in what he says: but a man who shows the opposite character gives me pain, and the better he seems to speak, the more I am pained, with the result, in this case, that I am judged a hater of discussion. Now of Socrates' words I have no experience, but formerly, I fancy, I have made trial of his deeds; and there I found him living up to any fine words however freely spoken. So if he has that gift as well, his wish is mine, and I should be very glad to be cross-examined by such a man, and should not chafe at learning; but I too agree with Solon,

---

- In the ordinary game, the speaker is supposed to tell the truth and the listener is supposed to be convinced; he learns the truth through what he hears.
- In this Socratic game, the listener has to speak, to speak about himself, to confront his own way of life to the principles of rational discourse; and then to recognize that he is unable to *didonai logon* of his own life, so that he has to learn."

> while adding just one word to his saying: I should like, as I grow old, to learn more and more, but only from honest folk. Let him concede to me that my teacher is himself good—else I shall dislike my lessons and be judged a dunce—but if you say that my teacher is to be a younger man, or one who so far has no reputation, or anything of that sort, I care not a jot. I therefore invite you, Socrates, both to teach and to refute me as much as you please, and to learn too what I on my part know; such is the position you hold in my eyes since that day on which you came through the same danger with me, and gave a proof of your own valor which is to be expected of anyone who hopes to justify his good name. So say whatever you like, leaving out of account the difference of our ages.[18]

So there's Laches' speech. As you see, this speech answers the question: what are the personal qualities and what are the visible criteria that entitle Socrates to play this game, to be the *basanos* of other people's lives, and to be accepted by other people's life as a *basanos* for their own lives? From some previous information given at the beginning of the dialogue, we have learned that, first, Socrates was not well known, that he was not one among the most eminent citizens, and that he has no special competence in the field of military training, with the exception of having taken part in certain battles in which Laches played the role of the general.[19] We have also learned—and this is important—that Socrates was younger than Nicias and Laches. So why should Nicias and Laches agree to submit themselves to the Socratic game? I think that in this text Laches gives the answer. As an old soldier, he is supposed to not be very smart, to not be very much interested in discussions, in political or philosophical discussions and so on. So the reason why Laches agrees to play this game with the Socratic *logos* is because there is a harmonic relation between what Socrates says and what he does. You remember that this was also the point in Nicias's speech, the problem of the relation between *logos* and *bios*. You remember that in Nicias's speech, the Socratic game appeared to be: are you able to give account of your life? Well, Socrates appears as someone who is able to give account of his life, or, better than that, he doesn't even need to give account of his life since it is quite visible in his behavior that there is not the slightest, the smallest discrepancy between what he is and what he does. He is a *mousikos anēr,* and the meaning of the word here is very interesting because in some of the Platonic texts *mousikos anēr* denotes the man who has a culture, a liberal culture. Here the *mousikos anēr* is someone who has a kind of ontological harmony since his *logos* and his *bios* exist in a certain harmonic relation. This *harmonia* is not only a *harmonia,* but the good *harmonia,* since, as you know, there were four kinds of harmony in Greek music: the Lydian one, which was despised by Plato because it was too graceful; the Phrygian one, which was despised by Plato because it was the harmony of the passions, it was a passionate harmony; the Ionian one was an effeminate harmony; and the Dorian one was virile and courageous. It is this kind of harmony that Socrates reveals, precisely through his courage, the courage he manifested in the battle where Laches was general.

That's the reason why Laches says about Socrates that he is capable of *logōn kalōn kai pasēs parrēsias.* Where is it? *Axion onta logōn kalōn kai pasēs parrēsias,* and the translation is: "there I found him living up to any fine words however freely spoken." More precisely, the text says that Socrates, since he shows this harmony in his existence, is able, first, to use *logoi kaloi,* the beautiful discourses—"beautiful," that means "ethically valuable," "reasonable," and so on—and that he can accept *parrēsia,* which means that he says exactly what he thinks, and what he thinks will be exactly what he does. That's the first aspect of *parrēsia.* And then, as a consequence, Laches is able to accept that this man who is much younger than him—Socrates, even if he isn't a youth anymore—he accepts that Socrates interrogates him. And he accepts—in spite of the fact that he is general and Socrates is almost nothing in the city—being interrogated and cross-examined by Socrates.* Those are the reasons

* The manuscript specifies: "It is worthwhile to note that, in order to substantiate his assertion about Socrates, Laches gives as an example Socrates' courage at the battlefield.

And this example means a lot:

why Socrates is recognized by his interlocutors as a parrhesiastic figure.

A few words about all of this. You see that we may recognize in this parrhesiastic game, of course, a lot of differences with the parrhesiastic game that we find in political life, and also some analogies and some proximities. As you see, the parrhesiastic figure here is still, as was the case in the political field, the man who is able, by a certain verbal activity, to make truth appear. He is able to do that insofar as he is courageous, courageous in his speech, courageous also in his life, but he is able to do that insofar as he is courageous and able to confront his listener's opinion or to criticize him if it is necessary. But as you see also, the game is somehow different from the parrhesiastic game. The differences are, first, the fact that it is a personal relation between two guys. The difference is also in the fact that between the elements of the parrhesiastic game we have noticed in the political context—between *logos*, truth, and courage—a new element now emerges, and this new element is *bios*. *Bios* now appears as the main element in the parrhesiastic game. In the political parrhesiastic game, you had the one who was supposed to know

---

a) Laches was well known for his courage; and as a general he is the best possible judge of Socrates' courage.

b) The problem which is at stake in the present discussion is the nature of courage.

c) And as we know courage is necessary for *parrēsia*.

That's the reason why Laches says very explicitly that he considers that Socrates is able to say beautiful things and that he is able to use *parrēsia*.

And we see by the following lines what he means by *parrēsia*: the fact that Socrates' discourses are rooted in, and [guaranteed] by his own life.

Socrates' life shows:

- that Socrates is sincere,
- that what he says is true (because it takes place in a real life),
- and that Socrates is courageous to [show] a style of life, a type of behavior that conforms to the beautiful things he says.

And then [Laches] accepts the parrhesiastic game with its consequences: the cross-examination and the possible discovery by Laches himself that he has still a lot of things to learn."

the truth, who had to tell this truth even if it was dangerous for him, and on the other side there were the listeners. Here you have something different: two people, only two people, [confront each other through] *logos*, truth, courage, and *bios*, the *bios* of one and the *bios* of the other. On the speaker's [side], on the philosopher's side, on the Socratic side, the relation between *logos* and *bios* is a harmonic relation, which entitles him to exercise the parrhesiastic function. And on the other side, on the interlocutor's side, the relation between *logos* and *bios* is a problematic relation. Problematic, first, in this sense that the listener or the interlocutor has to give an account of his life and has to show whether or not his life conforms to *logos*, and also in that sense that the work, the target, the aim of the parrhesiastic game is to lead the interlocutor to choose a kind of life which will be in conformity to *logos*.* The harmonic relation of *logos* and *bios* is, on the one hand, the ground of the parrhesiastic role of Socrates, and at the same time the visible criterion of the parrhesiastic function. And on the other hand, the harmonic relation of *logos* and *bios* is the final objective or target of the parrhesiastic activity and of the parrhesiastic game. From this perspective, the parrhesiast is not the man who is able to become a good leader for the city, the parrhesiast now is the one who is able to be a real *basanos*, a real touchstone, and that means that he himself has the qualities that are to be tested by the interlocutor. His own relation to truth allows him to make the relation to truth in others' existences appear.**[20]

Well, I would like to stop there and only point out one or two more things. We have seen the problematization of *parrēsia* as a game between *logos*, truth, and *genos* (birth). We have seen that in Euripides' *Ion*, and we have seen this game between *logos*, truth, and *genos* in the field of relations between gods and human beings. Then

* The manuscript adds: "And the parrhesiastic game has as its target to show at which point the listener, the disciple, is able or unable to harmonize his *bios* and his *logos*."

** The manuscript adds: "In the *Gorgias* there is another characterization of Socrates as a *basanos*. And Socrates explains very clearly that in order to be a *basanos* one needs to have *parrēsia*, *epistēmē* and *eunoia*."

we have seen the problematization of *parrēsia* as a game, not between *logos,* truth, and *genos,* but between *logos,* truth, and *nomos* (law), and we have seen that in the field of the political institutions, and precisely in the field of the *isonomia,* which is equality of people before the law. And whereas in the first case *parrēsia* appeared as the right of well-born citizens, *parrēsia* in the political field now appears to be the personal qualities of the good leader. With Socrates we now see a third kind of problematization of *parrēsia,* we see *parrēsia* problematized as a game between *logos,* truth, and *bios.* It's no longer *logos,* truth, and *genos,* and it's no longer *logos,* truth, and *nomos;* it is *logos,* truth, and *bios,* and we see that in the field of personal relations and of educative relations. This *parrēsia* is no longer a right of well-born citizens, it's no longer the personal qualities of a good political leader, it is the ontological and ethical quality of the *basanos,* of the touchstone for others' existence. And, as you remember, in the first case, in Euripides' *Ion, parrēsia* was opposed to the god's silence. In the second problematic of *parrēsia,* in the political one, *parrēsia* was opposed to the *dēmos*'s will and to those who flattered the desires of the mob. And in the third type of *parrēsia,* the Socratic parrhesiastic game, *parrēsia* is opposed to self-ignorance and it is opposed also to the bad teaching of the sophists. It is interesting to note that this parrhesiastic role—this role of *basanos,* of touchstone—that appears very clearly here is presented in other Platonic texts (and in particular in the *Apology*) as a mission which has been assigned to Socrates by the oracular deity, Phoebus, who in *Ion* kept silent.[21]

What I would like to show you next time, maybe, will be that in the Platonic tradition, the problem will be to define the possibility of a coincidence between political *parrēsia* and ethical *parrēsia*—between the political game between *logos,* truth, and *nomos,* and the ethical game between *logos,* truth, and *bios.* On the contrary, in the Cynic tradition, which also derives from Socrates, the opposition, I think, will be complete. Or more precisely the philosopher, the Cynic philosopher, will be considered in this tradition as the only one who is able to play the parrhesiastic game, and he has to play this game in a permanent negative attitude, in permanent critique of any kind of political institution and of any kind of *nomos*. So that's it. It was not too long, for once. Are there any questions?

—*I just have a question about terms. I'm not sure if I know what the words* genos *and* nomos *mean . . .*

—*Genos*, it's the race, it's the family, it denotes the kind of birth that characterizes you. And *nomos* is law. Are there any other questions?

—*Is there the same kind of truth in each of the three examples you gave?*

—The same kind of truth? No, not at all. It's quite clear that in Euripides, in *Ion*, the truth was this legendary, mythic genealogy on which were founded Ion's rights, but also the rights of Athens as being the city [endowed with] a kind of pan-Hellenic role in the context of its rivalry with Delphi. That was the kind of truth which had to appear. In the political game, the kind of truth which must be disclosed through *logos* is what is useful for the city, what can ensure the salvation of the city, *sōzein tēn polin*, and *sōzein* means "help the city to escape a danger," which also means "the maintenance of its own being," or "assure its welfare." That's the role of the discourse [in the political game]. And here [in the Socratic game] truth is, of course, what parrhesiastic *logos* discloses, it's the truth of someone, but this truth—and maybe it was not clear when I [spoke]—is not the different events of his life, the truth of someone's life is the kind of relation he has to truth, and how he constitutes himself as someone who must try to know the truth through *mathēsis*. That is the ontological object of the Socratic touchstone and the Socratic cross-examination. The truth is an ontological one and not a political one; it is the relation of someone to truth.

—*Is that true of* logos *too? Is* logos *going to vary in each of the three cases?*

—Sure, since you could say that in the first case, *logos* is very, very close to the myth, the *muthos*. Here in the second case, *logos* is much closer to any kind of discourse, and the main problem is the difference or use of rhetoric in the field of politics. In the case of the third kind of *logos*, we can see that the question of rhetoric is evacuated—not completely evacuated, but [*logos* is] polemically differentiated from rhetoric. In any case, it can't be the rhetoric that helps Socrates, or Socrates cannot use rhetoric as a way to play this role of touchstone. Yes?

—*These three forms, do you mean to suggest any kind of strict chronological progression?*

—No, you see, Euripides died just before the end of the fifth century, Socrates was put to death in 399. No, for a lot of reasons: first, it's rather difficult to know the precise chronology; second, you know very well that in the ancient culture philosophical themes, philosophical problematics, and so on were much more permanent than they have been since, and anyway we have rather few documents from those periods. So it's a fact that the first [form of *parrēsia*] that appears in Euripides is something which, I think, didn't establish a long tradition. The problem of political *parrēsia*, because of the institutional changes and the development of the Hellenistic monarchies, took more and more the form of the personal relation between the king and his advisers; in this case, of course, the problem of moral value, and of the moral education of the prince, leads to something which is close to Socratic teaching. And Socratic teaching had later a very long tradition through the Cynics and through other philosophers. So [the three forms of *parrēsia*] were nearly contemporary when they appeared and when they were formulated, but in fact the historical destiny of the three was not the same.

—*Do you see a collision between the* logos-*truth*-bios *triptych and the* logos-*truth*-nomos, *for instance in Socrates' fate, when he challenges the city?*

—I am not sure, but I had an idea when reading the Cynics these last few weeks.[22] I had the impression that *parrēsia* had been so important for the Cynics, who had been real parrhesiasts for centuries and centuries, but that for them the problem was to play a parrhesiastic game which was always characterized—not always, not through to the end, but still for a rather long time—by a polemical attitude toward political institutions. On the contrary, Plato, and what we know of Socrates through Plato, seems to indicate an attempt to make the political parrhesiastic role and the ethical one coincide:

what kind of relations can this philosophical *logos* have with *nomos*? You see that in the *Apology*, you see that in the *Crito*, you see that also, of course, in the *Republic* and in the *Laws*. In the *Laws*, there is a very strange, very interesting text where you find the word *parrēsia*. I don't know if you remember this small passage. It is just before the explanation of the sexual rules for young people, and Plato says: in the city, [alongside]* the role of the laws, of the good laws, we need someone who is able to tell everyone exactly the kind of moral conduct that they should observe. And he calls this man the parrhesiast.[23] Alongside the lawgivers and the wardens of the laws, he feels the need for someone else who does not play the role of giving the laws, or surveying and observing how they are applied; someone must tell the truth and give advice about the purely moral, ethical field, and this person is called a parrhesiast. As far as I know, it's the only text, either in the *Republic* or in the *Laws*, where he speaks of the parrhesiast as a kind of political figure in the field of the [law].**

—*In your discussion of the relationship between* bios *and* logos, *you spoke of them each as something that was concretely present in the touchstone, that is, Socrates himself, and also as the goal of his dialogue or his method. But there seems to be a contradiction between these two aspects: one serves as the foundation for the exchange, and the other one is its end.*

—The Socratic game consists in showing to certain people like Laches or Nicias that in spite of the fact that they are courageous, they are not able to know what courage is. They are not able to give an account, a reasonable account of their own life. So there is no harmonic relation between *logos* and *bios*. That's the Socratic game. Then the problem becomes: why can Socrates be the one through whom, and by which, other people are led to recognize that their existence is not harmonic from this point of view? Well, to this question Laches—who was a general, who saw that Socrates could be courageous in his conduct—says: I accept Socrates as a touchstone for the relation between *logos* and *bios*, since I know that his life is in

* This exchange was difficult to hear, so the phrasing in brackets is conjectural.

** Foucault does not conclude this sentence.

harmony with what he says. That's the difference—maybe I was not clear enough—between Socrates and a sophist. The sophist has very beautiful discourses, *kaloi logoi,* about courage, but he is not courageous himself. This coincidence or this harmony between *logos* and *bios* is, from Laches' point of view, is the reason why Socrates can be accepted as a parrhesiast and why this old general agrees to be cross-examined like a child by Socrates.

—*You've made a distinction between* parrēsia *as described by Euripides in* Ion *and that of Socrates, and it seems to me that the oracular function in* Ion, *that of the god dispensing truth, is pretty similar to that of Socrates. How do they differ from one another?*

—If I mentioned the fact that Socrates, in the *Apology,* presents himself as having a mission assigned by Phoebus—to be a parrhesiast—it is because, of course, there is a relation [between the two]; in a way, Socrates plays a role that is not completely different from the oracular role. But I think that there are very large, important differences. There is at least one point which can be considered as common between the two: it is the fact that with the oracular answer, you cannot really understand this obscure and enigmatic answer without knowing yourself, or without knowing exactly the kind of questions you ask and the meaning which the oracle can take in your own life, in your own behavior, in your own situation.[24] On the other hand, I think that the difference is that the oracle must say what will happen to you, so that you can learn and discover through Socratic *parrēsia* what you are—not your relation to the future or to a chain of events, but your relation to truth. It is another kind of relation to the truth.

—*This is going way back to when you talked early on about the aristocratic attack on Athenian democracy. There, the main thrust of the aristocratic argument seemed to be that* parrēsia *within Athenian democracy could only be the bad sort of parrēsia. My question is that there seem to be two sorts of ways that the democratic opposition to that view could support the idea of democracy. One would be to have an ideal sort of a* polis *where* parrēsia *and criticism could actually be heard and understood and taken into account. Another would be one where the opposition between the people and the* polis *wasn't there or wasn't as strong so that* parrēsia *in the full, critical role would not be needed. In other words, people might need advice, they might need almost a sort of technical advice, but the fundamental opposition between* demos *and* polis *wouldn't be there. My question is, do you think those two are real alternatives? And also, what do you think would have been the ideal defended by the democrats at the time, even though we don't have those texts?*

—We have said very few things about the attitude of the democrats. Do you have any ideas?

—*When you read Pericles' speech in Thucydides, I think that might be the closest that you might get.*

—You see, what is interesting about this problem of the *dēmos*'s will, the *dēmos*'s desire—and I cannot give you any real answer—is that there wasn't any political theory like, for instance, Rousseau's theory, which said that since it was the will of the *dēmos*, it was the will of the city. I don't know if there is something like that [with the Greeks], because this notion of *dēmos* is very ambiguous, at least in the texts which have been preserved and which for the most part come from the aristocratic tradition. *Dēmos* corresponds to both the people in the city and the worst part [of the city], since they are the most numerous. I think that this was very deeply embedded in the Greek mentality, and I am not sure there was any kind of political theory implying that since it was the *dēmos*'s will, it was also the city's will. With the Cynics, we'll see something very interesting from the political point of view, but much later on [in history]. The transcendence of the city in regard to the citizens is something, I think, that is essential in Greek political thought. So for us, what does "the city" mean? It's not the totality of its inhabitants, I think, or of its citizens. I think that this question could not appear in Greece. The city was of course something different even if... We should correct [this claim] because of Aristotle, but Aristotle is a kind of monster in the Greek culture, he is not at all typical.[25] But here, in these theories about *parrēsia*, it's quite clear that the *dēmos* is not entitled to impose its own will on the city.

—*Do you see any challenge to this description of a kind of* parrēsia *which you have predicated on a correspondence between word and deed in the description of Socrates, by other descriptions of Socrates in which there is a radical disjunction between word and deed? In the* Alcibiades, *for example he is described as a lecher, and other descriptions underline the contrast between exterior (his ugliness) and interior (his philosophy); still others describe him as a liar and the one that wears a mask.*

—Yes, but that opposition between physical appearance and the reality of the man is not the problem of *bios*. *Bios* is not a biological reality, it's not the body; *bios* is the style you give to your existence, your life, and it's a question of choice and of freedom. I don't think you can find anywhere a contradiction between Socrates' discourses and Socrates' life.

—*Not in the use of irony, for example?*

—*Aristotle says that in the* Nicomachean Ethics, *in fact in the same passage that you cited about* parrēsia.[26]

—How do you understand this rather obscure passage about irony in Aristotle's text about *megalopsuchia*? Because the translation didn't get exactly the same meaning.

—*It's a very interesting moment . . .*

—But anyway it has nothing to do with . . .

—*They don't go together, where someone says one thing but does the other, that's not* parrēsia. . .

—*But I'm asking if they can be reconciled, these two . . .*

—*But the question of Socratic irony may not mean exactly that, it may not be quite the exact use of* eiron, *the ironic figure. It's really tricky.*

—I think that irony, Socratic irony, is a game inside *logos*; I don't think it is ever a contradiction, even an apparent contradiction, between *bios* and *logos*.

NOVEMBER 21, 1983

YOU RECALL THAT THE LAST time we met, and analyzed the text from the *Laches*, we saw the emergence with Socrates of a new type of *parrēsia*, a type of *parrēsia* that is, I think, very different from the political *parrēsia* we have studied through Euripides and other texts. I think that this text from the *Laches* dramatizes very clearly a certain displacement in the parrhesiastic role. Remember that in the *Laches* we had a game with five people, or five partners. Two of them were very well born, wealthy citizens, but they were not able to use *parrēsia* and to play the parrhesiastic role, and they did not know how to teach their own children. So they turned back to two other types of men—two famous citizens, a general and a political figure, one of whom was Laches and the other Nicias—and those two were also unable to play the parrhesiastic game, and they were obliged to turn to Socrates, who appears as the real parrhesiastic figure. You see through this case the move from political *parrēsia* to philosophical [*parrēsia*]. I also think that we saw at the very beginning of this dialogue a characterization of the parrhesiast; this characterization was determined not by birth and social status, but by a certain harmony, a certain relation between what the parrhesiast says and what he does, and the way he lives. And third, at the very end of the dialogue, we have seen just how far this parrhesiastic game was able to go. Of course, the parrhesiastic game played by Socrates did not define courage, but everybody agreed at the end of the dialogue that Socrates, in spite of the fact that he was unable to give a good, clear definition of courage, should help others to take care of themselves.

So I think that taking this text as a point of departure, we can observe through Greco-Roman culture the rise and the development of a new type of *parrēsia*, a new kind of *parrēsia* that we could characterize in the following way.

First, this *parrēsia* can be characterized as a philosophical *parrēsia*. I say that it is a philosophical *parrēsia* because it has been put into practice during centuries and centuries by the philosophers, and also because a large part of philosophical activity in Greco-Roman culture has been devoted to the parrhesiastic game. Very schematically, I think that we could say that the philosophical role entailed in Greco-Roman culture three different kinds of games, each related to one another. [It has an] epistemic game or role, insofar as philosophy has to discover and to teach some truth about the world and about nature. The philosophical role entails also the political game, insofar as the philosopher has to take a position towards the city, towards *nomos*, towards the institutions, and so on. There is also a parrhesiastic game in the philosophical activity in the Greco-Roman culture from the fourth century until early Christianity. This third role is a parrhesiastic activity that does not exactly raise the question of the relation between the *logos* and the *nomos*, but has as its main target the elaborations of the relationships between truth and life, truth and style of life, and truth and what we could call the aesthetics and the ethics of the self.[1] I think that we have to consider *parrēsia* in the field of the philosophical activity, of the philosophical role in Greco-Roman culture. We have to consider this *parrēsia*, not as an idea, not as a theme, but as a practice, and as a practice that has tried to give shape to the relations individuals could have to themselves. I think that our moral subjectivity is at least partially rooted in this practice. That's the first point about this characterization of *parrēsia* in philosophical activity. More precisely, we could say that in this practice, the criterion of the parrhesiast must be found, not in his birth, not in his citizenship, not in his competence, but in his life, in his *bios*, or more precisely in the harmony between his *bios* and his *logos*.

Second, we could say that the target of this *parrēsia* is not to persuade the city or the Assembly or the fellow citizens to make the best possible decisions for themselves and for the city, but the target, the aim, of this new kind of *parrēsia*, of this *parrēsia* as philosophical activity, is to convince someone that he must care for himself and change his life. I think that this problem of "changing one's life," this theme of conversion, becomes something very important in Greco-Roman culture from the fourth century onward, and this theme of "changing one's life" is essential through parrhesiastic or, more generally, philosophical practice. Of course this idea of changing one's life, this theme of conversion as an aim for *parrēsia*, is not completely different or remote from what happened in political life when an orator, using his *parrēsia*, asked his fellow citizens to wake up, to change their mind, to change their decision, to refuse what they had previously accepted or to accept what they had previously refused. But I think that this notion of changing one's mind takes on a more profound or larger meaning in parrhesiastic practice since it is not only a question of changing one's opinion, but of changing completely one's life, one's style of life, one's relations to others, and one's relations to oneself.

Now the third point about this kind of new parrhesiastic practice as opposed to the political one. As you see, this parrhesiastic practice implies a complex relationship between truth and the self. Through this parrhesiastic practice, one is supposed to be capable of recognizing who he is, and through this self-knowledge he is, or should become, able to get access to truth. With philosophical *parrēsia*, I think that the question is: how is the individual, how is the subject able to know himself, and through this knowledge to get access to truth and knowledge? So, as you see, there is a kind of circle, and this kind of circle between knowing the truth about yourself in order to make yourself able to know the truth is characteristic of parrhesiastic practice since the fourth century. As you know, this has been one of the permanent principles or the permanent enigma of Western philosophy—think of Descartes or Kant.

And the last point I would like to underscore about this new philosophical *parrēsia* in Greco-Roman culture is that this new *parrēsia* is no longer linked to the *agora* as the public place where political discussions and decisions take place, but this *parrēsia* can be used in a lot of other places. This *parrēsia* implies relations different from the relations between orator and citizen, and this new kind of *parrēsia* has recourse to many techniques that are very different from the techniques of persuasive discourse in political life.

Those are the aspects [of *parrēsia*] that I would like to analyze this evening and in the next, and final, seminar. So I would like to give a brief analysis of this kind of philosophical *parrēsia* from the point of view of its practices, its parrhesiastic practices. By this expression "parrhesiastic practices," I mean two things. First, the problem of the parrhesiastic relation, which I intend to deal with this evening; and [then] the parrhesiastic procedures and techniques about which I'll try to give you a brief survey in our next meeting.

So tonight [we'll discuss] the problem of the new parrhesiastic relation, or the parrhesiastic relation through these new practices, the emergence of which we could observe in the *Laches*' beginning. I would say that we can recognize or distinguish three main forms of relations which are implied in this new philosophical *parrēsia*. But of course this is rather schematic, and you can see that there are several intermediate forms. For clarity of presentation, I would like to distinguish what we could call the community relationship or, better yet, the *parrēsia* as an activity within the framework of a small group of people, or within the framework of community life. The second type of relationship which is implied by the parrhesiastic relationship is *parrēsia* as an activity or as an attitude in the framework of public life. Then, third aspect, third kind of relationship, *parrēsia* in the framework of individual or personal relationships. And I'll be still more schematic, saying that the *parrēsia* as a feature of the community life, of a group life, this *parrēsia* seems mostly to have been very important and very highly evaluated in Epicurean philosophy or in the Epicurean way of life. On the contrary, *parrēsia* as a public activity, as a public demonstration, has been, I think, one of the main aspects of Cynicism—or this kind of life was at the borderline of Cynicism and Stoicism. *Parrēsia* as an aspect of personal relationships, *parrēsia* as it is put to work in some personal, individual relationships, is to be found more frequently either in Stoicism or in this form of generalized or common Stoicism that is visible even in writers who are not real Stoics, like Plutarch.[2]

But of course all that is simply schematic, it's only aimed at—because of the brevity of time—the clarity of the presentation. We could find several intermediate forms. For instance, if I think it's true that community life, because of the importance given to friendship, was more often practiced by the Epicureans, it's also true that you could find some Stoic groups organized around a philosopher. Or at least—for instance, in Rome—you can find several Stoics or Stoico-Cynic philosophers who were the moral and political advisers of a few small groups of people, of aristocratic circles, groups, or clubs. For instance, Musonius Rufus or Demetrius, who was a Cynic and who was the adviser of a kind of liberal anti-autocratic group around Thrasea Paetus, who committed suicide under Nero (and Demetrius, a philosopher, was his adviser and I would say *le régisseur*, the director, of Thrasea Paetus's suicide). You have also other intermediate forms; for instance you have the case, very interesting, of Epictetus. Epictetus was, as you know, a Stoic. Epictetus, for whom the notion and the practice of *parrēsia* was very important, also had some connections and acquaintance with Cynicism.* He directed a school about which we know only a few things through the *Discourses* collected by Arrian. Through those *Discourses,* we know that, first, this school directed by Epictetus had a permanent structure that made possible a real community life for the students. In this school were also public lectures that people from the outside were allowed to attend. Those people coming from the outside could ask questions and sometimes they were mocked and twitted by the master. In this school, it is also possible to find some private and personal interviews between Epictetus and one of his disciples; some of these conversations were public and held in front of the class, and some of them were really personal conversations and interviews. We also know that this school was a training place for those who wanted to become philosophers and who needed to be taught how to take care of others and how to become in turn good moral advisers. It was a kind of *école normale* for the direction of conscience.[3] So you see there were several institutions and practices around this parrhesiastic practice. When I say that I'll analyze *parrēsia* within collectives through the example of the Epicureans, or the problem of *parrēsia* in public life through the example of the Cynics, or the problem of personal *parrēsia* through the example of the Stoics, I should be very clear that these are only examples. I use them as a guideline, and real practice was much more complicated and intricate.

First, the problem of *parrēsia* in community life through the example of Epicurean groups. Unfortunately—or fortunately, for the brevity of my presentation—we know very little about Epicurean communities, and especially the parrhesiastic practices in those communities. But we have one text written by Philodemus. Philodemus was an Epicurean author of the first half of the first century BCE, and Philodemus wrote a book on the precise topic of *parrēsia*: *Peri parrēsias*.[4] We don't have this book or this treatise in its entirety. Parts of it have been rediscovered in Herculaneum's ruins at the end of the nineteenth century, and what has been preserved is very frag-

* Foucault actually says "with Stoicism"; this has been corrected in line with the original manuscript for the lecture.

mentary and rather obscure. I confess that without the commentary of an Italian scholar, I wouldn't have been able to understand the few Greek words which remain. An Italian scholar, [Marcello] Gigante, published a commentary on this text a few years ago, maybe ten years ago.[5] Well, what I would like to underline in this text are the following three points.

First, in this text, we see that the *parrēsia* is considered and characterized by Philodemus not only as a quality, not only as a virtue or as a personal attitude, it is, more than that, presented, analyzed, or at least characterized as a *technē*. *Technē*, technique. Well, this *technē* is compared by Philodemus both to medicine and the medical art of curing patients, and to piloting a boat. The comparison of medicine and sailing is, as you know, something that is very traditional in the Greek culture. This comparison in itself, without the reference to *parrēsia*, is interesting for two reasons. The first one is this. The reason why the pilot's *technē* (sailing) and the physician's *technē* (medicine) were so often compared to each other was that in both of them, first, a certain knowledge was necessary, and this knowledge could not be useful without a certain practical training, exercises, and so on. In those two techniques, the common point is that if you want to put those two *technai*, two techniques, into operation, then you must take into account not only the general rules and principles that you have learned during your training, but you also must take into account some pieces of information which are specific to a given individual situation. You must take [into] account, first, the circumstances, which mean that, for instance, if your patient has a certain constitution, you have to use a specific type of medicine, and so on; but you also must take into account, not only the circumstances, but also the best moment to intervene and give this medicine, or make this decision if you are the pilot. This necessity of taking into account the circumstances and the moment, what the Greeks called *kairos*, is something which is very important and which always is considered by the Greeks as the common point between piloting and curing patients. This problem of *kairos*, the best moment for doing something, has always had great importance in Greek thought from an epistemological point of view, from a moral one, and from a technical one. What is interesting is that since *parrēsia* is brought together with piloting and medicine, that means then that *parrēsia* is also something that, like medicine and piloting, is a technique which deals with individual cases, with individual circumstances, and with the choice of a good moment. In a way, we could say in our vocabulary that piloting, medicine, and parrhesiastic practice are "clinical techniques."

The second reason why the Greeks so often brought together medicine and piloting is that with these two kinds of techniques, medicine and piloting, one has to decide, to give orders, and to exercise power, and the others—the patients, the crew, and the people on the boat—have to obey. As you can easily infer, piloting and medicine are of course related to politics in which, of course, you also have to choose the best moment, and in which there is someone who is supposed to be more competent than the others, who has the right to give orders, and who others must obey. In politics, there is an indispensable *technē* which must take into account circumstances, *kairos*, [a] certain type of power relations through which one decides and the others obey. So we have in these kinds of techniques three *technai*—medicine, piloting, and politics—and I think this comparison between medicine, piloting, and politics, which is very present in the Greek texts, is at the root of a very important kind of reflection which is so often formulated by the theoreticians of politics, one not about the law, the constitution, or *politeia*, but about the art of governing people.[6]

But anyway, to come back to this text [of Philodemus], if I mention here this old affinity between medicine, piloting, and medicine, it's in order to indicate that the parrhesiastic activity by which one leads someone else to discover who he is, this *technē*, this "spiritual guidance" (to use [a word] which is obviously anachronistic), is integrated into the field of some other well-known techniques such as piloting, medicine, and politics during the Hellenistic period. Now we have a body of four *technai*, four clinical and political *technai*: piloting, medicine, politics, and taking care of oneself or of others through the *parrēsia*. Of course, the first one of these four techniques, piloting, is only a metaphoric reference, but the three others—medicine, politics, and *parrēsia* or taking care of oneself or of others—constitute a corpus, a body of techniques, which have, from the point of view of the Greco-Roman culture, very close relationships to one another. I think it would be something important to study, to analyze those relations, the way the Greeks and the Romans have analyzed the relations between those three clinical and political activities—governing people in the city, governing patients through medical techniques, and governing the life of people through philosophical *parrēsia*. As you know, several centuries later, Gregory of Nazianzus will call this spiritual guidance *technē technon, ars artium,* the "technique of techniques," an expression which is really important since during the Roman Empire, the political *technē* which was considered as the *technē technōn,* the royal art.[7] And from the fourth century until the seventeenth century in Europe, when you find the expression *ars artium, technē technōn,* most of the time it refers to spiritual guidance as the most important of those different techniques by which, choosing the best moment and taking into account the circumstances, you are able to govern other people, either if they are patients and you are their physician, or because you are king and they are your subjects, or because you are their spiritual guide and they must be guided. All of that, of course, is very implicit in this text by Philodemus, but the characterization of *parrēsia* as a *technē* in relation to medicine and piloting is something characteristic of this move of *parrēsia* towards this new field of techniques and practices.

There is also a second element that appears in the text of Philodemus, which is the relation between *parrēsia* and a certain hierarchical structure in Epicurean communities.[8] Of course, commentators disagree about the form and the complexity of this hierarchy. Some of them think that this hierarchy was very well established, complex, and so on, and the others—Gigante, for instance—consider it to be much more simple than that. Anyway, it seems that there were at least two categories of teachers and two kinds of teaching in Epicurean communities. I think that's interesting. There was teaching in the form of a class, where the teacher addresses a group of students, and there was also teaching in the form of a personal interview with advice and precepts given to one of the community members by one of the teachers. The lower-ranked teachers had to teach a class, but the higher-level teachers could both teach classes and also give personal advice.

—*Sounds like Oxford.*

—Yes, sure. Our university system derives from that [model]. The school ruled by Epictetus would be a very good "public school" for England.

—*Can I ask you one question really quick before you go on? What is the relation of these four arts of governing to* phronēsis?

—Yes, you are right to [ask that question]. *Phronēsis* is this kind of knowledge by which you can make the best decision within the domain of those four kinds of *technē*, since the usual form of *ēpistemē* can give you the general rules, for instance, to make a mathematical proof. But when you have to take into account particular elements, and you cannot be sure of the result, there is something like a probability, and then you must use *phronēsis*. That's quite clear in Aristotle.

—*To a certain extent that concerns the law as well.*

—The law? Yes, if you must apply a law to an individual case, you must also use *phronēsis*. But as far as I know, [the Greeks] never consider applying law to an individual case as a *technē*.

—*What is* phronēsis?

—*Phronēsis* is translated in French by *prudence.*

ANYWAY, YOU SEE IN THIS organization of these Epicurean groups that it seems likely that there was a distinction between general teaching and personal guidance. And, first point, I think that we must outline that the difference was not the difference between theoretical teaching, for instance about logic and physics, as opposed to practical teaching about ethics, since there were classes about ethics, and since also, as you know, physics, cosmology, natural laws had an ethical meaning for the Epicureans.* The distinction is not between the "content" of theoretical and practical teaching, it is much

* The manuscript adds: "and the reason to study those fields of knowledge was precisely to catch this ethical meaning."

more between two types of pedagogical or psychagogical relation between truth, teacher, and disciple. And what is interesting, and this is the second point, is that in the Socratic dialogue and, I think, in the Socratic context, there was only one procedure by which the interlocutor was led to discover the truth about himself,* to care for the self, and to discover the truth about the world, about the Forms, about the nature of the *psukhē*, and so on and so on. So there was only one procedure, one way, one path to get to the truth, to discover the truth about oneself and the truth about the world. It seems that according to this Epicurean text, [there were two types of pedagogical relationship in Epicurean schools: a relationship]** that took the form of an authoritative teaching in which someone told the truth to the others, and another type of relationship by which the master was obliged to help the disciple to discover and disclose the truth about himself.*** Anyway, these two kinds of teaching have been, I think, something permanent in our culture, and you can find them, for instance, in the early modern period of the seventeenth to eighteenth centuries—at least in France, and I think also in England and Protestant countries—where in the educational system you always find those two kinds of relationship between the master and the disciple: the collective relationship in the form of a class and the [relationship of] spiritual guidance. The third point I would like to underline about this organization of Epicurean schools is that the second role, spiritual guidance, was much more valued than the other.

I don't want to conclude what I wanted to say about Philodemus without pointing out some indications of what we could call the

* The manuscript adds: "([that is] he did not know anything)."

** This passage is missing and so this phrase is speculative.

*** The manuscript specifies: "It seems through this Epicurean text that a certain type of relationship to the master became necessary in order to learn how to take care of oneself. And, maybe, we can see there the point of departure of those specific forms of spiritual guidance which have been always in a close relation to pedagogy and to the learning of truth, but which took a specific form [here].

A gap between accessing the truth [and] taking care of the self, although the one [is] absolutely indispensable to the other."

"mutual confession." Through some words of the text it seems that there were some sort of sessions, of meetings in which community members each recounted their misdeeds, their faults, their failures, and so on, and that they did so at a kind of community meeting. We know very few things about this practice, but there is a very interesting expression that you find in this text by Philodemus, which is the expression *di' allēlōn sōzesthai*, that means "the salvation by one another."[9] Of course, salvation does not have the meaning we now give to the word; it doesn't refer to any kind of after-death life or to any kind of judgment by the divinity. *Sōzesthai*, to save oneself—in the Epicurean vocabulary, and in the Stoic or Cynic vocabulary—means to have access to a good, a beautiful, and a happy life. In this salvation, others—the friends, or the members of the community—played a decisive role: they were the agents for truth, or for the truth of the self. All of that, of course, refers to the very important role of friendship in these Epicurean groups. That's it for *parrēsia* in community groups and Epicurean communities. Are there any questions about the Epicureans?

—*Is there a strain between the hierarchical structure of these groups and these public confessions?*

—I don't know. There are only a few words [in them]; you know how smart classicists are, and from two halves of a word, or the half of two words, [they can arrive at various interpretations] . . . *

[I would now like to speak about] public *parrēsia* in the Cynics. As I have told you, we know very few things about the real life of Epicurean communities, but we have some idea of their thought through several texts. I think that the situation is exactly the reverse for the Cynics, since we know very little about the Cynic doctrine, if there was any Cynic doctrine, but we have a lot of information, or at least numerous testimonies, about their way of life. There is nothing very surprising in that claim, since, in spite of the fact that the Cynics have written books like any other philosophers, they were interested in choosing and practicing a certain way of life more than anything else.[10]

* This passage is partly inaudible, and so this passage is speculative.

The historical problem of Cynicism is this one. All the Cynics from the second to the first century BCE and of course all the Cynics afterwards refer to Diogenes and sometimes to Antisthenes as the founders of the Cynic movement and of Cynic philosophy. Through Diogenes and Antisthenes, they relate themselves back to Socrates. In fact it seems—and here I follow an American scholar, Farrand Sayre, who wrote an interesting book about the Cynics in the late 1940s or early 1950s—that the Cynics, as a philosophical sect, appear only in the second century BCE, and so more than two centuries after Socrates' death.[11] Sayre explains the appearance of the Cynics on the Greek scene as a consequence of the constitution of the Macedonian Empire in two ways. First—and I think we can be a little skeptical about this explanation that has been given so many times for so many different phenomena—that with the decadence of the political structures of the ancient world, a bad, critical, aggressive individualism arose as a failure of Greek philosophy. And Sayre gives another explanation that may also be problematic but that is much more interesting. It is that the Greeks for centuries and centuries before Alexander have been aware of the existence of Indian philosophy. Through Alexander and Alexander's conquests, Indian philosophy became more familiar, and Sayre considers that we can find in the Cynic movement several aspects of the Indian monasticism and asceticism.

Anyway, whatever we can discern about the origin of Cynicism, it is a fact that the Cynics were very numerous and influential from the end of the first century BCE to the fourth century CE. A writer like Lucian, who didn't much like the philosophers, wrote about the Cynics: "The city swarms with these vermin, particularly those who profess the tenets of Diogenes, Antisthenes, and Crates."[12] In fact, the Cynics were numerous and influential to the point that Emperor Julian, in his attempt to revive classical culture, wrote a lampoon of the Cynics, scorning their ignorance and their coarseness, and he presented them as a danger for the empire and for Greco-Roman culture.[13] One of the reasons why Julian so bitterly addressed himself to the Cynics was that there were some similarities and affinities between them and Christianity. Some of these similarities that so scared Julian may not have been more than mere appearance. For instance Peregrinus, who was a great figure within Cynicism at the end of the second century and was satirized by Lucian, seems to have been a Christian who was converted to Cynicism.[14] It is obvious that some of the early Christian ascetics used to live in the same way as the Cynics.

Well, the high value those Cynics attributed to ways of living did not mean at all that they had no real interest in theory; this interest in different ways of life meant, I think, that they considered that life, human life, and any way of life could be defined as a certain relation to truth, and that the way people lived served as the touchstone for their relations to truth. As you see, this is something you could find in the Socratic tradition. But—and this may be something more specific to [the Cynics], and the conclusion they drew from this Socratic principle—they believed that their teaching should be a kind of interconnection between a visible, spectacular, provocative, and sometimes scandalous way of life and a truth which could be made accessible to everyone by examples and the explanations associated with those examples. The Cynics wanted those truths, those fundamental truths, to become the rules or at least the guidelines for their own existence and for all human existence; they wanted their own lives to be the blazon of those essential truths. As you see, there is nothing here that is particularly remote from the Greek conception of philosophy as an art of life. That's the reason why, even if we accept the hypothesis about Buddhist influence, we must recognize that the Cynic attitude in its general form is, in principle, a radical version of the Greek conception of relations between life and truth. We could say that it is the most radical version of the Greek principle of relations between knowledge of the truth and the way of life. That is, I think, the explanation for the importance of *parrēsia* and of *parrēsia* as a public activity.

As a consequence of this attitude, we can understand to what kind of tradition the Cynics referred in their teaching, in their way of life, and in their *parrēsia*, and in their way of life as a public *parrēsia*. We could say that in the Platonic, in the Aristotelian, or in the Stoic tradition, people refer to a doctrine, refer to certain texts, or at least to certain quotations and theoretical principles. In the Epicurean tradition, Epicureans refer to a doctrine but also to the personal example of Epicurus, whom every Epicurean had to imitate. Epicurus provided the doctrine and Epicurus was the model.* In the Cynic tradition, I think that the main references were not to a text, or to a doctrine, but the main references were to examples. Of course I do not deny the importance of examples in other philosophical schools, but I think that in the Cynic movement there were no texts, no established and recognized doctrine; there was a theoretical tradition, but the reference was to various people, real or mythic, who were the sources of Cynicism as a way of life. Those examples who were the real sources of reflection, of commentary, those people were either mythical characters like Hercules, Odysseus, and Diogenes. Diogenes was a historical figure but also a mythical one. As a historical figure, we know very few things about Diogenes,** but this historical figure became a mythical figure in the Cynic tradition through a number of anecdotes, of gestures, of provocative attitudes, scandals, and so on, which have been added to the initial, originary elements [of the Cynic tradition]. Diogenes became a kind of philosophical hero. I think that's important to understanding Cynicism and the relation to truth it presumed between a way of life and truth. For instance, Plato and Aristotle, and maybe also Zeno in the Stoic tradition, were philosophical authors and authorities—they were not clearly heroes. Epicurus was both an author and a hero, and Diogenes was a "pure hero."[15] This idea of a philosophy or a way of life which refers to a hero is something that is really important, and you can see what might have been, at a certain moment, the relation between Cynicism and Christianity: the reference not to a text but to a hero, to a heroic figure.***

* The manuscript adds: "to such an extent that creativity, in the Epicurean tradition, was very much restrained by making Epicurus a sacred figure."

** The manuscript specifies: "a philosopher who had, through Antisthenes, some relation to the Socratic movement."

*** The manuscript adds: "The truth-teller as a hero:

- Socrates?
- Diogenes

We now come to the problem of Cynical *parrēsia*. [I believe—and once again I will be rather schematic—that the Cynics used three types of parrhesiastic practice.]* The Cynics used preaching, critical preaching as a parrhesiastic practice; they also used scandalous behavior; and they used dialogue, what I would like to call provocative dialogue.[16]

First, the critical preaching. Preaching is a form of continuous discourse, and as you know, most philosophers, and especially the Stoics, delivered speeches where they gave a presentation of their doctrines. Most of the time, they gave those lectures in front of a rather small audience. The Cynics, on the contrary, disliked this kind of elitism, and they preferred to address numerous crowds; they liked to speak, for instance, in a theater or a place where people gathered for feasts, religious events, and so on. In his great portrayal of the good Cynic, Epictetus evokes those people who in a theater stood up in the middle of the crowd and began a speech.[17] This public preaching was not new. We have testimonies of this kind of preaching as early as the fifth century BCE. The sophists, for instance, were from a certain point of view a kind of preacher, and some of the sophists we see in the Platonic dialogues are a kind of preachers. I think that the Cynic preaching was historically important and had its own specificities. It was historically important because it was the way in which certain philosophical themes—about the way of life, freedom, renouncing luxury, the criticism of political institutions, moral rules, and so on—were diffused far beyond the limits of the philosophical elite and became something popular. From this point of view, Cynic preaching opened the path to various Christian themes. Not only were the themes and form of Cynic preaching taken over by Christian proselytism, but, as you know, for centuries and centuries preaching was one of the main forms of truth-telling and *parrēsia* in our society. Truth was to be told and

---

- the martyr
- and then in modern society, the revolutionary leaders."

* This passage was missing from the lecture and reestablished from Foucault's lecture notes.

taught not only to the elite, as most philosophers presumed, but it also should be told and taught to everybody. Beyond this problem of elitism or unpopularity, I think that in Cynic preaching there was also something important and specific connected to the themes of this preaching. It seems that there in this preaching were very few positive teachings—no direct definition of what is good or bad, but the permanent use or reference to freedom and to *autarkeia*, or autarky, as a criterion to judge any kind of existence and behavior. Most of this preaching using freedom and *autarkeia* as a permanent, constant, general criterion seems to have been oriented toward the arbitrariness of the rules, of law, of social institutions, and against any kind of existence that was dependent on these laws and institutions.* In few words, this preaching has been a permanent criticism against institutions and the social game insofar as they are opposed to freedom, independence, and nature. This is [true] for preaching as a critical *parrēsia*.

Beside popular and proselytic preaching, I think that the Cynics also had recourse—I don't know if you would call it bad jokes or scandalous practices—to what you could call a scandalous attitude. I think that is also quite typical for Cynic forms of *parrēsia*. Most of the time, those practical parrhesiastic attitudes were a way to call into question a rule, an institution, a collective habit, an opinion, and so on. In order to be very schematic and brief, we could say that they used several techniques, several types of scandalous behavior.

One of [these techniques] was the inversion of roles. For instance, we'll see this in Dio's discourse about Alexander.[18] The famous encounter between Alexander and Diogenes has been very important and frequently referred to by the Cynics because it was a typical inversion of roles. The encounter between Alexander and Diogenes doesn't take place in the palace, or in the court, it takes place in the street. The king is standing up and Diogenes is sitting

* The manuscript adds: "both against people who try to draw profit from those institutions and [laws] and against those who bow before those laws and institutions."

back in his barrel. The king is ordered by Diogenes to move, in order to let Diogenes see the sun. Saying that and ordering the king to move in order for the sun to touch him was, of course, an affirmation of the direct, natural relations between the sun and the philosopher in contrast to a mythical genealogy by which the king was supposed to come from a god. Against this mythology of the king and the god [stood] the natural relationship between a man and the sun. That was an example of this technique and of this inversion of roles.

There was also the technique of displacing the rule from a domain where it was accepted to another domain where it was not accepted, in order to show how arbitrary this rule, practice, or habit was. For instance, once, during the Isthmian Games, Diogenes, who was bothering everybody with his permanent scandals, took a crown and put it on his head as if he has been victorious in a football game or something like that. The magistrates were very happy about that because they thought that it was, at last, a good occasion to punish him, to exclude him, and to get rid of him. But he explained that if he put a crown on his head, it was because he had won a much more glorious and difficult victory against his own vices than the athletes when they claimed victory.[19] Later in those same games, he took a crown and, having watched two horses competing with one another, he gave the crown to the horse which was the winner.[20] So you see two symmetric displacements: if the crown is supposed to be a reward for someone who has won a real victory, either it is a moral victory—and then Diogenes, since he is a philosopher who has won victory over all vices, deserves it—or it is only a question of physical strength, and in this case there is no reason why a horse should not be crowned as victorious. It is a question of practices.

There is also another type of scandalous behavior as a form of *parrēsia*. Sometimes the Cynics used practical *parrēsia* by bringing together two types of rules which seem contradictory or remote to one another. For instance, the problem of the satisfaction of bodily needs. You eat; there is no scandal in eating. Since there is no scandal in eating, you can eat in public, in spite of the fact that in Greece that practice was not quite so straightforward. Anyway Diogenes used to eat in the *agora*. And since he ate in the *agora*, there was no reason why he shouldn't masturbate in the *agora*, because in both cases it was the satisfaction of a bodily need. There were a lot of other techniques, but I don't want . . . no, I don't want to try to conceal, to hide another of those niceties.

Besides this preaching, and beside those practical scandals, I think that the Cynics also used another kind of parrhesiastic method, about which I would like to give you some more precise information, and that is the provocative dialogue. In order to give you a more precise example of this kind of dialogue—which is interesting because it both derives from Socratic *parrēsia* but it is different from Socratic *parrēsia*—I'll take an example from the *Fourth Discourse* by Dio of Prusa about monarchy.

Dio of Prusa, do you know who he is? He is a very interesting guy from the last half of the first century and the beginning of the second century. He was born in Asia Minor to a wealthy family that had played a political role in the city's life.* Dio's family was typical for this class of provincial notables that gave to the Roman Empire so many writers, so many civil servants, so many officers, generals, and sometimes emperors. Anyway, Dio of Prusa came to Rome, maybe as a professional rhetor, but there are debates about this. An American scholar has written a very interesting book about Dio of Prusa. There are very few things about his thought and the philosophical background, because as a good historian he writes social history and he doesn't worry about ideas, but anyway it is a very good picture of the social life of intellectuals like Dio of Prusa in the Roman Empire at this moment. The book is *The Roman World of Dio Chrysostom* and the author is C. P. Jones, Christopher Prestige Jones.[21] The book is good.

In Rome, Dio became acquainted with Musonius Rufus, the Stoic philosopher, and maybe through him he became involved in some political circles that were more or less liberal and more or less opposed to personal power. He was exiled by Domitian and he was even forbidden to stay in his own country-land. Thus began for him a wandering life, and he seems to have been converted either to philosophy or at least to the Cynic attitude, to the Cynic lifestyle,* and he took up the customs and the attitude of the Cynics for several years. When he was authorized to return to Rome, he started a new career as a wealthy, famous teacher. Anyway, for a while he had the life and the attitude, the habits and the philosophical references or background of a Cynic philosopher. His discourse, *Seventh Discourse* is called the *Euboean Discourse,* and there is a very interesting description of a small community of peasants which, I think, is the first ethnico-philosophical description. I think you should read that, it's very, very interesting. It is the *Seventh Discourse,* and is in the first volume of Dio's works in the Loeb Classical Library.[22] In a way it's a kind of utopia, it's also a kind of pastoral close to all those themes you find in Virgil about the beautiful life in the country. But it is also a social description, and it presents itself as a social description of a community, and he explains, for instance, the rituals of marriage, and also a conflict about property between two landowners and so on. All of that is very interesting, and for the history of anthropology, I think that the point of departure is, of course, not Rousseau . . .**

* The manuscript adds: "(although he always remained close to Stoicism)."

** The manuscript specifies: "During one of his travels, he visited some countries more or less preserved from Greco-Roman civilization; and of those people he gave a description which is very interesting: it is one of the first examples of what we could call the ethno-philosophical primitivism—a portrayal which does not present itself as a myth, nor as an evocation of the first ages of mankind, nor as the revival of the good old days, but as an accurate report of a real society which still exists but which is not Greco-Roman, life in a state of nature as a kind of reasonable existence which is to be found outside the limits of our civilization (he describes a marriage, the behavior of the bride and bridegroom, the rituals . . .). And through this 'realistic' description he intends to teach a lesson to his fellow citizens of the Greco-Roman world. He wants to show them how human society can live in freedom and happiness by following a handful of natural laws.

This text is worth being analyzed from the point of view of a history of anthropology."

Well, I will put aside this *Seventh Discourse* and turn to the fourth one, in which, I think, you find the three forms of Cynic *parrēsia*. It is a discourse, a preaching.* You also find some references to Diogenes' scandalous behavior, and there is a narrative of the encounter between Alexander and Diogenes.[23] There is also an example of provocative dialogue, the provocative dialogue between Alexander and Diogenes.** This discourse is devoted to narrative of this famous encounter, which seems to be a historical fact, between Alexander and Diogenes.*** Dio's discourse has three parts, beginning with some considerations about this encounter, then a narrative of fictional dialogue, and then a long discourse. In the very beginning of the speech, in the first part, Dio criticizes those who present the meeting between Alexander, the famous king and conqueror, and Diogenes as a kind of egalitarian encounter between one who was famous for his military victories and another who was famous for his virtues. Dio of Prusa does not want people to praise Alexander because he did not disregard a poor guy like Diogenes. Dio insists on the point that Alexander felt himself to be in a position of inferiority toward Diogenes. Alexander felt himself inferior and jealous because of Diogenes' reputation. Diogenes did not need anything in order to do what he wanted to do, whereas Alexander, in order to do what he wanted to do—conquer the world—needed money, soldiers, allies. And whereas Alexander was obliged to lie and to flatter his allies, Diogenes could tell the truth to everyone. Alexander, writes Dio, "if he expected to keep the Macedonian and the other Greeks submissive, must time and again curry the favor of their rulers and the general populace by words and gifts (*logois te kai dōrois*); whereas

* The manuscript specifies: "It is in itself a discourse, and in this discourse Dio reports a speech that Diogenes is supposed to have delivered in front of Alexander."

** The manuscript adds: "which seems to be a Cynic version of the Socratic game of questions and answers."

*** The manuscript adds: "And following the Cynic way of teaching, [Dio] gives about this meeting a lot of details which are completely fictional, but which throw some light on the philosophical meaning Dio attributes to this scene."

Diogenes cajoled no man by flattery, but told everybody the truth (*alla talēthē pros apantas legōn*)."[24] So it's quite clear that Diogenes appears here as the master of truth, and from this point of view Alexander is inferior to him, and Alexander feels this inferiority. But in spite of the fact that Alexander feels this inferiority, Alexander accepts the game, he accepts the game of the *parrēsia*. Alexander had some vices and some faults, of course, but he was not a bad tyrant and he agrees to play the parrhesiastic game: "So the king came up to him as he sat there and greeted him, whereas the other looked up at him with a terrible glare like that of a lion and ordered him to step aside a little, for Diogenes happened to be warming himself in the sun." A nice little anecdote. "Now Alexander was at once delighted with the man's boldness and composure in not being awestruck in his presence. For it is somehow natural for the courageous to love the courageous." This courage at the root of *parrēsia* is recognized by the military courage of Alexander, and that's why Alexander accepts *parrēsia*: "For it is somehow natural for the courageous to love the courageous, while cowards eye them with misgiving and hate them as enemies, but welcome the base and like them. And so to the one class truth and frankness [there you find the word *parrēsia, alētheia kai parrēsia*—M. F.] are the most agreeable things in the world [for the courageous, even if they are kings, because courage admires courage. So *parrēsia* is the most agreeable thing in the world—M. F.], to the other, the cowards, flattery and deceit. The latter lend a willing ear to those who in their intercourse seek to please, the former [the courageous one—M. F.], to those who have regard for the truth."[25]

Now the parrhesiastic game can begin. Alexander agreed to play this game despite the rudeness of Diogenes. The parrhesiastic game begins, and in some respects, it is not very far from the Socratic game, since it is a game with questions and answers. But there are at least two important differences.[26] First, in this parrhesiastic game, it is Alexander who asks the questions and Diogenes who answers, which, of course, is the reverse of the Socratic dialogue. There is another, more important difference, I think, and this second difference is typical for Cynic *parrēsia*. As you remember, Socrates played with his interlocutor's ignorance. Diogenes doesn't play with Alexander's ignorance. Diogenes plays with something else: he plays with Alexander's pride. Diogenes wants to hurt his pride. For instance, from the beginning, he calls Alexander a bastard or he tells him that a king is not different from those children who put a crown on their head and proclaim that they are king. He also says that Alexander's victories on the battlefield are much less important than the war that the same Alexander has to fight against his own vices. All of that is not very pleasant to hear. But that's Diogenes' game. Hitting his interlocutor's pride, forcing him to recognize that he is not what he claims to be, is something that is, as you see, different from showing him that he ignores what he thinks he knows.[27] Of course there are some relations between the Socratic and the Cynic games, since often in a Socratic dialogue you see that someone is hit by his pride, or by the fact that he is obliged to acknowledge what he does not know. That is very clear, for instance, with Callicles, who at a certain moment refuses to debate because his pride has been really hurt.[28] This is only a by-product of the main parrhesiastic game, which is: I'll show you that you don't know what you think you know. In the case of Diogenes, the pride-game is most essential, and the ignorance-and-knowledge-game is only a by-product of this game, which is, I think, different.

Through this attack against the interlocutor's pride, you see that the interlocutor is led exactly to the frontier, to the limits of the first parrhesiastic agreement.* You have seen that Alexander was willing to play this game, to accept this kind of insolence characterized by insults on the part of Diogenes, but there are certain limits. Every time Alexander is insulted by Diogenes, he becomes angry and he comes close to quitting or even to brutalizing Diogenes. So that you see that the parrhesiastic game is always at the frontier of the *parrēsia*-contract, always close to a transgression either because the parrhesiast has said too many bad things, or because the interlocutor becomes angry. You have [here] an example of this game at the limit of the rule: "Do you know," asks Diogenes, "that it is a sign of fear

* The manuscript adds: "(I'll tell you the truth but you won't punish me)."

in a man for him to carry arms?[29] [And no man who is afraid would ever have a chance to become king, any more than a slave would." At these words, Alexander came close to hurling his spear.[30] And then, when the dialogue got to this point, there were two possibilities]* for bringing the interlocutor back into the game, and Diogenes uses them both.

Either the challenge: Diogenes says: "Well, okay, I know that you are outraged, and you are free to, you have the material and legal possibility of killing me. Will you be courageous enough, or cowardly enough, to kill me?" And for instance, after a few insults, Diogenes says to Alexander: "In view of what I say, rage and prance about, think me the greatest blackguard, and slander me to the world and, if it be your pleasure, run me through with your spear; for I am the only man from whom you will get the truth, and you will learn it from no one else. For all are less honest than I and more servile."[31] So you see very clearly Diogenes' [gambit]: he willfully makes Alexander angry, and then he says: "Now, you kill me, but you must know that if you kill me, nobody else will tell you the truth." And there is an exchange, a new form of parrhesiastic contract: either you kill me or you'll know truth. And, of course, this kind of courage and this kind of blackmail to truth has as a consequence that Alexander is very favorably impressed. Alexander agrees to keep playing the game and there is a new parrhesiastic contract, a new parrhesiastic agreement inside the game. Alexander, says Dio, "was at once delighted with the man's boldness and composure in not being awestruck in his presence."[32] And later on, he says: "Then was Alexander amazed at the courage and the fearlessness of the man."[33] That was the first way to bring back Alexander to the game.

But there is also another way, which is not the challenge "either you kill me or [agree to hear] the truth."** It's something that is more subtle: the trick. This trickery is, I think, different from Socratic irony. I'm sure that you remember very well that the Socratic irony

* Several phrases missing from the recording of the lecture were restored based on the manuscript.

** This passage was difficult to hear and so this phrase is speculative.

consists in this: that Socrates feigned to be as ignorant as his interlocutor so that the interlocutor was not ashamed to show his own ignorance. That was, at least, the principle of Socratic irony. Diogenes' trick is somewhat different. Diogenes, at the very moment when his interlocutor bursts out, says something nice or something that his interlocutor supposes to be nice. For instance, after having said to Alexander that he is a bastard—which, of course, was not very well received by Alexander—Diogenes says: "Well, I'll tell you what I mean when I say you are a bastard; I mean that you are Zeus's son." This, of course, pleases Alexander because Alexander does not know yet what conclusion Diogenes will draw. Anyway, Alexander is pleased and he keeps dialoguing with Diogenes.[34]

So you see, there are two possibilities, either the challenge "kill me and then you won't know the truth" or something nice that pleases Alexander and makes him willing to keep dialoguing. But whereas the Socratic dialogue takes a circuitous path from ignorant knowledge to the knowledge of ignorance, you can see that the Cynic dialogue is much more like a fight, a battle, a war, with peaks of great aggression and some moments of peaceful calm, of nice exchanges—which, of course, are traps for the interlocutors. But this kind of Cynic game, differently, I think, from the Socratic one, is explained very clearly by Dio as a kind of strategy within dialogue. After he said very nasty things to Alexander, I don't remember what, Diogenes says: "Well, do you want me to tell you the Libyan myth?"[35] This myth touched on a question posed by Alexander. And the king replied that he did not know this myth. "Then Diogenes told it to him with zest and charm, because he wanted to put him [to put Alexander—M. F.] in a good mood, just as nurses, after giving the children a whipping, tell them a story to comfort and please them."[36] And a little later on, [Dio] gave the same explanation for this kind of game: "When Diogenes perceived that [Alexander] was greatly excited and quite keyed up in mind with expectancy, he toyed with him and pulled him about in the hope that somehow he might be moved from his pride and thirst for glory and be able to sober up a little. For he noticed that at one moment he was [Alexander—M. F.] delighted, and at another grieved, at the same thing, and that his soul was as unsettled as the weather at the solstice when both rain and sunshine come from the very same cloud."[37] But of course, this sweetness is on the side of Diogenes only a way to go further in his aggression. And for instance, when Diogenes, having pleased Alexander in saying that Alexander is a bastard (that is, the son of Zeus), then Diogenes goes further. Alexander, of course, is happy and proud, but Diogenes says: "Well, when Zeus has a son, he gives him some marks of his divine birth." And of course Alexander thinks that he has those marks, and Diogenes says: "Well, I'll indicate to you the marks of divine birth." Those marks prove to be a purely moral portrayal of the royal figure. Then he says: "No one can be a bad king any more than he can be a bad good man; for the king is the best one among men, since he is most brave and righteous and humane, and cannot be overcome by any toil or by any appetite. Or do you think a man is a charioteer if he cannot drive, or that one is a pilot if he is ignorant of steering, or is a physician if he knows not how to cure?"[38] Note those three metaphors: medicine, piloting, steering. "Therefore, just as one cannot pilot except after the manner of pilots, so no one can be a king except in a kingly way."[39] So you see Alexander, as a son of a god, thought that he had marks in his body to show he was divinely born. The answer is: no, there is only one way to be a king, and that is to behave as a king. Afterwards, Alexander asks how he could learn this way of being a king, and the answer from Diogenes is: "there is no way to learn to be a king, you are king by nature, and you recognize that you are king by nature if you play [. . .]."[40]

So as you see, the game comes to a head when Alexander does not discover who he is, as in a Socratic dialogue, he discovers that he is not in any way who he thought himself to be, that is to say, a king of royal birth, and that there is only one way to become a real king: that is to live the same type of life, or to have the same type of character, of *ethos*, as a Cynic philosopher.* And there is a point in the dia-

* The manuscript specifies: "Alexander understands very well that this royal character is something which is different from the institutional definition of monarchy. But Dio goes further and tells him that this royal character

logue where there is nothing more to say. You remember that in the Socratic dialogues, in those moments when the interlocutors feel too embarrassed and do not know what to say, Socrates is obliged to begin or to recall the discourse of somebody else. And most of the time, at the end of the dialogue, when this continuous discursivity begins, then a positive thesis appears.* In this text by Dio of Prusa, you have the same thing: when Alexander feels too embarrassed,** then Diogenes starts a discourse, a continuous discourse,*** but in this discourse it's not a question of saying something which might be the truth of a positive thesis. Diogenes contents himself with giving a precise description of three main faults that are always linked to royal character. These are: the inclination and desire for pleasure; the appetite for richness; and the disorder in ambition within political life [. . .].****

What's interesting is that there is no positive teaching at the end of the dialogue, no positive teaching, only the analysis or the indication of the targets of a permanent spiritual fight. Of course the phrase "spiritual fight," "spiritual struggle" doesn't exist yet here, but what's interesting is that there is no metaphysical thesis, no metaphysical statement, no theoretical affirmation, only the description of the faults with which Alexander will have to fight all his life. I think that you can see in this dialogue the same practice which takes the form of a struggle or a fight between Alexander and Diogenes.

---

cannot be taught; and that Alexander is not able to learn it through any kind of lessons, but only through a certain relation to himself. And he describes the king as a philosopher, a Cynic philosopher."

* The manuscript adds: "It is the moment of the direct teaching."

** The manuscript adds: "But it is not the discomfort of someone who does not know what to say because he discovers that he does not know. It is the discomfort, the distress of someone who oscillates between pride and depression, joy and anguish, who does not know which kind of being he is."

*** The manuscript adds: "Doing this long speech, Diogenes wants to show Alexander that he—Diogenes —is able to compete with the Sophists and the rhetors; and he also wants to please Alexander who is fond of this kind of teaching (that's not very far from Socrates' behavior in the *Phaedrus*)."

**** The last words of this sentence are not audible.

It is not this kind of irony by which the leader leads the other to a certain point that the other doesn't suspect. It's something else; it is a fight between two kinds of power, between political power and the power of truth. In this fight there is a permanent danger and the parrhesiast accepts this danger, confronting Alexander himself from beginning to end. The effect of this parrhesiastic fight is not to lead the interlocutor to a certain truth, to get him to discover the truth. It leads him to internalize this kind of fight, and to fight within himself against his faults, his desires, and to become with himself what Diogenes had been with him. I don't mean to say that the Cynics invented this important category of the spiritual fight, because you find it in Plato, you find [in his texts]* some very important elements of this idea of spiritual fight. But I think that you have here, in this kind of Cynic matrix, a type of *parrēsia* that is different from the Socratic game. Those formal characteristics, you will also find them in Christian institutions, but [in Cynicism] there is also not only the form but the content, which consists in a specific purpose: this notion of parrhesiastic fight, which is a way to render someone able to fight a spiritual war against himself, without any theoretical reference to a philosophical [doctrine].**

—*Something interests me in the second category, the one of the scandal, and in the provocation that I thought was interesting, which was the theatrical nature of the provocation, away from speech and toward gesture and a full mise en scène. So what would you say about the entrance of this sort of visualization, this sort of theater of provocation, which isn't speech?*

—Yes, you're quite right. What's interesting in this entire Cynic attitude is the fact that it is always something which is public, which needs an audience and which is theatrical.[41] Even this encounter between Alexander and Diogenes took place, of course, in the street with a lot of people watching. I think it's something very interesting. Anyway, you have to take into account the fact that Dio of Prusa—

* This phrase is not entirely audible.

** The last word of this sentence is not audible and so this word is speculative.

who for a while lived a Cynic existence, a Cynic way of life—is not a pure Cynic. I don't know if anything like pure Cynicism ever existed. We know very well that in the Greco-Roman world of first centuries there were a sort of precursor to monks who were beggars, and they would say nasty things to people, and who engaged in scandalous behavior. It's easy to call that the pure Cynic, but there were very few with a theoretical background. In the case of Dio of Prusa, who had a very good philosophical education, [it's very different]. I'm not quite sure then that this parrhesiastic game, which is so very well explained in this form of discourse, is not closer to the Socratic tradition than most of the Cynic practices. Maybe it's a combination of the Socratic form and some Cynic [features].

—*When did the negative connotations of the term "Cynic" appear?*

—Very early, because, as you know, the word means "the dog" and Diogenes was called "the dog." The first historical reference to Diogenes is to be found in Aristotle, where Aristotle does not even name Diogenes, he says "the Dog."[42] So, very quickly there was something scandalous [in Cynicism]. I understand very well why Sayre said that it was something completely foreign or that came from outside Greek culture or from India. I think that it's most ambiguous. In a way, I think that they were very close—this idea that someone is nothing other than his own relation to truth, and that this relation to truth must take form and shape in life, was completely Greek. But there has been always something scandalous, at least for this kind of philosophy which in Greece was at the same time something very familiar, something very well-received, but always something very elitist. So you have, maybe more than the problem of Greece versus India, the problem of popular philosophy and of the popular attitude towards an elitist philosophy, and an elitist attitude. Anyway, the noble philosopher always very much disregarded the Cynic. I think the problem of Julian is very interesting. As an emperor, Julian had written a pamphlet against the Cynics, both because he thought that they were too close to the Christians but also—and this is another interpretation, which is not completely congruent with the other—because he thought that this kind of philosophical movement and popular philosophy could be competitive against Christianity. So he was disappointed by the fact that Cynicism and the Cynics had no real culture, and were not able to be representative of the old Greco-Roman culture. He was disappointed because they were too close to the Christians, but he hoped, he expected that it could be something like a popular philosophy.

—Since the cynics had no doctrine, it's very hard to tell whether it's a reform movement or not; your descriptions could go either way.

—It's difficult to answer [that question], I think, since we have very little information about what might be the true Cynicism. For instance, there is a philosopher, Demetrius, who lived at the beginning of the first century, and who is considered by Seneca as a Cynic; Seneca analyzes and praises him a lot.[43] Demetrius lived in the court or in the best society in Rome. But we don't know anything about him—or just a few things through Seneca—and it is difficult to know the political theory of those people.

—Do you see the Cynical mission of delineating the faults of character in this game as the background to the developing Christian delineation of sin in a confessional framework?

—Well, I haven't had the time to describe the faults that Alexander had to fight against. It is interesting because in this text he says that there are three ways of life: one is devoted to pleasure, the other to richness, and the third to political power. He says that those three types of life are, in a way, personified by three spirits, three *daimones*.[44] All that is something very interesting, and very complicated. This conception of the *daimones* seems have been a popular conception of spirits in Greek culture, and became a philosophical concept which you can find in Plutarch, for instance, and which has great importance in Greek culture. The fight against bad spirits, the bad *daimones* in the Christian asceticism, that seems to have some *précurseurs* (precursors) in Greek culture.*

—I think what you're talking about are the medieval sin lists—the listings of various sins—that came much later, about the fifth century, with Evagrius and Cassian, where you have this notion of the daimones *and the elaboration of eight sins by Evagrius and seven sins by Cassian.*

* Foucault expresses himself in French.

—Cassian borrows this conception from Evagrius, and Evagrius, we know very few things about him.* He had a very strong philosophical background, this Evagrius, as Cassian had. Anyway there is a very good article about this notion of *daimōn*, of *esprit*, in the *Dictionnaire de spiritualité*.[45] Anyway, we can be sure that this notion of *daimōn* is a figure that is very important in the Christian notion of spiritual struggle. This notion, you find it in Plutarch, you find it also discussed in several [. . .].** I cannot give you exactly the historical stages, but only some elements of that [evolution].*** Anyway, there is also something which has never been much studied, and that is this notion of spiritual struggle, which is incredibly important for the form of subjectivity we have now. You cannot understand psychoanalysis and the psychic dynamic if you don't have in mind the old tradition of the spiritual struggle. I'm sure that, or at least I believe that there are no books on this notion.

—*Doesn't Hadot write about them in his recent book on spiritual exercises?*[46]

—No, he speaks sometimes about spiritual struggle but it's not this one. He analyzes Marcus Aurelius and some of the Stoic texts which are mostly interpreted as theoretical texts, and he tries to interpret them as forming a matrix for various spiritual exercises. It's very amazing, but . . .

—*It sounds to me from your description of the Cynic tradition that it is actually a tradition of replacing truth with insults, in that these philosophers are willfully misleading the interlocutor and replacing revelations of truth with insults and traps. Is that the end of these practices?*

—You are quite right to ask the question because really I have not been able to say what I want to say yet. The problem is not to substitute truth for insults or insults for truth. In order to help someone, for instance Alexander, to understand that the real royal character is not linked to a status, to birth, to fame, or power but to certain natural qualities which are visible in Diogenes, he uses this method

* The next sentence is inaudible.

** The last few words of this sentence are inaudible.

*** This last word is inaudible and so this phrase is speculative.

which I would call a kind of Cynical ethical reduction. The scandalous practices we spoke of have this effect. What are you doing when you do something, when you give a crown to someone [...]?* What do you really want to reward? [...]** You say that you are a king, I know that you worry about your birth because it was a rumor in Greece that Alexander was not the son of Philip, but a bastard. What does that mean? Is it important to be a bastard or not? You say that that you are the son of Zeus. What does that mean? And what are the indispensable qualities of a king? So, you see, [the aim] was not to put insults in place of truth. It was a phenomenology, an aggressivo-phenomenological reduction. It was exactly this type of reduction. The fool, the monarch as a fool, the Cynic as fool, the fool as a fool...

—*You mentioned the hypothesis about the origins of cynicism in India?*

—No, I am completely incompetent in this field. I know that some very serious scholars have offered this hypothesis; what I wanted to show is exactly the contrary, not in order to criticize their thesis, but to show, even if there is a historical origin in India, there is something that is exactly in line with the Greek conception of philosophy as way of life, an art of living, a technique of life, and so on.

NOVEMBER 30, 1983***

PERHAPS YOU REMEMBER THAT LAST week when we met, my intention was to analyze three kinds of the parrhesiastic game: the first in the framework of group relations, and I took the example of the Epicurean groups; I also wanted to analyze the parrhesiastic

* The next sentence is inaudible.

** The next sentence is inaudible.

*** The last session, originally scheduled for Monday, November 28, 1983, was pushed back to Wednesday, November 30, since Foucault was feeling ill. Before beginning his lecture, Foucault apologized to his audience: "I would like to apologize for not being able to give the lecture last Monday. I will try to give it today, but I'm not quite sure that I will be able to succeed... If I collapse before the end of my presentation, you'll..." The audience responded: "We'll pick you up."

game in the framework of public life, and I took the example of Dio of Prusa and Cynicism; and I also had the intention of analyzing the parrhesiastic game in the framework of personal relations, and my intention was to take some examples from Plutarch and from Galen. But once more I was out of time, so I had no time to give you any information about Plutarch and Galen. I would like to give you very briefly now some indications about those two texts, which, I think, are rather good examples of some of the technical problems which can arise in the framework of personal relations, that is, in the framework of the parrhesiastic game within personal relations.

Very briefly, only few references, first about Plutarch. In Plutarch there is a text which is very precisely and explicitly devoted to the problem of *parrēsia* and to a certain aspect of the parrhesiastic problem.* This text tries to answer the question: how is it possible to recognize a parrhesiast, a real, a true parrhesiast? And how is it possible to distinguish between a parrhesiast and a flatterer? You find this text in the first volume of the Loeb edition, in the first volume of Plutarch's *Moralia*; the exact title of the pamphlet is *How to Tell a Flatterer from a Friend*.[1] In this text, I think we must underline several points.

First, why do we need to have some friends in our personal lives who play the role of a parrhesiast? The reason that Plutarch gives for the necessity of having a parrhesiast lies in the kind of relations we have to ourselves. This relation that we have to ourselves is a relation of love, of self-love, of *philautia*. This relation of self-love is for us the ground of a permanent illusion about who we really are, about ourselves, such that the first flatterer against whom we have to struggle and fight is ourselves. We are our own flatterers.[2] And it is in order to disconnect this kind of relation we have spontaneously to ourselves, it is in order to get rid of this *philautia*, that we need a parrhesiast.**

* The manuscript adds: "or, I should say, to a technical problem in *parrēsia*."

** The manuscript adds: "But if we need a parrhesiast, in order to fight this self-flattery, we must take care to pick a real parrhesiast and not a flatterer (the real flatterer is not the one who obviously 'flatters,' but the one who be-

Of course you can understand that it is very difficult, first, to accept a parrhesiast, and also to recognize a parrhesiast, for two sets of reasons. The first one is, of course, that a parrhesiast is not easy to recognize since through our *philautia* we are interested in not recognizing the true parrhesiast. So there is at stake in this text the problem of the uncontested criteria through which we are made able to discover the true parrhesiast we need so badly in order to get rid of our *philautia*. To pick a real parrhesiast, and not a flatterer, implies that we are in possession of a kind of semiology of the real parrhesiast. And how can we recognize the true parrhesiast? Plutarch proposes two major criteria in order to recognize the true parrhesiast. Those two criteria are: first, the conformity of what the so-called or the supposed parrhesiast says with the way he behaves. Here you recognize very easily the Socratic harmony that was described and defined at the beginning of the *Laches*, when Laches said that he could trust Socrates as a parrhesiast about courage since he had seen that Socrates was truly courageous and that there was a harmony between what he said and the way he behaves. So for Plutarch this criterion of conformity between what the parrhesiast says and the way he behaves, this conformity is the first criterion. But there is a second one, the permanence, the continuity, the stability, the steadiness of the parrhesiast, of the man who is supposed to be the parrhesiast, the stability, the steadiness of his choices, of opinions, of his thoughts.[3]

Of course, there are a lot of other very interesting things in this text. But I'd like to underscore those two major themes. First, the theme of the self-deception, and its link with *philautia*. Of course, the theme of the self-deception is not something completely new, but as you see in Plutarch's text, it's something which is clearly different from the Platonic or the Socratic [theme of] ignorance of our own ignorance. It is the fact that we are not able, not only to know that we know nothing, but we are also not able to know who exactly we are. I think that this theme of self-deception has become

---

haves like a parrhesiast blaming you, rebuking you, and reproaching you for the way you act)."

more and more important in Hellenistic culture; and in the imperial period, in Plutarch, it is something which is really important.

There is a second theme that I would like to underline in this text. It is the theme of stability, the steadiness of mind that is evaluated, which is valued as something very important, very highly prized in life. Stability, steadiness, *firmitas*. That's not something which is new, but in late Stoicism, this notion of *firmitas*, of steadiness, takes on great importance, and there are obvious relations between the theme of the self-deception and the theme of the mobility of mind. Destroying self-deception and acquiring and keeping the steadiness of mind are two ethical, moral behaviors which are linked to one another. Self-deception makes you unable to know who you are, and all those movements in your thoughts, in your opinions, in your feelings, which force you to move from one opinion to another, from one feeling to another, those two things are related to one another, since if you are able to grasp exactly who you are, then you stay in the same place and you won't be moved by anything. If you are moved by any kind of stimulation, perception, feeling, passion, and so on, then you are not able to stay in close contact with yourself, you are dependent on something else, you are driven to a lot of different things, and you are not able to be in complete possession, in perfect possession of yourself. Those two elements—having self-deception and being moved by anything from the external world—those two elements, self-deception and the mobility of mind, became something important in the Christian tradition.[4] In early Christian spirituality, Satan, the Devil, is always represented as the agent both of *philautia*, self-indulgence, self-deception, as opposed to the renunciation of the self, and Satan is also the agent of the mobility of mind, of this instability, of this unsteadiness, as opposed to the steadiness, to the immobility of contemplation. And on the contrary, fastening one's own mind to God is a way, first, to renounce oneself and to destroy any kind of self-deception, and it is also a way to acquire an ethical and an ontological steadiness. So I think that you can see through Plutarch's text, this analysis of the relation between *parrēsia* and flattery and the difficulty of recognizing a parrhesiast, certain elements which will become so important in the Christian tradition.

I would also refer very briefly to Galen's text, where you see the same problem: how is it possible to recognize and to choose a real parrhesiast? This text written by Galen, the famous physician, at the end of the second century CE, this text is to be found in the pamphlet about the passions and the way to cure the passions of the soul.[5] And Galen explains that the reason why we need a parrhesiast in order to cure our passions is the same as Plutarch gave a century earlier: it is the *philautia*, the self-love, which is at the root of all the kinds of self-deception.[6] But it is worthwhile to note that in this text the parrhesiast that everybody needs in order to get rid of his own *philautia*, this parrhesiast does not need to be a friend, he does not need to be someone we know, someone with whom we are acquainted, and that, I think, is a very important difference between what you can find in Galen and what we can find in Plutarch. In Plutarch, exactly as in Seneca, and in a very old tradition which derives at least from Socrates, the parrhesiast always needs to be a friend, and the friendship relation is at the root of this parrhesiastic game. As far as I know, it's the first time you see that the parrhesiast does not need to be a friend. It's even much better that the parrhesiast be someone that you do not know in order for him to be completely neutral. A good parrhesiast does not hate you, but a good parrhesiast does not love you either. The good parrhesiast is someone with whom you have previously no particular relation, someone who is neutral,* but of course you cannot choose him at random. You must, of course, review certain criteria in order to know if he is really a good parrhesiast. And to do that, you must have heard something about him. Does he have a good reputation? Is he old enough? And

* The manuscript adds: "And maybe we can see one of the signs of a certain decline of friendship as social, cultural and ethical form in the Greco-Roman world.

(This decline has not been something sudden: Marcus Aurelius/Fronto. But it seems likely that the new pattern of political structure, the 'rise of bureaucracy,' [and] a new style of family life and family relations have been important factors in the decrease of friendship's value in the Ancient world.

And it is a fact that Christianity, and Christian asceticism [have] been distrustful towards friendship)."

is he rich enough? Because it is very important that the parrhesiast, or the one you want to play the role of parrhesiast, it is very important that he isn't poorer than you are, because if he is poor and if you are rich, of course he has every likelihood of being a flatterer. But if he is at least as rich as you are, and if he is richer than you are, then he has no interest in flattering you and he has good chances of being a parrhesiast.[7]

It's very interesting also to note that in this text the parrhesiast does not need to be a physician or a doctor. In spite of the fact that Galen himself is a doctor, in spite of the fact that he explains that as a physician he has been very frequently obliged to cure passions and that he has succeeded in curing passions, in spite of that, it's interesting to note that Galen does not ask this as a condition for being a parrhesiast. Someone can help you in curing your passions if he is able to tell you the truth about yourself. But it's not enough to know that he has a good reputation, that he is old enough, that he is rich enough; you also have to test him, and Galen gives a kind of program for testing a possible parrhesiast. You have to ask him questions about yourself and to see how he answers those questions, if he is severe enough with you. You have to be very suspicious when the supposed parrhesiast congratulates you, or when he is not severe enough, and so on. Galen does not elaborate the precise role of this parrhesiast in the cure of passions, he gives only few examples of the advice he happens to give himself as a parrhesiast, but it's interesting to see that in this text the relation between *parrēsia* and friendship seems to be disconnected, and that there is a kind of trial of the parrhesiast through a sort of examination of the future parrhesiast by, I wouldn't say the *client,* since it's not a paying activity, but there is something like that in this text. Anyway, I apologize if I am so brief in speaking about those two texts which are important.*

* Foucault goes on to say, "I think that you can read them; they are not very difficult to read, they are difficult to find in this library. All of the works of Galen are to be found only in the Biology Department. I don't really know what they do with Galen in this department, but you can't find them in the main library."

[What I just said] was supposed to be the third part of last week's lecture, the problem of the parrhesiastic game in the framework of personal relations, of group relations, and of public life and personal relations.* That would have been the third part. The lecture tonight

* Foucault had prepared, for the lecture on November 21, a preliminary version of this third part of the lecture, which he didn't have time to present. He presents, then, a rather different, new version on November 30. Below is the first version of that lecture:

"A. Plutarch: *How to Tell a Flatterer from a Friend*. In this text appears very clearly what is the opposite of *parrēsia*: it is flattery (you have to remember [the] importance of flattery in this type of society, clients and patrons and so on). The flatterer tells lies in order to please his interlocutor, and to give him a deceptive, misleading image of himself. It is of course the most dangerous thing for the care of the self. Plutarch: the worst enemy of the *gnōthi seauton* is the flatterer. That's the reason why we have to rely upon a parrhesiast and not upon a flatterer.

But the problem is: how to recognize a parrhesiast? The problem is not so simple as it looks at first glance, because a flatterer who shows that he is a flatterer is not dangerous. A real flatterer is the one who hides that he is a flatterer.

All the first part of Plutarch's treatise deals with this problem: 'the semiotic of flattery.' And the solution is to be found in the fact that the flatterer is changing in his opinion, in his behavior, in his way of life, according to people with whom he is. You can be sure that he who rebukes you is not a flatterer if his own choices for himself are the same: the same as the choices he suggests to other people, the same in his own life.

The signs of the parrhesiast are the conformity of what he says to the others to the way he behaves himself, and the conformity of his behavior to a permanent scheme. From this you can see that the behavior of the supposed [parrhesiast] is evidence both for the truth of what he thinks and for the sincerity of what he says. There are, in fact, two problems: the sincerity and the truth. Both are solved at the same time by the correlation, the conformity of what he says to what he is. [Plutarch, "How to Tell a Flatterer from a Friend," 52A–E—Ed.]

The adequate correlation between what he says and what he is, is the problem, the duty of the master. In the avowal, this adequation is the problem of the disciple, or of the penitent. But in another form:

– For the penitent, what he says is supposed to show what he is. And the sincerity is proved by his attitude.

– For the parrhesiast, the evidence that he is sincere, and that he tells the truth, is given by the way he lives, by what he is.

[B.] Galen.

The treatise is an answer to an Epicurean treatise about passions. To this treatise, Galen objects that there is no clear analysis of what is meant by 'guarding,' protecting oneself against the passions. [There is] no clear difference between watchfulness, diagnosis, [and] correction. His own treatise will be a technical treatise about those questions.

Three main principles:

– Passions and errors are different from each other, and passions are at the root of errors, which is something quite different from Stoicism.

– But even if the passions are not errors, knowledge is necessary in order to cure the passions. Truth as medicine. *Gnōthi seauton*.

– This self-knowledge is not possible without the help of somebody else. The reason is the self-love which makes one blind to his own faults.

'Neither love nor hate': emotional neutrality. That's the only case where such an indication is to be found. [See Galen, *On the Passions and Errors of the Soul*, pp. 31–33.—Ed.]

– *Philia* as a requisite for the care of the self:

– *Eros*

– *Eunoia*

– *Dilectio* (Seneca).

– The disappearance of *philia*?

– Professionalization? But [the parrhesiast] is not a specialist.

'Judge from your own experience.' *Basanizein*. The problem of the proof, of the trial of the other. [See Galen, *On the Passions and Errors of the Soul*, pp. 31–33.—Ed.]

– Epictetus: the pupil [has] to give evidence that he is able to choose to listen to the master.

– Galen: the trial of the master. Cf. Plutarch.

What's interesting in the trial of the master as a parrhesiast is that:

– it is not a question of professional competence;

– the trial is a rather complex game between the director and the directed.

One point which deserves attention is the principle of the indefinite struggle and the principle of a perpetual distrust towards oneself.

is supposed to be about the practices of the parrhesiastic game, the kind of parrhesiastic game we find in the philosophical and moral literature in the two first centuries of our era.

Of course I won't present all those practices, which are very numerous. I will begin only with two short remarks. First, I think that in those techniques, you see something which is interesting and important, and that is a shift from a truth game that, in the classical conception of *parrēsia*, was constituted by someone courageous enough to tell the truth to other people,* towards another truth game consisting in being courageous enough to disclose the truth about oneself.** That's a general remark about those practices.

Second, the framework in which [we find] this new parrhesiastic game, where the problem is to tell the truth about oneself, is what the Greeks called *askēsis*, from which derives our word asceticism. But it has to be very clear that the Greek *askēsis* does not have the same meaning as our asceticism, which has been modeled by and through Christian practices. *Askēsis* in Greek has a very broad meaning: it denotes any kind of practical exercise or training.[8] For instance, it was a commonplace to say that any kind of art, of aptitude, of technique, had to be learned by *mathēsis* and by *askēsis*, by a theoretical learning [or *mathēsis*], and by a practical training or *askēsis*. Musonius Rufus, repeating a traditional teaching, said that the art of living (*tou biou*) was, like the other arts, an art which one could learn only from theoretical teaching. This *technē tou biou*, this art of living, demanded practice and training, *askēsis*.[9] So *askēsis* does not mean anything more than a practical training. And, as you see, this *askēsis* is different from Christian asceticism on two major points. The first one is that in Christian asceticism the ultimate aim, the ultimate target is the renunciation of the self, whereas in Greek and Greco-Roman philosophy, moral *askēsis* has as its target the formation of a

---

The political and social problem of flattery. [These last three lines are crossed out on the lecture manuscript.—Ed.]"

* The manuscript adds: "about themselves."

** The manuscript specifies: "The discourse of the self."

relation with oneself, a relationship of possession and of sovereignty. The second great difference is this one, that Christian asceticism takes as its principal theme the detachment from the world, whereas philosophical, Greco-Roman asceticism is concerned to endow the individual with the preparation, the baggage, the equipment which permit him to confront the world. That's the second remark.

Third, this *askēsis* implied numerous different forms of exercises. They were rather well specified, but they have never been, as they will be later in Christian institutions, analyzed and described. Some of them have been discussed, criticized, as the *praemeditatio malorum*, but most of them were known by everybody, so that the people used those kinds of exercises without offering any precise theory about them. Everybody could recognize them, but the fact is that often in Greek and Latin texts you'll find some passages which are mostly read by us as more or less interesting theoretical considerations about death, life, the world, necessity, time, and so on, [when] in fact those texts are not at all a kind of theoretical consideration about those general topics, [but rather] they are schemas, they are matrices for spiritual exercises. We must not forget that most of those texts written in late antiquity about ethics were not at all theories about the foundations of ethics but practical books with recipes and exercises which one had to read, to reread, to meditate, to learn, in order to make of them a kind of permanent matrix for one's own behavior.

So after those three preliminary remarks, I would like to turn to the kind of exercises where someone has to examine the truth about himself and to tell someone else this truth. Most of the time, when we refer to this kind of exercise, by which one has to tell the truth about himself, most of the time, we call those exercises "examination of conscience," and we consider them as belonging to the same genre, to the same form. But I think that it is an oversimplification, and I am afraid that the term of "examination of conscience," which has been often used and that I have used also for those different exercises, may be misleading. In fact, I think that we have to very precisely define the different truth games which have been put to work, which have been applied in those exercises in the Greco-Roman tradition. I would like to analyze, through four examples, maybe five if I have enough time, some of those truth games which are commonly called the "examination of conscience" in order to show you how different those exercises were from one another, to show you also what kinds of elements of behavior, of mind, and of feelings were considered relevant for those different exercises. I would also like to show you that those exercises, in spite of these differences, implied a type of relation to truth, a kind of relation between truth and the self, that is in general very different from what we find in our Christian tradition.*

The first text I would like to analyze briefly is a short text by Seneca from *De ira*:

> Sextius had this habit, and when the day was over and he had retired to his nightly rest, he would put these questions to his soul: "What bad habit have you cured today? What fault have you resisted? In what respect are you better?" Anger will cease and become more controllable if it finds that it must appear before a judge every day. Can anything be more excellent than this practice of thoroughly sifting the whole day? And how delightful the sleep that follows this self-examination—how tranquil it is, how deep and untroubled, when the soul has either praised or admonished itself, and when this secret examiner and critic of self has given report of its own character (*speculator sui censorque secretus cognovit de moribus suis*)! I avail myself of this privilege, and every day I plead my cause before the bar of self (*cotidie apud me causam dico*). When the light has been removed from sight, and my wife, long aware of my habit, has become silent, I scan the whole of my day and retrace all my deeds and words (*totum diem meum scrutor factaque ac dicta mea remetior*). I conceal nothing from myself, I omit nothing. For why should I shrink from any of my mistakes (*erroribus*), when I may commune thus with myself? "See that you never do that again; I will pardon you this time. In that dispute, you spoke too offensively; after this

* The manuscript adds: "and from what we could call the hermeneutics of the self."

> don't have encounters with ignorant people; those who have never learned do not want to learn. You reproved that man more frankly than you ought, and consequently you have, not so much mended him as offended him. In the future, consider not only the truth of what you say, but also whether the man to whom you are speaking can endure the truth. A good man accepts reproof gladly; the worse a man is the more bitterly he resents it."*[10]

First point: We know from several sources that this kind of exercise was a rule, or at least was a habit, in the Pythagorean tradition, in the Pythagorean sect. Before they went to sleep, the Pythagoreans had to conduct this kind of examination which consisted in the recollection of the errors they committed during the day, errors against the rules of behavior, which, as you know, were very strict in the Pythagorean school. In this Pythagorean tradition, the purpose of this examination was a purification of soul, and this purification of soul was made necessary by the fact that, for the Pythagoreans, sleep was considered as a state of being where the soul or mind could be in contact with divinity, with gods, through dreams; of course, one had to keep one's soul as pure as possible to have beautiful dreams and contact with benevolent divinities. So that was the meaning of the old self-examination you can find in the Pythagorean tradition, and you have testimonies about this tradition for instance in Diogenes Laërtius. In several other texts, in Cicero, in the *De senectute*,[11] you find references to this kind of practice in the Pythagorean movement. It is quite clear that in this text we still have some traces of these kinds of practices through the idea that Seneca expresses very clearly when he says that with this habit we are able to have a good and delightful sleep: "How delightful the sleep that follows this self-examination—how tranquil it is, how deep and untroubled." And you find here this very old and very deep conception of sleep and

* Certain passages in this text having produced laughter from the audience, Foucault adds: "I am really surprised that you laughed at this text. When you read it to a Catholic audience, people do not laugh. You are rather dull (*ennuyeux*)."

dreams as possible contact with divinity. You find also an expression of this theme in Plato, in *The Republic*, and you see that self-examination has this kind of effect, of impact: it is supposed to be a purification of soul.[12] We know from Seneca himself that his first training was Pythagorean; for a while he tried to eat only vegetarian food, and so on.[13] So this Pythagorean background is clear in this text.

But I think that it is worth noting that Seneca relates this practice of self-examination not to the Pythagorean tradition, in spite of those traces in this text, but to Sextius, who was a typical Stoic and one of the great originators of Stoicism, a representative of Stoicism in Rome at the end of the first century BCE.[14] In fact it seems that this exercise, in spite of its purely Pythagorean origin, was used and praised in several philosophical sects or movements, by Epicureans, Stoics, Cynicism, and so on. You find, for instance, in Epictetus some references to this kind of exercise.

It would be, of course, useless to deny that Seneca's self-examination is very close to Christian practice, which has been so highly praised during centuries and centuries in the Christian tradition.* But if we look at the text a little more closely, I think that we can see some very interesting differences. I would like to draw your attention to three points.

First point: the question of Seneca's attitude toward himself. What kind of procedure is Seneca really using in this examination? To what model does he refer in this text? What practical matrix does he use and apply in his relation to himself? Of course, at first glance, it seems to be judicial practice, and very close to the Christian confession. There are faults, those faults are confessed, there is an accused (who is Seneca), there is an accusator or a prosecutor (who is also Seneca), there is a judge (who is also Seneca), and it seems that there is a verdict. The entire scene seems to be judicial. In fact, Seneca employs some of the most typical words of the [Latin] judicial vocabulary, for instance, *cognoscere de moribus suis, causam dico*. All of those are judicial terms. But if we look closely, we see that it is

* The manuscript adds: "and mainly in the Counter-Reformation."

a question of something rather different from a court or from a judicial decision. For instance, Seneca says that he is *speculator sui*: the word *speculator* means that he is an inspector, an inspector who inspects either the freight in a boat, or the work that has been done by people building a house, and so on. Seneca says also that he is *scrutator*, that he scrutates, *scrutatur totum diem suum*: that means that he inspects, that he examines his entire day. This word also belongs not to the judicial vocabulary, but to the vocabulary of administration. Seneca says again that he must *facta ac dicta sua remetiri*. That word, the verb *remetiri*, is again a technical term that is used for the bookkeeping: it serves to check whether there is any kind of mistake or fraud in the books. So with regard to himself, Seneca is not exactly a judge who has to punish, he is much more an administrator who, once the work has been done, or when the book has been written, or when the year's business is finished, settles up, takes stock of things, and sees if everything has been done correctly. It is much more an administrative scene than that of a court or a judicial scene.

[Second point:] we can now turn to the faults that Seneca recalls, and that he gives as examples in this examination. It is worthwhile to note that they are not the kind of faults that we should call "sins"; for instance, he does not confess that he has had too much to drink, or that he has committed sexual offenses, or that he has bad feelings for someone, or that he hates someone, or that he has committed financial fraud (the kind of faults that Seneca was in fact very familiar with, since he has been one of the great thieves of Nero's reign). But you find nothing like that in this kind of confession, because I think that the faults for which he blames himself are very different. For instance, he says that he has committed a fault insofar as he has criticized someone, and instead of correcting the man he criticized, he hurt him. Or again, he reproaches himself that he talked with people who were in no way capable of understanding him. In doing so, in conducting himself in this way, he has made what he calls *errores*, mistakes. And as you see, these are not sins with the meaning we are able to give to this word. What he calls *errores*, what he calls mistakes, are only poor adjustments between aims and means. What he reproaches himself for is that he didn't have in mind the ends about which he should have been thinking. For instance, he should have been thinking that it is useless and irrational to blame someone if he is not able to be corrected. You must blame someone only if you are able to correct him and to help him to improve himself. So I would say that these are not sins with the meaning of the word we use now. I would say that what [Seneca] calls mistakes, *errores,* are a kind of strategic, of tactical errors in conduct, and that he was not able to establish a rational relation between the principles he knew and the behavior he had. And that's exactly in what an error consists. It's not a transgression of a law, it is an incapacity, inability, or an unsuccessful attempt to coordinate precisely the rules he accepts, he recognizes, he knows, and his own conduct.

The third point will be this: In fact, Seneca does not react to his own errors, to his own mistakes as if they were sins, he does not punish himself, there is nothing like penance, or like "satisfaction." The memorization of his mistakes has for its object a reactivation of practical principles of conduct which are useful for the future. He says: "Well, see that you never do that again. I will pardon you this time. In that dispute you spoke too offensively. After this don't have encounters with ignorant people. Those who have never learned do not want to learn. In the future, consider not only the truth of what you say, but also whether the man to whom you are speaking can endure the truth. A good man accepts the truth gladly."[15] So in this examination, it's not at all a question of analyzing a responsibility, or of discovering a feeling of guilt, it's not even a question of purifying oneself from previous faults, it's a kind of administrative investigation, of administrative scrutinizing, which creates the possibility of reactivating some rules in order to make those rules more vivid, more active, more permanent, more efficient as a matrix for a future conduct. That's the first text I would like to analyze.

—*Is this examination of conscience just for men? Or can it also be practiced by women?*

—I think that the question is very important in the Pythagorean circles where, since the beginning, the role of women has been important. But I don't think that for any of the usual Greco-Roman philosophers the question of self-examination by women would be relevant. Women don't have to examine themselves. I have found in Dover,[16] I think—I'm not sure if it is Dover—something about the problem of sexual ethics at least in classical Greece. He said: of course women had to behave following the rules, but it was not a question of ethics, it was a question of legality; it was not a question of personal virtue, it was a question of the relation of women to the rules. It was not a question of their relation to themselves. For instance, to be truthful to their husbands was a rule, and they were punished if they transgressed this rule. It was not a question of ethics. On the contrary, for the man who was not obliged to be truthful to his wife, to be truthful to his wife was a question of ethics because it was a question of his relation to himself. We know that in Pythagorean circles women had a very important role, and there were texts written in the first two or three centuries of our era under the name of women, Pythagorean texts. We are not sure that they were really written by women, but the fact that they were supposed to be written by women proves that the women were integrated in those circles.

The second text [that I would now like to analyze with you] is a long text from *De tranquillitate*.[17] *De tranquillitate* is precisely one of those numerous texts written about the theme we encountered a few moments ago, the theme of firmness, steadiness, and so on. To put it very briefly, *tranquillitas* is a Latin word which is supposed to translate the Greek *euthumia*. This *tranquillitas* refers to, denotes a certain state of stability, of steadiness in mind; it denotes also that in this state, the self is independent of any kind of external event and of any kind of internal incitation which could induce an involuntary movement in the mind. So *tranquillitas* denotes not only a stability but a sovereignty, an independence, and *tranquillitas* refers also to a certain feeling of pleasure which has its source, its principle, in this sovereignty, in this possession of the self by itself.

The beginning of the *De tranquillitate*, written by Seneca, presents itself as a request for a "moral consultation." A young friend of Seneca, who belongs to the same family and who started a political career under Nero, asks Seneca to give him moral and philosophical advice. It is interesting to note that very obviously there is for Serenus, this young friend, and for Seneca no real incompatibility between a political career and a philosophical choice. The philosophical choice is not for them an alternative to political life; it had to go along with political life in order to give to this public activity what we could call its moral "armature," its moral framework, and to determine the relations between the individual and this kind of public activity. Serenus, who asks for this moral consultation, has been for a while attracted to and seduced by Epicurism, and then later turned towards Stoicism. But even after turning to Stoicism, he felt uncomfortable, he had the impression that he was not able to improve, he had the feeling that he was blocked. He didn't make any progress; this idea is very important since, as you know, for the early Stoics there couldn't be any kind of progress, since one becomes a sage once and for all. The idea of progress was relatively new in Stoicism.* Never mind. It is in this context that Serenus turns to Seneca and asks Seneca to help him. Of course, we cannot be sure that it is a true picture of the real Serenus; we can, on the contrary, be sure that Seneca himself has written this text, but this text is supposed to be the letter in which Serenus makes his request for a moral consultation. And in spite of the fact that it has been written by Seneca himself, it is a model, a pattern for a kind of self-examination. Serenus is supposed to examine what he has done or who he is at the moment he asks for this consultation. This kind of self-examination, at a moment which is very important in one's life, because you need philosophy—you have learned something about philosophy but not enough—at this very important moment, you have to conduct this self-examination. This self-examination is, of course, very different from the evening self-examination that Seneca practices every day like the Pythagoreans.

* The manuscript adds: "The idea has been challenged very early on; and you see that, in late Stoicism, the philosophical practice was at the same time the ethical framework for an active life and a spiritual itinerary which had to develop for its own sake."

So what is this self-examination?

> When I made examination of myself, it became evident, Seneca, that some of my vices are uncovered and displayed so openly that I can put my hand upon them, some are more hidden and lurk in a corner, some are not always present but recur at intervals; and I should say that the last are by far the most troublesome, being like roving enemies that spring upon one when the opportunity offers, and allow one neither to be ready as in war, nor to be off-guard as in peace.
>
> Nevertheless the state in which I find myself most of all—for why should I not admit the truth to you as to a physician [*quare enim non verum ut medico fatear*]?—is that I have neither been honestly set free from the things that I hated and feared, nor, on the other hand, am I in bondage to them; while the condition in which I am placed is not the worst, yet I am complaining and fretful—I am neither sick nor well.[18]

So that's the beginning of this request for a consultation. As you see, the demand by Serenus takes very explicitly the shape of a medical consultation on the state of his own soul: "Why should I not confess to you the truth, as to a doctor? [. . .] I don't feel altogether ill, but nor do I feel entirely in good health," and so on. All of those expressions are very clearly related to this famous metaphor, or at least this famous conception, of the philosophical and moral discomfort [as] physical illness. What is important also is to underline the fact that Serenus uses this expression, and says very explicitly that in order to get cured, he wants to *verum fateri*, that is, to confess the truth. And the problem is: what is the truth, what are those kind of thoughts, of secret faults, of shameful desires that Serenus has to confess? As you'll see a little later on, there are no secret faults, no shameful desires, nothing like that. Serenus's confession is something completely different and can be divided in two parts, first, a very general exposé about himself, and [second], an exposé of his attitude in different domains of activity and life.

First, a general presentation of his condition:

> There is no need for you to say that all the virtues are weakly at the beginning, that firmness and strength are added by time. I am well aware also that the virtues that struggle for outward show, I mean for position and the fame of eloquence and all that comes under the verdict of others, do grow stronger as time passes—both those that provide real strength and those that trick us out with a sort of dye with a view to pleasing, must wait long years until gradually length of time develops color—but I greatly fear that habit, which brings stability to most things, may cause this fault of mine to become more deeply implanted. Of things evil as well as good long intercourse induces love.
>
> The nature of this weakness of mind that halts between two things and inclines strongly neither to the right nor to the wrong, I cannot show you so well all at once as a part at a time; I shall tell you what befalls me . . .[19]

So those are the general issues [voiced] by Serenus about his own state. So as you see, Serenus considers first that this consultation is a kind of medical consultation, that he needs to tell the truth in order to be cured. This truth that he will expose is the description of a state of discomfort, of malaise that he feels; across this text and from some other indications later on, you see that this feeling of malaise is from the beginning to the end referred and compared to the situation of a boat, of a ship that does not advance anymore, but rolls and pitches. And Serenus fears staying at sea in this condition, in view of the firm land which remains for him inaccessible.[20]

In this description, with this implicit and at a certain moment explicit metaphor of the boat, we can recognize a very old and traditional theme, but I think that the organization of those themes has something very particular. The comparison to the boat is something which is traditional. You remember what I told you about the constant references in this moral philosophy both to medicine and to piloting, to medicine and to boats; here you have very explicitly those three elements: the problem of moral-philosophical needs, the metaphor or the reference to medicine, and the reference to piloting. Serenus is on the way to acquiring truth, he is as on a boat, and he sees from the boat the truth, but he lacks complete possession and mastery of himself. He has the feeling that he does not make progress anymore, maybe because he is too weak, maybe because his way is not the good one.* He does not know exactly the reason for this discomfort and this kind of immobility, but what is interesting is that the immobility, which he describes as a malaise, is explained by the fact that he is in a kind of perpetual mobility. It is a mobility without any other movement than this kind of rocking. The boat is rocking and cannot advance because it is rocking. And the very specific problem of Serenus is this one: how can I substitute this movement of rocking caused by the instability, the unsteadiness of my mind for another movement which is one which might lead me to the coast and to firm land? It's a kind of problem of dynamics. I would say that it is something which is, as you see, very different from the Freudian dynamics of the soul, where the dynamics of the soul are defined by a conflict between two forces, inside the apparatus of the mind, *psukhē*. Here, you have a dynamic where you have the movement the mind seeks toward truth, toward steadiness, toward immobility, toward land, and this movement of oscillation, of rocking, which prevents it from advancing. And now we must see how this analysis—which in the beginning is only a metaphor—how this metaphor gives form to a precise description of Serenus himself, and how this dynamic grid can give place to a real description of oneself.

So we have now a long self-description of Serenus:

> I shall tell you what befalls me—you will find a name for my malady. I am possessed by the very greatest love of frugality, I must confess; I do not like (*placet*) a couch made up for display, nor clothing brought forth from a chest or pressed by weights and a thousand

* The manuscript adds: "As you see, this confession is a procedure of control which is concerned with the individual's position. [Serenus] has to explain his own position as if it were a ship's position. It is much more a question of ethical 'geography' in spiritual travel than a question of deep psychology and secret desire. Once more we meet these two comparisons of spiritual guidance with piloting and medicine."

mangles to make it glossy, but homely and cheap, that is neither preserved nor to be put on with anxious care; the food that I like (*placet cibus*) is neither prepared nor watched by a household of slaves, it does not need to be ordered many days before nor to be served by many hands, but is easy to get and abundant; there is nothing far-fetched or costly about it, nowhere will there be any lack of it, it is burdensome neither to the purse nor to the body, nor will it return by the way it entered; the servant that I like is a young home-born slave (*placet minister incultus*) without training or skill; the silver is my country-bred father's heavy plate bearing no stamp of the maker's name, and the table is not notable for the variety of its markings or known to the town from the many fashionable owners through whose hands it has passed, but one that stands for use, and will neither cause the eyes of any guest to linger upon it with pleasure nor fire them with envy.

Then after all these things have had my full approval (*Cum bene ista placuerunt*), my mind is dazzled by the magnificence of some training-school for pages (*praestringit animum apparatus alicuius paedagogii*), by the sight of slaves bedecked with gold and more carefully arrayed than the leaders of a public procession, and a whole regiment of glittering attendants; by the sight of a house where one even treads on precious stones and riches are scattered about in every corner, where the very roofs glitter, and the whole town pays court and escorts an inheritance on the road to ruin. And what shall I say of the waters, transparent to the bottom, that flow around the guests even as they banquet, what of the feasts that are worthy of their setting? Coming from a long abandonment to thrift, luxury has poured around me the wealth of its splendour, and echoed around me, on every side. My sight falters a little, for I can lift up my heart towards it more easily than my eyes. And so I come back, not worse, but sadder, and I do not walk among my paltry possessions with head erect as before, and there enters a secret sting and the doubt whether the other life is not better. None of these things changes me, yet none of them fails to disturb me.

I resolve to obey the commands of my teachers (*Placet vim praeceptorum sequi*) and plunge into the midst of public life; I resolve to try to gain office and the consulship (*placet honores fascesque*), attracted of course, not by the purple or by the lictor's rods, but by the desire to be more serviceable and useful to my friends and relatives and all my countrymen and then to all mankind. Ready and determined, I follow Zeno, Cleanthes, and Chrysippus, of whom none the less not one entered upon public life, and not one failed to urge others to do so. And then, whenever something upsets my mind (*Ubi aliquid animum insolitum arietari percussit*), which is unused to meeting shocks, whenever something happens that is either unworthy of me, and many such occur in the lives of all human beings, or that does not proceed very easily, or when things that are not to be accounted of great value demand much of my time, I turn back to my leisure, and just as wearied flocks too do, I quicken my pace towards home. I resolve (*placet*) to confine my life within its own walls: 'Let no one,' I say, 'who will make me no worthy return for such a loss rob me of a single day; let my mind be fixed upon itself, let it cultivate itself, let it busy itself with nothing outside, nothing that looks towards an umpire; let it love the tranquillity that is remote from public and private concern.' But when my mind has been aroused by reading of great bravery, and noble examples have applied the spur (*ubi lectio fortior erexit animum et aculeos subdiderunt exempla nobilia*), I want to rush into the forum, to lend my voice to one man; to offer such assistance to another as, even if it will not help, will be an effort to help; or to check the pride of someone in the forum who has been unfortunately puffed up by his successes.

And in my literary studies I think (*In studiis puto mehercules*) that it is surely better to fix my eyes on the theme itself, and, keeping this uppermost when I speak, to trust meanwhile to the theme to supply the words so that unstudied language may follow it wherever it leads. I say: 'What need is there to compose something that will last for centuries? Will you not give up striving to keep posterity from being silent about you? You were born for death; a silent funeral is less troublesome! And so to pass the time, write something in simple style, for your own use, not for publication; they that study for the day have less need to labor.' Then again, when my mind has been uplifted by the greatness of its thoughts (*Rursus, ubi*

> *se animus cogitationum magnitudine levavit*), it becomes ambitious of words, and with higher aspirations it desires higher expression, and language issues forth to match the dignity of the theme; forgetful then of my rule and of my more restrained judgement, I am swept to loftier heights by an utterance that is no longer my own.[21]

I hope you are convinced that there is nothing very interesting in this confession. I hope you believe that because it's not quite true. It's in fact rather interesting. Of course the text appears as a pure accumulation of relatively unimportant details about, as you see, what Serenus likes, what pleases him, what on the contrary doesn't matter to him. All that about very small, tiny things, for instance to agree to eat from plates inherited from his father, and things like that. Well, nothing very interesting. But it also seems to be a great disorder, a great mess of details like that. In fact I think that behind this apparent disorder, it's rather easy to discover the real organization of the text. There are three parts in the discourse. One is devoted to Serenus's relations to wealth, to possessions, to domestic life, to private life, to home, and so on. The other part, which begins, "I resolve to obey the commands of my teachers and plunge into the middle of public life,"[22] this paragraph is devoted to Serenus's relations to public life, to his political career. There is a third paragraph which starts at, in the English text, "And in my literary studies . . . ,"[23] and in this third part Serenus speaks about his literary activity, the speeches he likes to deliver, and so on. But in fact, under those questions, you recognize very easily the great problem of glory, of immortality, of the relation between death and immortality, the question of life after death in the memory of men. So we have very clearly in this text three important domains of activity: private life, domestic life first, [then] public life, and [finally] immortality.

In each of those three paragraphs, you can very easily find two parts. In the first part, Serenus explains not only what he does, but more precisely what it pleases him to do. That's why in the beginnings of those three paragraphs he often uses the word *placet*, meaning "that pleases me," and he explains what he is used to doing, what he is willing to do, what he likes to do, and so on. In so doing, he shows how indifferent he is to other things which really are not important. All those descriptions are quite positive. He gives a picture, a very positive image of who he is. He explains, first, that he does not have great needs (that's the description about his private life that was just read), and he is not attached to luxury. In the second paragraph, he explains that he does not want to have a great political career, that he is not willing to sacrifice anything important for a great political career. And in the third paragraph about immortality, he says that he is not seduced by rhetoric, that he prefers to deliver good and useful speeches instead of having a purely literary success. So in a way you see that he writes a balance sheet for his freedom, and this balance, as you see, is not bad at all. It is quite positive. Serenus is attached to what is natural, to what is necessary, to what is useful, either for himself or for his friends, and he is indifferent to the rest. In the three domains of life (private life, public life, immortality), well, things are not bad at all, Serenus is a good fellow. He shows that on these specific, important topics—to what is he indifferent and what is important for him?—he considers as important those things which are truly important and he is indifferent to the rest.

But in those three paragraphs, after having explained how he is indifferent to indifferent things and what kind of importance he attributes to important things, he poses certain kinds of objections to himself. You can find those objections in the three paragraphs at the moment when he started to use the word *animus*. For instance, in the first part of the first paragraph, you find the word *placet cibus, placet minister*, and so on. And then, after *Cum bene ista placuerunt*, you find *praestringit animum apparatus alicuius paedagogii*. In the second paragraph, *placet imperia vim praeceptorum* . . . (I resolve to obey the commands of my teachers and plunge into the midst of public life,), the paragraph about public life, you also find *placet imperia vim, placet honores fascesque*, and then *ubi lectio fortior erexit animum et aculeos subdiderunt exempla*. And the same in the third paragraph, which starts "And in my literary studies" (*In studiis puto mehercules*), you also find *rursus, ubi se animus cogitationum magnitudine levavit*. So you see that all of these three paragraphs are organized in the same way, and that on those three topics—private life, public life, immortality—Serenus explains the following situation: In spite of making good choices, being independent of those things which are not important, he feels in his mind, *animus*, involuntary movements which do not exactly incline him to behave in another way, but that make him feel pleasure in seeing or thinking of certain things which are unimportant. These feelings of pleasure are the sign that his *animus*, his mind, his soul, is not completely stable, that he is not yet solidly settled and steady, and that maybe one day he can be pushed, and pulled, and tossed, and rocked, and so on. So in the three fields of his conduct there is an opposition. This opposition is not between the act and the intention. The opposition that Serenus outlines and which is the real reason of his consultation is not between acts and intentions, it is not between the acts and intentions on one side and desires on the other side, this opposition is not these. It is the opposition between a practice, a use of freedom, which is rather satisfactory, since this use of freedom by Serenus conforms to Stoic teaching, to the Stoic rules of conduct, but there is an opposition between this practice, which is good and conforms to the rules, and a certain instability, unsteadiness of the soul, of *animus*, an instability of the soul that is very important and that makes Serenus feel uncomfortable and anxious insofar as *animus* is the principle of conduct. Briefly, Serenus knows the rules, he is able to put them into operation, he enjoys doing so, but those rules, he feels that they are not yet for him a permanent matrix for his conduct, for his feelings, for his pleasures. He conforms to the rules, he has the will to conform to them, but he doesn't yet have this *tranquillitas*, this *firmitas*, this steadiness which entails the permanence of ethical structure, complete sovereignty over himself, and the kind of pleasure which has no other sources than himself.

So when Serenus compares himself to a ship, it is, as I told you, a very conventional, very traditional metaphor, but this metaphor operates, as you see, as a permanent guide for his analysis, or at least we can say that it fits this analysis perfectly. Serenus sees the port, he sees the land, he sees truth, the rules he has to observe, he knows how to sail, he is a good pilot, there is no storm which might threaten him, but he is tossed, and he cannot go further as a consequence of the instability of *animus*. Seneca's answer will be precisely the exploration of this stability. We could say, as I told you a few minutes ago, that we recognize here something like a set of dynamics and a *topos* (topic).[24] This topic is not at all the topic borrowed from the physiological model as in Freud; it is the geographical topic with the sea, the shore, the earth, and the boat that is the implicit and explicit metaphor of the text. There is a dynamic here as well, but this dynamic is not at all the thermodynamics you can find in Freud's texts, it is the dynamic of piloting, of sailing, with those two movements I earlier discussed, the movement toward the earth and the movement of rolling. Those two great metaphors, the geographical topic and the piloting's dynamic, form the grid of this self-observation.

That's [what I have] for Seneca and this kind of assessment of freedom that I wanted to [speak to you about]. And now [let's move on to] Epictetus. But maybe there are questions about [what I just said].

—*Isn't there also a military metaphor in this text with its themes of the sea and piloting? It sounds like naval warfare.*

—First, this metaphor of warfare, of struggle with enemies is very frequent in the Greek tradition, but I don't think that this metaphor really organizes the perception of the self in this text. The military metaphor as organizing self-perception can be very clearly found in early Christian spirituality. Some of Seneca's texts are much more precise; he says, for instance, that you have to organize your self and your soul as a very robust army, but I don't think that in this text you can find an organizing function for the metaphor, despite its presence.

—*I would like to ask a little bit about in exactly what way the person seeking some guidance felt there was some insufficiency in the matrix that he used. In some sense, it sounds like he <u>had</u> incorporated or embodied in himself some philosophy, some more or less complete way of life, and that he felt there were certain insufficiencies in the Stoic philosophy.*

—I don't think that there is something from Stoic doctrine or Stoic philosophy he lacks, it is his own relation to this philosophy which is not sufficiently elaborated. You must keep in mind that you have here an example of late Stoicism. It's quite obvious that for the first Stoicism, for Zeno, when somebody knew the principles of the philosophy, that was enough, and he didn't need to make any other progress. What's interesting here is that in the general framework of Stoic doctrine you have new elements which have been brought about by this evolution of Stoicism. And here, you have someone who knows the principles, who knows the rules, the *dogmata,* and also the practical rules, the theoretical foundations for the doctrine and the practical rules, and in spite of that, there is something he lacks. And he wonders, he would like to know what that is.

—*And the answer is . . .*

—It is *tranquillitas.*[25] And *tranquillitas,* as far as I can understand from this text and from the others, holds that there is a moment in which the rules, the theoretical rules and the practical rules, the theoretical principles and the practical rules, are embedded in the soul to such an extent that the soul cannot be moved by anything else. You see, that is not something related to the doctrine itself. And that is *tranquillitas.*

—*Is it rather that instability is an essential part of his dynamic, and therefore, the only situation in which one might imagine stability in this scenario is after death, as Christians and Augustine thought in their use of the same boat-imagery?*

—No. What's interesting is that more and more in this literature from late antiquity, the theme of instability and unsteadiness becomes more and more important. Of course, that is linked to the human condition, but much more to opinion and to the imagination than to a kind of situation linked to a fault or something similar. It's not the fact that we live in historical time which is the root of this unsteadiness. Anyway, we are able, through theoretical study and through exercises and practical attitudes, to stand completely firm within this [human] world. So we don't need to wait until after death to attain this stability. That's quite clear.

SO, ONE MORE TEXT. I am afraid I won't be able to read the five texts I wanted to read.

I think you can find in Epictetus a third type of self-examination, very different from the two I have mentioned and quoted from Seneca. In Epictetus, you find references to several types of self-examination. You find references to the evening examination, you find also references to this type of general self-examination we have encountered with Serenus, but there is another type of self-examination that is, I think, much more specific to Stoicism, and also more specific to Epictetus himself.* This self-examination in Epictetus takes the form of a permanent trial for our representations.[26] This technique is also related to the problem of stability and steadiness. This exercise, this practice tries to give an answer to the question: since a permanent flow of representations flows through the mind, how is it possible to avoid being disturbed, moved, pushed, tossed by those representations? Or, if you like: how could we accept into our minds the representations we are able to control, and dismiss, exclude, expel those representations which. on the contrary, induce us to involuntary movements, emotions, and feelings? How can we discriminate in our consciousness, in our mind, between the representations we can control and the representations which are dangerous for our self-control? In order to solve this very practical problem—which, as you see, is linked to the problem of the flux of representations and the permanent agitation of our mind**—we must adopt an attitude of permanent surveillance with regard to representations which may enter our thoughts. Epictetus explains this attitude of permanent surveillance through two metaphors: first, the metaphor of the night watchman who does not admit anyone into the house or into the town without checking his identity.[27] He uses also the metaphor of the money changer, who verifies the authenticity of the currency, what the Greeks called the *argurognōmōn*, who, when a coin is presented to him, looks at it, weighs it, and verifies the metal and the effigy.[28]

* The manuscript specifies: "But among those different types of self examination, there is one which is important, both because it is an elaboration by Epictetus of some specifically Stoic themes, and because it had a great influence on Christian spirituality."

** A few words here are inaudible.

Those two metaphors of the watchman and of the money changer are to be found in early Christian texts, and people like Cassian ask the monks to survey their own representations like a watchman at the door of the house, or like a money changer.[29] On Monday we read some texts from Evagrius where this metaphor was also used.[30] But I think that what is important to note is that in this Christian conception of the self-surveillance, in the Christian metaphor of the mind who must be the watchman of his own representations, in this Christian metaphor the examination of representations has an objective. It is to try to decipher whether or not, behind an apparently innocent representation, the Devil, the Seducer, is hiding himself, and whether an apparently innocent representation is a trap, a lie. We must decipher where this representation comes from, the relation between the apparent value of this representation and its real value, all those operations that a good money changer does when he is presented with money.

For Epictetus, the metaphor of the watchman and the metaphor of the money changer have, I think, a completely different meaning. For Epictetus, the problem is not to know where this representation comes from, the problem is not to know whether or not the Devil hides behind this representation; it is the question of whether or not this representation represents something which depends upon us, whether or not it represents something which is accessible to our will. I would say that in Christian spirituality, the verification, the trial raises the question of the origin of representations, and it was intended to dispel, to clear away delusions. In the Stoic practice, the testing of representations raises the question of their objective content, and this practice of self-surveillance, this practice of watching over our representations, is supposed to guarantee, to insure the mastery of oneself.

Epictetus proposes two types of exercises on the self in order to reinforce this attitude of mistrust toward our representations. One form of the game, directly borrowed from sophistic games, is the following. In the traditional games played in philosophy schools, one of the students asked a question with an obviously sophistic structure and the other student had to answer without being trapped in the sophistry. The classical example—it is not exactly stupid—but the most famous example in the schools, the most elementary sophistic game was this one: "Can a chariot pass through someone's mouth?" There were two possibilities, either "No, a chariot cannot pass through a mouth," and then the other answer was "Yes, you just said the word 'chariot,' and so a chariot passed through your mouth."[31] Of course, this game was rather elementary; it was an obvious exercise in order to distinguish between the word and its *Bedeutung* [(meaning)].

Anyway, Epictetus criticizes this type of exercise because he said that they were not useful, and he proposes us another type of exercise, or the same type of exercise but about moral training, and designed to offer a better moral training. In this game with two partners, one person evokes an event or fact, and the other has to answer quickly whether this fact, this event, this kind of conduct is good or bad, or if it is something which is indifferent, which is beyond our own decision.* As an example of this type of exercise, Epictetus quotes this dialogue. One of the partners says: "So and so's son is dead." And the other must answer: "We can change nothing about that, it is not our responsibility, so it is not an ill." Question: "A certain person's father has disinherited him." Answer: "It is not our responsibility, it is not an evil." Question: "He is suffering from having been disinherited." Answer: "That's his responsibility, that's an evil." Question: "He has put up with it valiantly." And the answer is: "That lies within the scope of responsibility, and that's a good."[32]

So that is an exercise with two partners. But there is another exercise, a little different from this one. It has the same object but the form is much closer to various meditations that have been used later on in Christianity.[33] This second exercise consists of walking through the streets, and, regarding any representation you encounter, you must answer whether that which comes to your mind or your eyes or your ears depends on you or not, and you must reject all representations in the instances where the object does not depend on you:

* The manuscript adds: "will and freedom."

> Go out of the house at early dawn, and no matter whom you see or whom you hear, examine him and then answer as you would to a question. What did you see? A handsome man or a handsome woman? Apply your rule. Is it outside the province of the moral purpose, or inside? Outside. Away with it. What did you see? A man in grief over the death of his child? Apply your rule. Death lies outside the province of the moral purpose. Out of the way with it. Did a Consul meet you? Apply your rule. What sort of thing is a consulship? Outside the province of the moral purpose, or inside? Outside. Away with it, too, it does not meet the test; throw it away, it does not concern you. If we had kept doing this and had exercised ourselves from dawn till dark with this principle in mind,—by the gods, something would have been achieved![34]

As you see, this exercise must become a permanent attitude and this attitude seeks to clear the mind of any kind of representation which could be dangerous because it represents something which is not under our own sovereignty. In a way, it is a kind of "purification" of the mind from those dangerous representations. But this purification, as you see, doesn't deal with purity and impurity. It is a question of sovereignty, it is a question of mastery. Epictetus wants us to constitute a world of representations in which nothing could intrude which is not under the control and sovereignty of our will. And that, I think, is the game and the principle of this kind of self-examination.

Well, I would have liked to analyze two other texts by Marc Aurelius, but obviously I have no time for that and I feel rather tired.* So I would like to jump to my conclusions very briefly.

* One finds in the lecture manuscript notes for only one of the two texts on which Foucault intended to speak. These notes offer commentary on a passage from the *Meditations* (4.3) dedicated to the retreat to the self (*la retraite en soi-même*):

"'*The meditations with himself* (*eis heauton*).'

Some of those texts are quotations, thoughts, aphorisms, precepts that [Marcus Aurelius] gives to himself. But some are exercises that he has to practice more or less regularly; and he gives the principles, the general rules and examples of those exercises.

One of those texts is to be found in the Book IV, §3:

["Men look for retreats for themselves, the country, the sea-shore, the hills; and you yourself, too, are peculiarly accustomed to feel the same want. Yet all this is very unlike (*idiōtikōtaton*) a philosopher, when you may at any hour you please retreat into yourself (*eis heauton anachōrein*). For nowhere does a man retreat into more quiet or more privacy than into his own mind, especially one who has within such things that he has only to look into, and become at once in perfect ease; and by ease I mean nothing else but good behavior. Continually, therefore, grant yourself this retreat and repair yourself. But let them be brief and fundamental truths, which will suffice at once by their presence to wash away all sorrow, and to send you back without repugnance to the life to which you return.

For what is it that shall move your repugnance? The wickedness of men? Recall the judgment (*krima*) that reasonable creatures have come into the world for the sake of one another; that patience is a part of justice; that men do wrong involuntarily; and how many at last, after enmity, suspicion, hatred, warfare, have been laid out on their death-beds and come to dust. This should make you pause. But shall what is assigned from Universal Nature be repugnant to you? Revive the alternative: 'either Providence or blind atoms,' and the many proofs that the Universe is a kind of Commonwealth. Shall then the things of the flesh still have hold upon you? Reflect that the understanding (*dianoia*), when once it takes control of itself and recognizes its own power, does not mingle with the vital spirit, be its current smooth or broken, and finally reflect upon all that you have heard and consented to about pain and pleasure.

Well, then, shall mere glory (*doxarion*) distract you? Look at the swiftness of the oblivion of all men; the gulf of endless time, behind and before; the hollowness of applause, the fickleness and folly of those who seem to speak well of you, and the narrow room in which it is confined. This should make you pause. For the entire earth is a point in space, and how small a corner thereof is this your dwelling place, and how few and how paltry those who will sing your praises here!

Finally, therefore, remember your retreat into this little domain which is yourself, and above all be not disturbed nor on the rack, but be free and look at things as a man, a human being, a citizen, a creature that must die. And among what is most ready to hand into which you will look have these two: the one, that things do not take hold upon the mind, but stand without unmoved, and that disturbances come only from the judgment within; the second, that all that your eyes behold will change in a moment and be no more; and of how many things you have already witnessed the changes, think continually of that.

The Universe is change, life is opinion."

Marcus Aurelius, *Meditations,* trans. Arthur Spenser Loat Farquharson (New York: Knopf [Everyman's Library], 1992), 18–19.—Ed.]

Farquharson interprets this text as a trace of Neoplatonism in Marcus Aurelius' thought. And he brings together other texts from Marcus Aurelius which seem to sound equally neoplatonist. Marcus Aurelius speaks of 'drawing inward into the self' (VII, 28; VIII, 48; IX, 42), of 'finding the foundation of good within the soul' (VII, 59), of "making himself simple." [Farquharson's interpretation is in *Marcus Aurelius, His Life and His World* (Oxford: Blackwell, 1951).—Ed.]

I think that this passage does not refer to the soul contemplating itself in its reality and in its simplicity. It refers to a very precise type of self-examination. Unlike to Seneca's self-examination, this one is not an attempt to turn back to the previous deeds, or to give an assessment of freedom; it is a control, a verification of the rules of conduct that we have in mind and are ready to use as soon as it is necessary.

In the exercises I mentioned [a] few moments ago, Epictetus was checking his ability to get rid of any kind of dangerous representations. Here Marcus Aurelius is checking the rules he must keep in mind in order to rid himself of those representations.

A kit check.

The word '*anachoresis*.'

(It will be used in Christianity to denote the kind of monastic life in which the monk lived alone, in the country or in the desert, apart from city life).

– In classical Greek, the word belongs to a military vocabulary: it refers to the retreat of an army. The word was also used to denote a slave escaping from his master's house and hiding in the country.

– In the Hellenistic period the word was used to mean the retreat people practiced at certain moments in their lives or at the end of their lives, when they renounced public activity, political affairs, and any kind of urban life.

This practice was strongly criticized by most Stoics: they argued that this renouncement was in fact an egoistic attitude (rich people leaving the city and living in their luxurious country houses in order to avoid the duties and also the expenses linked to citizenship and to political career).

And Dio of Prusa for instance, in a discourse entirely devoted to the problem of *anachoresis,* very clearly opposes the *anachoresis eis chōron* which he criticizes, and the *anachoresis eis heauton* which he praises. [John Chrysostom, *On Retirement,* in *Discourses,* trans. J. W. Cohoon (Cambridge, MA: Loeb Classical Library, 1956), 2: 246–69. Foucault also evokes this text in his January 20, 1982 lecture for the course *The Hermeneutics of the Subject.* See HS, 88, 100n31; HS (Eng.), 91, 103n31.—Ed.]

This traditional opposition between the two kinds of *anachoresis* is to be recognized in the beginning of Marcus Aurelius's text: *idiōtaton* = non-philosophical.

– Retreating to the country is the attitude of an *idiōtēs* (of someone who is not a philosopher and who does not feel that he has any duty towards other human beings).

– The philosophical attitude consists in retreating into oneself. But, as you see, this retreat is not only a general attitude; it is also an exercise that one has to practice as often as possible in order to regenerate. The regeneration consists in reactivating some elementary rules of conduct (the most elemental). They have to be stocked, if one wants to memorize them, and they have to be as general as possible if one wants to use them in any circumstances. And after having reactivated those principles, you are able to turn back to your activities; you are ready to face any kind of situation.

And as an example, Marcus Aurelius chooses the particular topic of discontent and irritation (something different from anger). He reviews the different categories of things which one can be irritated with:

– other people
– personal destiny
– body
– glory, reputation (*doxarion*), good name [in the most enterprises].

1) About other people, one must remember four reasons (*krima*): ["Reasonable creatures have come into the world for the sake of one another; that patience is a part of justice; that men do wrong involuntarily; and how many at last, after enmity, suspicion, hatred, warfare, have been laid out on their death-beds and come to dust."—Ed.]

2) About destiny:

– a well-known alternative: providence/atoms

– a set of evidence: Marcus Aurelius does not mention them since they are supposed to be well known.

3) About the body:

– a general principle about *dianoia*

– and the set of examples anybody is supposed to have in his memory about this topic.

4) About glory, the exercise consists in this kind of contemplation which was very highly praised among the Stoics:

– endless time

– oblivion of men

– uselessness of their activity

– and what is the main topic of the meditation: the fact that our place in the world is extremely narrow.

That is, you know, one of the most frequent exercises of contemplation in Marcus Aurelius: try to take such a perspective over the world that you can see yourself, and men in general, as they are: tiny little things compared to universe (the second theme of contemplation, a theme not mentioned here, is: try to see which are the small, unimportant and even dirty elements of which you are made). [On these exercises of contemplation in Marcus Aurelius, see HS, 293–94; HS (Eng.), 305–7. See also Pierre Hadot, *Philosophy as a Way of Life: Spiritual Exercises from Socrates to Foucault*, ed. and trans. Arnold I. Davidson (London: Blackwell, [1995] 2003).—Ed.]

Then comes the last part of the exercise: a review of the different aspects of what one is; the aspects constitute the framework which permits practitioners to memorize the main ethical principles. These aspects are:

– man

– human being

– citizen

– mortal being.

And Marcus Aurelius arrives at the top of the pyramid: the two main principles we must permanently have in mind:

– change in the universe

– the fact that our opinions are also changing.

And the end is precisely a *gnōmē*, this kind of short sentence, which can be recalled as a permanent matrix for conduct. This short and alliterative sentence has to be printed in mind. [On the concept of *gnōmē*, see among others

In reading those texts about self-examination and underlining the differences between those texts, what I wanted to do was, first, to show you that there is a shift in the parrhesiastic practice, or at least in the problem of *parrēsia* as a game between the master and the disciple. The master must still in this type of practice use *parrēsia*—that means frankness, free speech—with the disciple in order to help him to become aware of his faults, of his ignorance, and so on. Seneca uses *parrēsia* or frankness with Serenus, for instance, very explicitly. Epictetus is said to use *parrēsia* toward his disciples. That must be clear. But, as you see, the emphasis is increasingly placed on the disciple's duty. The disciple must become aware of the truth about himself and he has to tell the truth either to himself (for instance that was the first example [we saw] from Seneca) or he has to tell the truth to someone else—and that was the second example from Seneca with Serenus. He must test himself, to check if he is able to do what he wants to do, and that's the example from Epictetus.* The truth about the disciple does not emerge only through the master's discourse or through the ironic dialogue between the master and the disciple. The truth about the disciple emerges from personal relations that the disciple establishes with himself. That's the first point.

Second point: it would not be sufficient to analyze those relations as deriving from the general principle "know thyself." Of course, in a certain way they derive from this principle, but we cannot stop at this point. Those relations to oneself are embedded in very precise techniques which take the form of spiritual exercises, some of them dealing with deeds, others with the state of equilibrium of the soul, others with the flow of representations,** and so on.

Third point: in all those different exercises, what is at stake? It's not the disclosure of a secret thing which has to be excavated from

---

OHS, 50 and 51–52 n. a; ABHS, 75, 76–77 n. *; MFDV, 130; WDTT, 135.—Ed.]"

* The manuscript specifies: "(and those were the examples from Epictetus and Marcus Aurelius)."

** The manuscript adds: "others with the permanent equipment of rules."

the depth of the soul. What is at stake is the relation to truth or, I should say, to certain rational principles. The problem is: did I bring into play the principles of conduct that I have in mind? As you remember, this question was the real motif in Seneca's evening self-examination. What Seneca asked was: did I bring into play those principles of conduct that I know very well and I am familiar with, but it happens that sometimes I do not apply them because maybe I am not familiar enough with them? Another question: am I able to stick with those principles that I know very well, with which I agree, and I put into practice most of the time? That is Serenus's question when he gives this description about himself and when he notes that he is perfectly able to behave in a decent manner, but he feels despite that that there is a kind of internal instability. Or the question that Epictetus raises in those exercises I was just speaking about, this question: am I able to react in conformity with those rules to any kind of representation which shows up to me?*

I think, then, that we must underline that if the truth of the self is nothing else in those exercises than the relations of the self to truth, then this truth is not a purely theoretical truth. It is a set of rational principles, that, on the one hand, are grounded on some general statements about the world, human life, freedom, necessity, happiness, etc., and, on the other hand, give us rules for our conduct.[35] The question raised in these different exercises is oriented toward knowledge, and toward this problem: are we familiar enough with those principles, are they effective enough in our mind, to become real rules for our everyday behavior? As you see, the problem of memory is at the heart of those techniques, but in the form of an attempt to remind us of what we have done, or thought, or felt. This attempt to remind us of what we have done, or thought, or felt is only a means, a way to reactivate those principles and to make them as permanent, as effective as possible in our life. Very obviously those exercises are a part of what we could call an "aesthetics of the self."**

* The manuscript adds: "Am I familiar enough with those principles? Am I able to use them as soon and as often as it is necessary? (Marcus Aurelius)."

** The manuscript adds: "(and not of a hermeneutics of the self)."

One need not find oneself in the position, the role, the situation of a judge who declares his own guilt; one must find oneself in the role of a technician, of a craftsman, of an artist, who from time to time stops working, examines what he is doing, and recalls the rules of his art and compares those rules with what he is just now doing. And this metaphor of the artist who stops working sometimes, takes his distance, looks at what he is doing and compares it to the rules, this metaphor, you can find it in Plutarch in the beginning of the *Peri euthumias* ("On the Tranquility of the Mind").[36]

THAT WAS THE END OF today's seminar, of what I wanted to tell you today. May I still take up more of your time, and say very few words as a general conclusion for this seminar, or do you want to ask questions about the [material from] today?*

—*Tell the truth!*

—Don't expect that from me!

Well, anyway, a few words about this seminar.

The point of departure: my intention was not to deal with the problem of truth, but with the problem of the truth-teller or of truth-telling, or of the activity of truth-telling. I mean that it was not for me a question of analyzing the criteria, the internal or external criteria through which anyone, or through which the Greeks and the Romans, could recognize if a statement was true or not. It was a question for me of considering truth-telling as a specific activity, it was a question of considering truth-telling as a role. But even in the framework of this general question, there were several ways to consider the role of the truth-teller in a society. For instance, I could have compared truth-telling, the role and the status of truth-tellers in Greek society and in other Christian or non-Christian societies—for instance, the role of the prophet as a truth-teller, the role of the oracle as a truth-teller, or the role of the poet, of the expert, of the

* As the audience jokes with him, Foucault continues, "My intention was to give a general overview of [the seminars], but really I am so tired, exhausted by this flu, and perhaps I can answer some questions afterwards."

preacher, and so on. But in fact my intention was not a sociological description of those different roles for the truth-teller in different societies. What I wanted to analyze and to show you is how this truth-telling activity, how this truth-teller role has been problematized in the Greek philosophy. What I wanted to show you is: if, of course as everybody knows, Greek philosophy with Plato, Aristotle, Chrysippus, Sextus Empiricus, and so on has raised the question of truth from the point of view of the criteria for true statements and correct reasoning, this same Greek philosophy has also raised the question of truth from another point of view, from the point of view of truth-telling, and raised questions like: Who is able to tell the truth? What are the conditions, the moral, the ethical, the spiritual conditions which entitle someone to present himself and to be considered as a truth-teller? About what topic is it important to tell the truth? About the world? About nature? About the trees? About the animals? About man? About behavior? About the city? And so on. Other questions: What are the consequences, the positive effects that can be expected for telling the truth either for the city or for the city's rulers and for individuals? And finally: What are the relations between this activity of telling the truth and exercising power? Should they be made to coincide, or should they be completely independent? Do they need one another? And so on. These questions about truth-telling: who is able to tell the truth? About what truth should be told? What are the consequences of telling the truth? What kind of relation to power [does it imply]? All of these questions, these four types of question—who, about what, with what consequences, and with which relation to power?—those four sets of questions about truth-telling seem to have emerged at the end of the fifth century BCE as philosophical problems around Socrates, and through his discussions with the sophists about politics, rhetoric, and ethics.*

Briefly, I would say that the great problematization of truth, which characterizes the end of pre-Socratic philosophy and the be-

* The manuscript adds: "and were raised at the same time as the question of criteria for true statements and correct reasoning."

ginning of a kind of new philosophy which is still ours, this problematization of truth has two sides, two major aspects. One is concerned with the question of how to make sure that a statement is true, that its reasoning is correct, and that we are able to get access to truth. And the other is concerned with the question of the importance for individuals, for the community, for the city, for society, of telling the truth and of having people telling the truth and of recognizing which people are able to tell the truth. On one side, the question of how to make sure that a statement is true, I think that you find the foundation, the roots of a great tradition in Western philosophy, and I would call it the tradition of the analytics of truth. On the other [side], [you find] the tradition of the question: what is the importance of telling the truth, who is able to tell the truth, and why should we tell the truth, know the truth, and recognize who is able to tell the truth? I think that is at the root, at the foundation of what we could call the critical tradition of philosophy in our society.[37] From this point of view, you recognize one of my aims since the beginning of this seminar: to fashion a kind of genealogy of the critical attitude in philosophy. So that's the general objective and aim of this seminar.

From the methodological point of view, I would like to underline the following theme. As you may have noticed, I heavily insisted in this seminar on the word "problematization."[38] I used it thousands and thousands of times, without providing you with any necessary explanation. I told you very briefly that what I intended to analyze in most of my work is neither people's conduct, which is something that belongs to the field of social history, and nor did I want to analyze the representational value of ideas. But what I have tried to do from the beginning was to analyze "problematization," that is, how and why certain things, conducts, phenomena, processes, become a problem. Why some conducts were for a long time, for instance, characterized as "madness," while others were completely neglected, and why those different things, different conducts were at a certain moment problematized as mental illness? Same question for crime and delinquency, same question for sexuality.

This kind of analysis, some people have interpreted it as a kind of "historical idealism."* I think that this analysis of problematizations is completely different from any kind of historical idealism. When I say that I am studying the problematization of madness, or of sexuality, or of crime, it's not a way to deny the reality of those things—crime, sexuality, or madness. On the contrary, I have tried to show, for instance, the real existence of social deviations which were the target of social regulation at a certain moment. And I have tried to show how real these social deviations were when they were returned to those institutions in which the doctors played an increasingly important role from the seventeenth century to the nineteenth century. I do not deny the existence of suffering, anxiety, deviant behaviors, and all those types of reactions and feelings due to brain damage and other [such causes]. The question I raise is this one: how and why were those different things brought together, and characterized, and analyzed, and treated as mental diseases? Schematically, what are the elements of any problematization, which are the elements that are relevant for any problematization, what is the form, the principle, the rule of this problematization, and what is the importance, the impact, and the consequences, the effects of those problematizations? I think that has nothing to do with idealism, even if I won't say that what is characterized, for instance, as schizophrenia is a category to which something real in the world corresponds. I think that there is a correspondence . . . well, there is a relation between the thing which is problematized and the problematization. Anyway, the problematization is an answer to something which is real, but the way the problematization organizes the thing which is problematized is not, most of the time—or at least sometimes—able to be analyzed in terms of a direct relation of representation to that which is represented.

There is also, regarding these analyses of problematization, an interpretation according to which the analysis of problematization lacks any historical context, as if they were something spontaneous, arising from anywhere. In fact, I have tried on the contrary to show that the new problematization of, for instance, illness or physical

* The manuscript adds: "Madness does not exist; sexuality does not exist."

disease at the end of the eighteenth century was very directly linked to a modification in practices, or to the development of a new social reaction to diseases, or to the challenge of certain processes like urbanization* and so on. But we have to understand, I think, very clearly that a problematization is not an effect, a consequence of the context; or rather, the situation which constitutes the context of this problematization is not an effect, it is not a consequence, it is an answer. The fact that an answer is neither a representation nor the result of the thing which it answers does not mean, of course, that it answers to nothing, and it does not mean that it is a pure dream, or that it is entirely invented. The problematization is in a way always a kind of creation, but it is a creation in that sense that, given a certain situation, you can never infer that *this* kind of problematization will follow.** That's the task of the historian when he tries to analyze problematizations: the task of the historian is to make comprehensible why this form of problematization has been put into operation, why it appears as an answer to certain elements of reality. I think that it is possible to offer a historical analysis of problematization as a history of the answer, the original, specific, and singular answer of thought to a certain situation, and this answer to a certain real and concrete situation doesn't have any kind of ideological relation to the thing to which it responds. There is an original relation of thought and reality in the process of problematization. And it is this kind of original, specific, and singular relation between truth and reality that I try to analyze through these kinds of problematizations.***

* The manuscript adds: "(urbanization = hospitalization)."

** The manuscript adds: "and that this problematization belongs to another level of reality and that this problematization has certain goals, finalities.

For instance, the problem of vagrants, the problem of urban populations, of disorders in the city was well-known and described; it was a challenge to all sorts of regulations before the 17th century, when the great state apparatuses considered it their duty to control this situation, and to make of it a major issue."

*** Foucault, feeling ill, declines to speak the last words of his lecture. The manuscript adds: "And then we can come back to the problem of critics. The

NOW I WILL STOP.* I am exhausted but if you want to ask me some questions, I'll try to answer.

—*In the Cynic's relation to truth, was their asceticism a necessity of their relation to truth? Or was it only that they regarded other involvements as too trivial to be bothered with?*

—But that's what I have tried to tell you about asceticism, the notion of *askēsis*, in antiquity, and it fits exactly with the Cynic doctrine. In fact, the Cynics have insisted quite a bit on the importance of *askēsis*. *Askēsis* is not an asceticism in the meaning we give to this word; *askēsis* is an exercise in order to incorporate, internalize, get familiar with certain principles, which in the case of the Cynics were mostly just practical rules for conduct. So you cannot even ask whether asceticism was necessary for access to truth; it was the exercise by which you have access to truth insofar as access to truth means not only knowing the truth but being able to put those rules into practice, into operation.[39]

—*You said that, according to Galen, one should choose a* parrhesiast *who is wealthier than oneself. What would be the Cynic attitude about that practice?*

—The Cynic, the answer would be: "This guy is completely stupid." The Cynics would have said: "Somebody who is rich, that is to say, someone who has positive relations to wealth, cannot really be a sage. So it's not worthwhile to use him as a parrhesiast. The idea of picking a parrhesiast from those who are richer than you would have been, I think, for the Cynics something completely stupid and ridiculous.

—*I wanted to ask you a question that you can give a very short*

---

aim of critics is to change the problematization. There is no ['diatribe'], no [deconstruction]. But a task of permanent reproblematization."

* On the last page of the manuscript, Foucault notes a free translation of lines 168–80 from *Prometheus Unbound* by Aeschylus:

> "Prometheus: One day Zeus will 'have need of me.' But I will not speak 'until he shall release me from my cruel bonds.'
>
> Chorus: 'Bold art thou . . . and thou givest too much licence to thy tongue (*agan d'eleutherostomeis*).'"

answer to. You refer to problematization as a response, an answer. What or who is the subject giving that answer? Or is it ridiculous to locate such a subject?

—No, it's not at all ridiculous. Well, the one who answers is the author of the answer, and it's a fact that you find the same kind of answer in a series of texts.[40] And then you can see that most of the time those answers are more or less collective answers. At a certain moment—and that, I think, is the point you want to make—at a certain point these kinds of answer become so general that there is an *animus*, and the real answer comes from this general framework. But the answer is given by well-defined individuals. It's not a collective consciousness; for instance, to the problem of *parrēsia*—how to recognize someone who is a parrhesiast, what's the importance of having a parrhesiast for the city, what is the training of a good parrhesiast?—there is a Socratic answer, or at least a Socratic-Platonic answer that is given by Socrates, or at least by Plato. And so it is not at all something like a collective answer.*

* To conclude the seminar, the convener addresses Foucault, "I think you've done enough work today. I'd like to express on behalf of everyone my thanks for an extraordinarily interesting course, and we look forward to seeing you again, having taken care of yourself a little bit better."

NOTES

PARRĒSIA

1. See VS, 84–94; HIST, 63–70; OHS, 31–33; ABHS, 19–20; MFDV, 1–4; WDTT, 11–14.

2. See Michel Foucault, "L'évolution de la notion d''individu dangereux' dans la psychiatrie légale du XIXe siècle," in DE, II, no. 220, pp. 443–64; "About the Concept of the 'Dangerous Individual' in Nineteenth-Century Legal Psychiatry," EW, 3: 176–200; MFDV, 199–228; WDTT, 199–229.

3. See Michel Foucault, "Sexualité et solitude," in DE, II, no. 295, pp. 987–97; "Sexuality and Solitude," EW, 1: 175–76; "Le combat de la chasteté," in DE, II, no. 312, pp. 1124–27; "The Battle for Chastity," in EW, 1: 185–97.

4. On this form of confession, and its evolution from the twelfth century onward, see Michel Foucault, *Les anormaux. Cours au Collège de France. 1974–1975*, ed. Valerio Marchetti and Antonella Salomoni (Paris: Seuil-Gallimard, 1999), 161–80; *Abnormal: Lectures at the Collège de France, 1974–1975*, ed. Valerio Marchetti and Antonella Salomoni, trans. Graham Burchell (New York: Palgrave Macmillan, 2003), 174–94; VS, 27–30, 81; HIST, 18–21, 60–61; MFDV, 182–89; WDTT, 184–91.

5. Foucault studies *exomologēsis* in a more detailed fashion in GV, 189–210; GL, 193–215; OHS, 69–76; ABHS, 57–63; MFDV, 101–10; WDTT, 103–13. See also "Les techniques de soi," in DE, II, no. 363, pp. 1624–27; "Technologies of the Self," in *Technologies of the Self: A Seminar with Michel Foucault*, ed. Luther Martin, Huck Gutman, and Patrick Hutton (Amherst: University of Massachusetts Press, 1988), 40–43.

6. See Jean Cassien, "Première conférence de l'abbé Serenus: De la mobilité de l'âme et des esprits du mal," trans. Dom Eugène Pichery, *Conférences*, 3 vols. (Paris: Éditions du Cerf, 1955), 1: 247–49; John Cassian, "Seventh Conference: On the Changeableness of the Soul and on Evil Spirits," trans. Boniface Ramsey, in *The Conferences* (New York: Paulist Press, 1997), 249–51.

7. For a more detailed analysis of *exagoreusis*, see GV, 283–307; GL, 288–313; OHS, 74–88; ABHS, 61–74; MFDV, 123–50, 161–66; WDTT, 125–52, 163–68; "Technologies of the Self," 43–49.

8. On Greco-Roman philosophy as a *practice* that consists above all else in the work of the self on the self and the care for oneself, see HS, 4–19; HS (Eng), 1–19; GSA, 220–24; GSO, 238–42; SS, 57–85; CS, 43–68. On this point, Foucault was no doubt influenced by the work of Pierre Hadot, who considered ancient philosophy above all else as a manner of living, and one that seeks to effect a transformation in practitioners' modes of being by means of a series of spiritual exercises. See Pierre Hadot, *Exercices spirituels et philosophie antique* (Paris: Études augustiniennes, 1981); new ed. (Paris: Albin Michel, 2002). Pierre Hadot, *Philosophy as a Way of Life: Spiritual Exercises from Socrates to Foucault*, ed. Arnold Davidson (Oxford: Blackwell, 1995).

9. Foucault had "discovered" the notion of *parrēsia* several months earlier. He mentions it for the first time during his lecture on January 27, 1982, for the course *The Hermeneutics of the Subject*. When citing the text *Peri parrēsias* by Philodemus, Foucault defines *parrēsia* as a certain "quality" or a certain "ethics of speech" necessary for Epicurean moral guidance: "*Parrēsia* is opening the heart, the need for the two partners to conceal nothing of what they think from each other and to speak to each other frankly." See HS, 132; HS (Eng), 137. Foucault later returns to the practice of *parrēsia* at greater length at the end of his lecture on March 3, 1982 (see HS, 348–51; HS (Eng), 366–68), and he devotes the entire lecture of March 10, 1982, to the subject (see HS, 355–91; HS (Eng), 371–409). Nonetheless, his study of *parrēsia* in *The Hermeneutics of the Subject* does not have the historical and philosophical sweep that it will later have. In this course taught at the Collège de France between 1981 and 1982, Foucault limits himself to an exploration of the significance of *parrēsia* within the practices that supported the guidance of souls in the Hellenistic era and in ancient Rome.

10. Foucault studies in detail the rules for silence that characterize the ancient spiritual direction in his course *The Hermeneutics of the Subject*. See HS, 324–26, 348–51, 395–97; HS (Eng), 340–43, 366–68, 413–16.

11. See Plutarch, "Comment écouter," trans. André Philippon, *Œuvres mo-*

rales, vol. 1.2 (Paris: Les Belles Lettres, 1989); "On Listening to Lectures," trans. Frank C. Babbitt, in *Moralia*, vol. 1 (Cambridge: Harvard University Press, 2014). For a detailed analysis of this text, see HS, 318–19; HS (Eng), 334–36. See also "Technologies of the Self," 30–31.

12. See Philo of Alexandria, *De vita contemplativa*, trans. Pierre Miquel (Paris: Éditions du Cerf, 1963); *On the Contemplative Life*, trans. F. H. Colson, vol. 9 (Cambridge: Harvard University Press, 1941). For a more detailed analysis of this text, see HS, 326–29; HS (Eng), 343–45. See also "Technologies of the Self," 31.

13. See Philodemus, *Peri parrēsias*, ed. Alexander Olivieri (Leipzig: Teubner, 1914).

14. See Polybius, *Histoires*, trans. Paul Pédech, (Paris: Les Belles Lettres, 1970), 83 (2.38.6); *The Histories*, trans. W. R. Paton, (Cambridge, MA: Harvard University Press, 2010), 1: 369 (2.38.6): "One could not find a political system and principle so favorable to equality and freedom of speech, in a word so sincerely democratic, as that of the Achaean league." For a more detailed analysis of this text, see GSA, 69, 137–39, 145; GSO, 71, 149–51, 157.

15. This is the first time that Foucault studies *parrēsia* in Euripides. He will take up in turn, in a more developed fashion, an analysis of four Euripidean tragedies (*Ion, Hyppolytus, The Phoenician Women, The Bacchanals*) in his course at the Collège de France, *The Government of Self and Others* (see GSA, 71–155; GSO, 75–168), where he will add a reading of *Orestes*, as well as in the lectures given at the University of California at Berkeley (see *infra*, p. 74ff), where he will study *Electra*, among other plays. In his analysis of the usage of the term *parrēsia* by Euripides, Foucault leans on the work by Giuseppe Scarpat, *Parrhesia. Storia del termine e delle sue traduzioni in latino* (Brescia: Paideia, 1964) (available in a newly revised and augmented edition *Parrhesia greca, parrhesia cristiana* [Brescia: Paideia, 2001]), 29–37.

16. Euripides, *Ion*, trans. and ed. Léon Parmentier and Henri Grégoire, in *Tragédies* (Paris: Les Belles Lettres, 2002), 3: 211 (ll. 669–75); *Ion*, in *"The Bacchae" and Other Plays*, trans. Philip Vellacott (Harmondsworth: Penguin Books, 1973), 61–62: "I care nothing for all this, Father, unless I can find my mother. And, if I might choose, I would like her to be an Athenian; then I should have free speech in my blood! A foreigner, coming to a city of unmixed race, must curb his speech: the law can enfranchise his name, but not his tongue."

17. Euripides, *Hippolyte*, trans. L. Méridier (Paris: Les Belles Lettres, 1960), 2:45 (ll. 421–25); *Hippolytus*, in *Three Plays: "Alcestis," "Hippolytus," "Iphigenia in Taurus,"* trans. Philip Vellacott (Harmondsworth: Penguin Books, 1974), 96:

I want my two sons to go back and live
In glorious Athens, hold their heads high there, and speak
Their mind like free men, honoured for their mother's name.
One thing can make the most bold-spirited man a slave:
To know the secret of a parent's shameful act.

18. Euripides, *Les Phéniciennes,* trans. L. Méridier (Paris: Les Belles Lettres, 1961), 5:170 (ll. 388–94); *The Phoenician Women,* in *"Orestes" and Other Plays,* trans. Philip Vellacott (Harmondsworth: Penguin Books, 1972), 249:

JOCASTA: What is an exile's life? Is it great misery?
POLYNEICES: The greatest; worse in reality than in report.
JOCASTA: Worse in what way? What chiefly galls an exile's heart?
POLYNEICES: The worst is this: right of free speech does not exist.
JOCASTA: That's a slave's life—to be forbidden to speak one's mind.
POLYNEICES: One has to endure the idiocy of those who rule.
JOCASTA: To join fools in their foolishness—that makes one sick.

19. Euripides, *Les Bacchantes,* trans. H. Grégoire, in *Tragédies* (Paris: Les Belles Lettres, 2002), 6.2: 77 (ll. 668–73); *The Bacchae,* in *"The Bacchae" and Other Plays,* 215:

HERDSMAN:
But first I would learn whether
I may speak freely of what is going on there, or
If I should trim my words.
I fear your hastiness,
My lord, your anger, your too potent royalty.
PENTHEUS:
From me fear nothing.
Say all that you have to say;
Anger should not grow hot against the innocent.

20. Foucault introduces here for the first time the idea of a "parrhesiastic pact" as a kind of engagement, on the part of the stronger party, not to punish the weaker party for the hurtful truth he is about to speak. He will mention this idea again, and will give it comparable meaning, in *The Government of Self and Others* (see GSA, 149–50, 160–61, 187; GSO, 162–63, 176–77, 203), in *The Courage of Truth* (see CV, 13–14; CT, 12–13), as well as in the lectures *Discourse and Truth* given at the University of California at Berkeley (see *infra,* p. 74). During the lecture of March 10, 1982, for the course *The Hermeneutics of the Subject,*

Foucault had spoken about a "pact" and an "engagement" that constitute the condition for the work of spiritual direction in Seneca; this pact, however, is stipulated by the parrhesiast *with himself.* That is, it consists of an "*adaequatio* between the subject who speaks and says the truth, and the subject who conducts himself, who conducts himself as the truth demands," that is to say between the parrhesiast as enunciating subject and the parrhesiast as subject of conduct. See HS, 388; HS (Eng), 406. This is the "individual" pact that Foucault, at the end of his lecture at the University of Grenoble, also names the "parrhesiastic pact," while taking care to distinguish it from a "political" pact that he spoke about when reading Euripides (see *supra*, p. 31); it is this same "pact by the subject speaking to himself" that he analyzes anew in his lecture from January 12, 1983, in the course *The Government of Self and of Others* (see GSA, 62–66; GSO, 64–69). Foucault traces a third type of parrhesiastic pact, what he terms a "pact of frankness" (*pacte de franchise*), in Plato's *Laches*, and studies it in the lecture of February 22, 1983, in *The Courage of Truth*. See CV, 119–24, 131–33; CT, 128–33, 141–44.

21. See Plato, *La République*, trans. Émile Chambry, in *Œuvres complètes* (Paris: Les Belles Lettres, 1964), 7.2: 26 (8.557b); *Republic*, trans. Paul Shorey, *The Collected Dialogues of Plato Including the Letters*, trans. Lane Cooper et al., ed. Edith Hamilton and Huntington Cairns (Princeton: Princeton University Press, 1963), 785: "To begin with, are they [the people of the democratic city] not free? And is not the city chock-full of liberty and freedom of speech? And has not every man license to do as he likes (*kai eleutherias ē polis mestē kai parrēsias gignetai, kai exousia en autē poiein ho ti tis bouletai*)?—So it is said, he replied.—And where there is such license, it is obvious that everyone would arrange a plan for leading his own life in the way that pleases him (*dēlon oti idian ekastos an kataskeuēn tou hautou biou kataskeuazoito ēn autē, hētis hekaston areskoi*)." For a more developed analysis of this text, see GSA, 181–85; GSO, 197–201. See also the lecture from November 14, 1983, at the University of California at Berkeley (*infra*, p. 129ff).

22. See Plato, *Les Lois*, trans. Édouard des Places, in *Œuvres complètes* (Paris: Les Belles Lettres, 1975), 11.1: 35–36 (3.694a–b); *Laws*, trans. A. E. Taylor, *Collected Dialogues*, 1288: "While the Persians steered a middle course between subjection and liberty, in the time of Cyrus, they began by winning their own freedom and went on to make themselves masters of numerous peoples. As a government they gave these subjects their share of liberty and placed them on equal terms with themselves; their soldiers thus grew attached to their commanders, and showed themselves forward in danger. Again, if a subject was a man of wisdom and a capable adviser, the king showed no jealousy of him, but

permitted free speech (*parrēsian*) and bestowed distinctions on such competent counselors, so that the gift of wisdom was freely placed at the disposal of the public service. Hence the combination of liberty with amity and generally diffused intelligence led, for the time, to all-round progress (*di' eleutherian te kai philian kai nou koinōnian*)." For a more detailed analysis of this text, see GSA, 185–88; GSO, 201–204.

23. Isocrates, *À Nicoclès*, trans. G. Mathieu and É. Brémond, in *Discours* (Paris: Les Belles Lettres, 1956), 2: 105 (28); "To Nicocles," trans. George Norlin, in *Isocrates*, 3 vols. (Cambridge: Harvard University Press, 1928), 1: 55–57: "Regard as your most faithful friends, not those who praise everything you say or do, but those who criticize your mistakes. Grant freedom of speech to those who have good judgement, in order that when you are in doubt you may have friends who will help you to decide. Distinguish between those who artfully flatter and those who loyally serve you, that the base may not fare better than the good. Listen to what men say about each other and try to discern at the same time the character of those who speak and of those about whom they speak." For a brief commentary on this discourse by Isocrates, see CV, 59–60; CT, 62–63.

24. See Plato, *Les Lois*, 12.1: 75 (8.835b–c); *Laws*, trans. Taylor, 1401: "But there is a matter of vast moment, as to which it is truly hard to inspire conviction. The task, indeed, is one for God himself, were it actually possible to receive orders from him. As things are, it will probably need a bold man, a man who puts plain speaking (*parrēsian*) before everything, to declare his real belief about the true interest of state and citizens (*os parrēsian diapherontōs timōn erei ta dokounta arist' einai polei kai politais*), and make the regulations the whole social system requires and demands in a corrupt age—a man who will oppose the passions at their strongest, and stand alone in his loyalty to the voice of truth without one creature on earth to second him." For a more detailed analysis of this text, see GSA, 188–90; GSO, 204–6.

25. Plato, *Gorgias*, trans. A. Croiset, in *Œuvres complètes* (Paris: Les Belles Lettres, 1972), 3.2: 166–67 (486d–87a); *Gorgias*, trans. Lamb, 395–97:

> "SOCRATES: If my soul had happened to be made of gold, Callicles, do you not think I should have been delighted to find one of those stones with which they test gold, and the best one; which, if I applied it, and it confirmed to me that my soul had been properly tended, would give me full assurance that I am in a satisfactory state and have no need of other testing?
>
> CALLICLES: What is the point of that question, Socrates?

SOCRATES: I will tell you. I am just thinking what a lucky stroke I have had in striking up with you.

CALLICLES: How so?

SOCRATES: I am certain that whenever you agree with me in any view that my soul takes, this must be the very truth. For I conceive that whoever would sufficiently test a soul as to rectitude of life or the reverse should go to work with three things which are all in your possession—knowledge, goodwill, and frankness. I meet with many people who are unable to test me, because they are not wise as you are; while others, though wise . . ."

For a deeper analysis of this passage in the *Gorgias,* see GSA, 335–44; GSO, 364–74.

26. In this passage from the *Gorgias,* Socrates indicates the three qualities that must be possessed by the person claiming to be a touchstone, and attributes them ironically to Callicles, but Socrates is not himself (as in the *Laches,* see *infra,* p. 134ff). See CV, 134–35; CT, 145: "In the *Gorgias* . . . Socrates offers a sort of possible parrhesiastic pact to Callicles. In this pact Socrates puts things in a way to make it seem that Callicles will be a touchstone for him, whereas, of course, the opposite will be the case. Here [in the *Laches*] it is indeed the opposite, since Socrates is the *basanos* (touchstone), and by rubbing against him, through confrontation with him, one will be able to distinguish between what is and is not good in one's life."

27. See Quintilian, *Institution oratoire,* trans. Jean Cousin (Paris: Les Belles Lettres, 1978), 5: 177 (9.2.27); *The Institutio Oratoria,* trans. H. E. Butler (Cambridge: Harvard University Press, 1920), 3: 388–89; See also GSA, 53–54; GSO, 53–54.

28. Foucault will later return in greater detail to this passage that proceeds from "democratic *parrēsia*" (found in the fourth century BCE) to *parrēsia* as a verbal activity that can be exercised within the game of autocratic power, and notably on the soul of the prince. See GSA, 172–80, 268–73, 275–81; GSO, 187–96, 290–96, 299–305; CV, 54–62; CT, 57–66. See also the lecture from November 14, 1983, from the University of California at Berkeley (*infra,* p. 124).

29. In the course *The Hermeneutics of the Subject,* Foucault studied *parrēsia* only from within, that is to say, as a practice for spiritual direction in ancient Greece and Rome. See *supra,* p. 230, endnote 9. But Foucault quickly realizes that the notion of *parrēsia* "extends far beyond" the use and meaning it has for individual spiritual direction (see GSA, p. 45; GSO, p. 45); this is why, in the last courses given at the Collège de France, the references to *parrēsia* within an-

cient Greek and Roman spiritual direction tend to disappear. Foucault evokes this theme again in a structured fashion only in the lectures from November 21 and 30, given at the University of California, Berkeley (see *infra*, p. 159, p. 192).

30. See Marcello Gigante, "Philodème: Sur la liberté de parole," in *Actes du VIIIe Congrès de l'Association Guillaume Budé (Paris, 5–10 avril 1968)* (Paris: Les Belles Lettres, 1969), 196–217.

31. Philodemus, *Peri parrēsias*. Foucault studies this text in the March 10, 1982 lecture for the course *The Hermeneutics of the Subject* (see HS, 370–74; HS [Eng], 386–91) as well as in the November 21, 1983 lecture given at the University of California at Berkeley (see *infra*, pp. 159–65).

32. Robert Philippson (1858–1942) was a German scholar of Epicureanism.

33. In the Collège de France course *The Government of Self and Others*, and yet more clearly in the course given the following year, *The Courage of Truth*, Foucault more tightly links *parrēsia* and the philosophical mode of life. See *infra*, p. 230, endnote 9.

34. If Foucault, taking inspiration from J. L. Austin, suggests here that *parrēsia* be considered through the lens of a pragmatics of discourse, then he envisions it primarily in the context of ancient spiritual direction. See J. L. Austin, *Quand dire, c'est faire*, trans. G. Lane (Paris: Seuil, 1970); J. L. Austin, *How to Do Things with Words* (London: Oxford University Press, 1962). In this context, the parrhesiastic discourse of the master presents itself as an act, since he is an "ethopoetic" agent seeking to modify and transform the ethos of the disciple. See HS, 227–28; HS (Eng), 237–38. However, several months later, Foucault realizes that this description of *parrēsia* risks being too limited. As a result, in the January 12, 1983 lecture for *The Government of Self and Others*, he returns to the reference to Austin and clearly distinguishes *parrēsia* from the performative utterance and concludes that the study of *parrēsia* emerges not from a pragmatics of discourse (defined from now on as the analysis "that involves a whole series of facts or discourses in which it is not the real situation of the person speaking which affects or modifies the value of the statement"), but from a "dramatics of discourse," that is to say, "the analysis of these facts of discourse, which show how the very event of the enunciation may affect the enunciator's being." See GSA, 59–66; GSO, 61–69.

35. An allusion to the works of Ettore Bignone, who puts forward the hypothesis of an influence of the lost writings of Aristotle on Epicurus and the Epicureans. See Ettore Bignone, *L'Aristotele perduto e la formazione filosofica di Epicuro* (Florence: La Nuova Italia, 1936).

36. Arrian, "Arrien à Lucius Gellus," in Epictetus, *Entretiens*, trans. Joseph Souilhé (Paris: Les Belles Lettres, 1948), 1: 4; "Arrian to Lucius Gellius," in

Epictetus, *The Discourses as Reported by Arrian*, trans. W. A. Oldfather (Cambridge: Harvard University Press, 1925), 1: 5: "But whatever I heard him say I used to write down (*grapsamenos hupomnēmata*), word for word, as best I could, endeavoring to preserve it as a memorial, for my own future use, of his way of thinking and the frankness of his speech (*ekeinou dianoias kai parrēsias*). They are, accordingly, as you might expect, such remarks as one man might make off-hand to another, not such as he would compose for men to read in after time." For another commentary on this text, see HS, 349–50; HS (Eng), 367–68.

37. On the notion of *hupomnēmata*, see HS, 343–44; HS (Eng), 360–61; "L'écriture de soi," in DE II, no. 329, pp. 1237–42; "Self Writing," EW, 1: 207–14.

38. See Plutarch, "De la tranquillité de l'âme," in *Œuvres morales*, trans. Jean Dumortier (Paris: Les Belles Lettres, 1975), 7.1: 98 (464E–F); "On Tranquility of Mind," in *Moralia*, trans. W. C. Helmbold (Cambridge: Harvard University Press, 2014), 6: 166–67.

39. See Arrian, "Arrien à Lucius Gellus," 1: 4; "Arrian to Lucius Gellius," 1: 5. Foucault only says "hopote" (when, at the moment when); the full quotation is: "*autos hopote elegen autous*: when he himself [Epictetus] uttered them [his discourses]" or "when Epictetus himself spoke them."

40. See Galen, "Du diagnostic et du traitement des passions propres de l'âme de chacun," in *L'âme et ses passions*, trans. Vincent Barras, Terpsichore Birchler, and Anne-France Morand (Paris: Les Belles Lettres, 2004), 4–17; *On the Passions and Errors of the Soul*, trans. Paul W. Harkins (Columbus: Ohio State University Press, 1963), 29–41. Foucault also analyzes this text from the perspective of *parrēsia* at the beginning of the second hour of the March 10, 1982 lecture for the course *The Hermeneutics of the Subject* (see HS, 378–82; HS (Eng), 395–99) and in the November 30, 1983, lecture from the course *Discourse and Truth* given at the University of California at Berkeley (see *infra*, pp. 189–92).

41. Galen, *L'âme et ses passions*, 12; *On the Passions and Errors of the Soul*, trans. Harkins, 37: "Each of us needs almost a lifetime of training (*deitai gar askēseōs*) to become a perfect man (*teleios anēr*). Indeed, a man must not give up trying to make himself better even if, at the age of fifty, he should see that his soul has suffered damage which is not incurable but which has been left uncorrected." Galen, *L'âme et ses passions*, 16; *On the Passions and Errors of the Soul*, trans. Harkins, 41: "Even if you should not become much better, be satisfied if in the first year you have advanced and shown some small measure of improvement. If you continue to withstand your passion and to soften your anger, you will show more remarkable improvement during the second year;

then, if you still continue to take thought for yourself, you will notice a great increase in the dignity of your life in the third year, and after that, in the fourth year, the fifth, and so on."

42. Galen, *L'âme et ses passions*, 8–9; *On the Passions and Errors of the Soul*, trans. Harkins, 32–33:

> "Whenever you hear anyone in town being praised by many because he flatters no man, associate with that man and judge from your own experience whether he is the sort of man they say he is. First, if you see him going continually to the homes of the wealthy, the powerful, or even monarchs, be sure that you have heard falsely that this man always speaks the truth, for such adulation leads to lies. Second, be equally sure that his reputation is false if you see him greeting these people by name, visiting them, and even dining with them. Whoever has chosen such a life, not only does not speak the truth, but he is wholly evil, because he loves some or all of the following: wealth, rule, honors, reputation.
>
> When a man does not greet the powerful and wealthy by name, when he lives a disciplined life, expect that man to speak the truth; try, too, to come to a deeper knowledge of what kind of man he is (and this comes about through long association). If you find such a man, summon him and talk with him one day in private; ask him to reveal straightway whatever of the above-mentioned passions he may see in you. Tell him you will be most grateful for this service and that you will look on him as your deliverer more than if he had saved you from an illness of the body. Have him promise to reveal it whenever he sees you affected by any of the passions I mentioned.
>
> If, after several days, although he has obviously been spending time with you, he tells you nothing, reproach him and again urge him, still more earnestly than before, to reveal immediately whatever he sees you doing as the result of passion."

43. Galen, *L'âme et ses passions*, 15–16; *On the Passions and Errors of the Soul*, trans. Harkins, 40–41.

44. Foucault studies the opposition between *parrēsia* and flattery in detail during the March 10, 1982 lecture for the course *The Hermeneutics of the Subject* (see HS, 357–64; HS (Eng), 373–79), where he presents anger as the inverse and the complement to flattery, without, however, mentioning clemency. See also GSA, 278–79; GSO, 302–3.

45. Plutarch, "Les Moyens de distinguer le flatteur d'avec l'ami," trans. Jean Sirinelli, *Œuvres morales*, 1.2: 84–141; "How to Tell a Flatterer from a Friend,"

trans. Frank C. Babbitt, *Moralia* (Cambridge: Harvard University Press, 1927), 1: 291–395. Foucault offers a deeper analysis of this text in the lecture given on November 30, 1983, at the University of California at Berkeley (see *infra*, pp. 186–88).

46. See Galen, *L'âme et ses passions*, 33; *On the Passions and Errors of the Soul*, trans. Harkins, 29: "When I was a young man, I thought that the Pythian dictum to 'know thyself' was held in praise without good reason because it did not enjoin some great action. In later life, I discovered that this dictum was justly lauded."

47. On the essential link, traced by the Stoics, between the principle of *gnōthi seauton* and the distinction between what does and doesn't depend on us, see Foucault, "Débat au Département de Philosophie de l'Université de Californie à Berkeley," in CCS, 116–17.

48. See Epicurus, *Sentences vaticanes*, 29; see *Les Épicuriens*, ed. D. Delattre and J. Pigeaud, Bibliothèque de la Pléiade (Paris: Gallimard, 2010), 65; "Vatican Sayings," in *Letters, "Principal Doctrines," and "Vatican Sayings,"* trans. Russel M. Geer (Indianapolis: Bobbs-Merrill, 1964), 67–68: "To speak frankly, I would prefer as I study nature to speak in oracles that which is of advantage to all men even though it be understood by none, rather than to conform to popular opinion and thus gain the praise that is scattered, broadcast by the many."

49. On this point see GSA, 52–54; GSO, 52–55.

50. Foucault adds: "No, this isn't Epictetus, this is Dio of Prusa." In fact, it seems that this text to which Foucault makes allusion truly is from Epictetus. *Entretiens*, 73 (3.22); *Discourses as Reported by Arrian*, 139.

51. In May 1982, Foucault's interpretation of *parrēsia* remains very much influenced by the Stoics, and the Cynics are barely taken into consideration. But starting with the lecture series *The Government of Self and Others* (see GSA, 316; GSO, 344), and especially in the lectures *Discourse and Truth* given at the University of California, Berkeley (see *infra*, pp. 166–227), and then in the course *The Courage of Truth* (see CV, 256–57, 287, *et passim*; CT, 278–79, 313–14, *et passim*), Foucault also consider Cynic invective and provocation as forms of *parrēsia*.

52. See Seneca, letters 29, 38, and 40, *Lettres à Lucilius*, trans. Henri Noblot (Paris: Les Belles Lettres, 1995), 1: 124–28, 157–58, 161–66; *The Epistles of Seneca*, trans. Richard M. Gummere, 3 vols. (Cambridge: Harvard University Press, 2006), 1: 203–11, 257–59, 263–71. For another commentary on these letters, see HS, 382–84; HS (Eng), 401–4.

53. Foucault underlines the importance of *kairos* in the practice of *parrēsia* on many occasions, and notably in the lecture given on March 10, 1982, for

the course *The Hermeneutics of the Subject* (see HS, 367–68, 371–72; HS (Eng), 383–85, 387–89) as well as in the lecture given on November 21, 1983, at the University of California at Berkeley (*infra*, p. 160). He likewise insists on it in his analysis of Plato's *Seventh Letter* during his course *The Government of Self and Others* (see GSA, 201, 206–7; GSO, 217–18, 224–25).

54. Seneca, letter 25, *Lettres à Lucilius*, 1: 111–14; *Epistles of Seneca*, 1: 183–87. (Foucault mistakenly indicates letter 50.)

55. See Plutarch, "Les Moyens de distinguer le flatteur d'avec l'ami," 33–36; "How to Tell a Flatterer from a Friend," trans. Babbitt, 366–67. Actually, the anecdote reported by Plutarch concerns not Demetrius Poliorcetes but Demetrius of Phalerum, who governed Athens from 317 to 307 BCE and was driven out by Demetrius Poliorcetes: "It is said that when Demetrius of Phalerum had been banished from his native land and was living in obscurity and humble station near Thebes, he was not well pleased to see Crates approaching, anticipating some cynical frankness and harsh language. But Crates met him with all gentleness, and conversed with him concerning the subject of banishment, how there was nothing bad in it, nor any good cause to feel distress, since thus he was set free from a hazardous and insecure office; at the same time he urged him not to be discouraged over himself and his present condition. Whereupon Demetrius, becoming more cheerful and once more taking heart, said to his friends, 'What a pity that those activities and occupations of mine have kept me from knowing a man like this!'"

56. Plutarch, "Les Moyens de distinguer le flatteur d'avec l'ami," 140 (74C); "How to Tell a Flatterer from a Friend," trans. Babbitt, 393: "This is the reason why it is necessary to treat frankness as a fine art, inasmuch as it is the greatest and most potent medicine in friendship, always needing, however, all care to hit the right occasion, and a tempering with moderation (*eustochias te kairou malista kai kraseōs metron echousēs aei deomenēn*)."

57. See Galen, *Traité des passions de l'âme et de ses erreurs*, 37; *On the Passions and Errors of the Soul*, trans. Harkins, 34–35: "You must not believe the man who tells you he has seen you do nothing in passion; consider that he says this because he is unwilling to help you, or because he chooses not to observe the wrong you do, or because he wishes to make sure that you do not come to hate him. Perhaps, too, he has seen that you could not endure it in the past when someone censured your errors and passions; hence, he naturally remains silent because he does not believe you are telling the truth when you say that you wish to know every wrong action you commit."

58. See Epictetus, *Entretiens*, 2: 110–15 (2.24); *Discourses as Reported by*

Arrian, 413–21. For additional commentaries on this text by Foucault, see HS, 93, 329–31; HS (Eng), 96–97, 345–48; GSA, 296; GSO, 320–21.

59. Plutarch, "Comment écouter," 37–62, see *supra*, p. 230, endnote 11; "On Listening to Lectures," 205–59.

60. For the meaning of the word *proairesis*, see *supra*, p. 28.

61. For a detailed analysis of Socratic and Platonic erotics, see UP, 205–69; UP (Eng), 187–246. See also SV, 93–97; ST, 90–95.

62. See Plutarch, "Les Moyens de distinguer le flatteur d'avec l'ami," 85–89; "How to Tell a Flatterer from a Friend," trans. Babbitt, 268–79.

63. See Galen, *Traité des passions de l'âme et de ses erreurs*, 35–38; *On the Passions and Errors of the Soul*, trans. Harkins, 32–35.

64. On the notion of "stultitia," and notably in Seneca, see HS, 126–30; HS (Eng), 130–35; M. Foucault, "L'écriture de soi," in DE, II, pp. 1239–40; "Self Writing," EW, 1: 211–12.

65. See Plutarch, "Les Moyens de distinguer le flatteur d'avec l'ami," 91 (52a–b); "How to Tell a Flatterer from a Friend," trans. Babbitt, 281: "For such is the conduct of a friend. But the flatterer, since he has no abiding-place of character to dwell in, and since he leads a life not of his own choosing but another's, moulding and adapting himself to suit another, is not simple, not one, but variable and many in one, and, like water that is poured into one receptacle after another, he is constantly on the move from place to place, and changes his shape to fit his receiver."

66. Plutarch, "Les Moyens de distinguer le flatteur d'avec l'ami," 92 (52d–e); "How to Tell a Flatterer from a Friend," trans. Babbitt, 283–85: "A further testimony is to be found in the action of the great flatterers and the demagogues, of whom the greatest was Alcibiades. At Athens he indulged in frivolous jesting, kept a racing-stable, and led a life full of urbanity and agreeable enjoyment; in Lacedaemon he kept his hair cropped close, he wore the coarsest clothing, he bathed in cold water; in Thrace he was a fighter and a hard drinker; but when he came to Tissaphernes, he took to soft living, and luxury, and pretentiousness. So by making himself like to all these people and conforming his way to theirs he tried to conciliate them and win their favour. Not of this type, however, was Epameinondas or Agesilaus, who, although they had to do with a very large number of men and cities and modes of life, yet maintained everywhere their own proper character (*ēthos*) in dress, conduct (*diaitē*), language (*logō*), and life (*biō*)."

67. Foucault's translation of *oikeiō pathei* is indecipherable; the sense of the expression is "by experiencing a personal feeling." Plutarch, "Les Moyens de

distinguer le flatteur d'avec l'ami," 93 (53A); "How to Tell a Flatterer from a Friend," trans. Babbitt, 285: "The flatterer is nowhere constant, has no character of his own, that it is not because of his own feelings (*oikeiō pathei*) that he loves and hates, and rejoices and grieves, but that, like a mirror, he only catches the images of alien feelings, lives and movements."

68. Seneca, letter 75, *Lettres à Lucilius*, 3: 51–52; *Epistles of Seneca*, 2: 137, 139: "You have been complaining that my letters to you are rather carelessly written. Now who talks carefully unless he also desires to talk affectedly? I prefer that my letters should be just what my conversation would be if you and I were sitting in one another's company or taking walks together, spontaneous and easy; for my letters have nothing strained or artificial about them. If it were possible, I should prefer to show, rather than speak, my feelings. Even if I were arguing a point, I should not stamp my foot, or toss my arms about, or raise my voice; but I should leave that sort of thing to the orator, and should be content to have conveyed my feelings to you without having either embellished them or lowered their dignity. I should like to convince you entirely of this one fact, that I feel whatever I say, that I not only feel it, but am wedded to it. It is one sort of kiss which a man gives his mistress, and another which he gives his children; yet in the father's embrace also, holy and restrained as it is, plenty of affection is disclosed . . . Let this be the kernel of my idea: let us say what we feel, and feel what we say; let speech harmonize with life. That man has fulfilled his promise who is the same person both when you see him and when you hear him."

Foucault commented at length on this text during the second hour of the lecture given on March 10, 1982, in the course *The Hermeneutics of the Subject*, claiming that it is essentially "a complete presentation on how the Greeks consider libertas, or *parrēsia*." See HS, 384–89; HS (Eng), 401–7. If Foucault gives a great deal of importance to this text in 1982, and even considers it to be at the very heart of *parrēsia*, he broadens his understanding of *parrēsia* later in the year and expands his treatment of *parrēsia* to include other texts in his last two lecture series at the Collège de France, *The Government of Self and Others* and *The Courage of Truth*, as well as the 1983 lectures *Discourse and Truth* given at the University of California, Berkeley.

69. See *supra*, p. 235, endnote 9.

70. See Seneca, *Questions naturelles*, trans. P. Oltramare (Paris: Les Belles Lettres, 1929), 2: 178 (4.A20); Seneca, *Natural Questions*, trans. Thomas H. Corcoran (Cambridge: Harvard University Press, 1971–72), 2: 16–19: "From here I will mingle my talk with yours so that you may not feel alone. We will be together in the part of us where we are best. We will give advice to each other, advice that will not depend on the facial expression of the listener." Foucault

quickly mentions this passage during his March 21, 1984 lecture for the course *The Courage of Truth*. See CV, 249–50; CT, 272.

71. Two years later, in the last lecture for the course *The Courage of Truth*, Foucault proposes a brief analysis of *parrēsia* as found within early Christianity, but he does not return to this "inversion of mission." After the analysis of ancient Cynicism, the points of discontinuity between pagan and Christian asceticism are mostly located by Foucault in the relation to the "*other* world" (*l'autre monde*) and in the principle of obedience. If, in Christianity, there is an "inversion of the values of *parrēsia*," it's that in reality there is an opposition between "two matrices" of Christian experience promoting "a positive and a negative conception of *parrēsia*," respectively. On the one hand, the "parrhesiastic pole of Christianity" (the mystical tradition) valorizes *parrēsia* as faith in God. On the other hand, the "anti-parrhesiastic pole of Christianity" (the ascetic tradition), which was "historically and institutionally much more important," evacuates *parrēsia* as so much arrogant self-confidence and insists instead on the necessity of a scrupulous deciphering of the self within a relation of total obedience to the other. See CV, 289–308; CT, 315–38.

72. The text to which Foucault refers may be the passage in the *Nicomachean Ethics* where Aristotle speaks of the *megalopsuchos* (the magnanimous): "for he is free of speech because he is contemptuous, and he is given to telling the truth, except when he speaks in irony to the vulgar." Aristotle, *Éthique à Nicomaque*, trans. J. Tricot (Paris: Vrin, 2007), 206–7 (4.1124b); *Nicomachean Ethics*, trans. W. D. Ross, and J. O. Urmson, *The Complete Works of Aristotle: The Revised Oxford Translation*, ed. Jonathan Barnes, 2 vols. (Princeton: Princeton University Press, 1984), 2:1775. See also the November 14, 1983 lecture from *Discourse and Truth, infra* p. 133.

73. In May 1982, Foucault does not yet consider Socrates to be a parrhesiast, and he thinks of irony as beyond the parameters of *parrēsia*. This might explain his perplexity when faced with the description of Aristotle and the *megalopsuchos*. See *infra*, p. 133.

74. The passage in the *Rhetoric* to which Henri Joly alludes is perhaps Aristotle, *Rhetoric*, 2.5.1382b19–20; *Complete Works of Aristotle*, 2202: "Of those we have wronged, and of our enemies or rivals, it is not the passionate and outspoken whom we have to fear, but the quiet, dissembling, unscrupulous; since we never know when they are upon us, we can never be sure they are at a safe distance." Foucault had noted this reference in his bibliographic notes on *parrēsia*.

75. See Plato, *Republic*, trans. Shorey, 785 (557b). See *supra*, p. 233, endnote 21.

76. From *apolaustikos*, "someone who seeks material pleasures."

77. See André-Jean Festugière, "Les trois vies," *Études de philosophie grecque* (Paris: Vrin, 2010), 117–56.

78. Lysias, *Sur le meurtre d'Ératosthène, Discours*, trans. L. Gernet and M. Bizos (Paris: Les Belles Lettres, 1964), vol. 1, pp. 30–40; "On the Murder of Eratosthenes," *Lysias*, trans. W. R. M. Lamb (Cambridge, MA: Harvard University Press, 1930), 5–27. A trial for *moicheia* is a trial for adultery.

79. See Lysias, *Sur le meurtre d'Ératosthène*, 31; "On the Murder of Eratosthenes," 7: "I shall therefore set forth to you the whole of my story from the beginning; I shall omit nothing, but will tell the whole truth"; "I will therefore resume from the very beginning of my affair (*ta hemautou pragmata*); I will omit nothing and I will tell the whole truth (*ouden paraleipōn, alla legōn talēthē*)."

80. See Lysias, *Sur le meurtre d'Ératosthène*, 30; "On the Murder of Eratosthenes," 13: "'So it is open to you,' I said, 'to choose as you please between two things,—either to be whipped and thrown into a mill, never to have any rest from miseries of that sort, or else to speak out the whole truth and, instead of suffering any harm, obtain my pardon for your transgressions. Tell no lies, but speak the whole truth (*pseusēi de mēden, alla panta talēthē lege*).'"

81. See Samuel 2:12. Quoted in Robert Alter, *The David Story: A Translation with Commentary of 1 and 2 Samuel* (New York: W. W. Norton, 2000), 257–59: "And the LORD sent Nathan to David, and he came to him and said to him: 'Two men there were in a single town, one was rich and the other poor. The rich man had sheep and cattle, in great abundance. And the poor man had nothing save one little ewe that he had bought. And he nurtured her and raised her with him together with his sons. From his crust she would eat and from his cup she would drink and in his lap she would lie, and she was to him like a daughter. And a wayfarer came to the rich man, and it seemed a pity to him to take from his own sheep and cattle to prepare for the traveler who had come to him, and he took the poor man's ewe and prepared it for the man who had come to him.' And David's anger flared hot against the man, and he said to Nathan, As the LORD lives, doomed is the man who has done this! And the poor man's ewe he shall pay back fourfold, in as much as he has done this thing, and because he has no pity!' And Nathan said to David, 'You are the man!'"

82. For a more developed analysis of the relations and the differences between prophetic speech and *parrēsia*, see CV, 16–17 *et passim*; CT, 15–16 *et passim*. See also the lecture given on October 24, 1983, at the University of California at Berkeley (*infra*, pp. 64–67).

DISCOURSE & TRUTH

OCTOBER 24, 1983

1. Lucian, *The Dead Come to Life or The Fishermen*, trans. A. M. Harmon (Cambridge: Harvard University Press, 1921), 3: 1–82. For a brief commentary on this text, see GSA, 283–84; GSO, 306–8.

2. This is the only place where Foucault proposes a systematic discussion of the "general" meaning of the concept of *parrēsia*, which he defines by emphasizing five fundamental characteristics: sincerity or frankness (the parrhesiast says what he thinks); truth (the parrhesiast "says what he knows to be true"); risk-taking (there is danger for the parrhesiast in speaking the truth); critical function (the truth that the parrhesiast enunciates is susceptible of hurting or angering his interlocutor, or it functions as a form of autocritique); and obligation (speaking the truth is, for the parrhesiast, at once an exercise of liberty and the expression of moral duty).

3. On the distinction between good and bad *parrēsia*, see GSA, 164–68, 176–77; GSO, 181–84, 192–93.

4. Plato, *Republic*, trans. Shorey, 785 (557b). See also *Phaedrus*, trans. R. Hackforth, *Collected Dialogues*, 488 (240e); *The Laws*, trans. Taylor, 1249, 1267–68 (649b, 671b). See GSA, 181–88; GSO, 197–205.

5. Foucault returns in more detail to the pejorative meaning of *parrēsia* within Christianity (from the fourth century onward) in the final lecture of his course *The Courage of Truth*. Cf. CV, 304–8; CT, 333–38.

6. Foucault insists on the difference between parrhesiastic truth-telling and the truth-telling of a teacher (or a professor, or an "expert") in the first lecture for the course *The Courage of Truth*. See CV, 23–25; CT, 23–25. On this difference, see also GSA, 54; GSO, 54.

7. Plato, *Letter VII*, trans. L. A. Post, in *Collected Dialogues*, 1574–98.

8. Plutarch, *Plutarch's Lives*, trans. Bernadotte Perrin (Cambridge: Harvard University Press, 1961), 6: 1–117.

9. With the exception of a brief commentary on a passage from Plato's *Seventh Letter* (*see infra*, p. 108), in these lectures at Berkeley Foucault never returns to these texts. He speaks about them at greater length in his 1982–1983 course at the Collège de France, *The Government of Self and Others*. See GSA, 47–52, 197–259; GSO, 47–52, 214–80. See also CV, 57–9; CT, 61–62.

10. Euripides, *The Phoenician Maidens*, trans. Arthur S. Way, in *The Tragedies of Euripides in English Verse* (London: Macmillan, 1894–98), 3: 57–61 (ll. 1011–99).

11. Foucault suggests many times in his comments on *parrēsia* that it must also be considered as a duty, but rarely in a manner so clear and sustained. See, for example: "It is his duty, obligation, responsibility, and task to speak, and he has no right to shirk this task" (CV, 19; CT, 18).

12. See *supra* p. **PAGE PROOFS.

13. Euripides, *Ion,* trans. Arthur S. Way, in *Tragedies of Euripides in English Verse,* 1: 299 (ll. 595–606).

14. Euripides, *The Bacchanals,* trans. Arthur S. Way, in *Tragedies of Euripides in English Verse,* 3: 400 (ll. 664–73).

15. See *supra,* p. 42.

16. In the autumn of 1983, Foucault does not yet consider Cynic life as such, or even its structure, as a parrhesiastic practice; he speaks only about certain scandalous behaviors (see *infra,* pp. 167–74). In the Collège de France course *The Courage of Truth,* by contrast, the *bios* of Cynic philosophy is considered part and parcel of parrhesiastic practices, through the theme of the "true life" led by Cynics as a "life apart." See CV, 200–264; CT, 217–87.

17. See CV, 302; CT, 332: "The martyr is the parrhesiast *par excellence.*" See also CV, 159–61; CT, 172–74.

18. In *The Government of Self and Others,* Foucault seems to argue a different point, when he affirms that Galileo, in writing his *Dialogues,* makes use of *parrēsia* "in a demonstrative text" (even if "it is not the demonstration or the rational structure of the discourse that defines *parrēsia*"). See GSA, 52–3, 61; GSO, 53, 63.

19. See HS, 221–28; HS (Eng), 230–38. See also CV, 191; CT, 205–6.

20. See notably Seneca, *Natural Questions,* trans. Corcoran, 2: 16–19 (4A, 20).

21. Euripides, *Bacchanals,* trans. Way, 400 (ll. 668–71).

22. Euripides, *Electra,* trans. Arthur S. Way, in *Tragedies of Euripides in English Verse,* 2: 235 (ll. 1055–59).

23. Thucydides, *History of the Peloponnesian War,* trans. R. Warner (London: Penguin, 1972), 118–23. For an analysis of *parrēsia* in the three discourses of Pericles recounted by Thucydides, see GSA, 158–64; GSO, 174–80.

24. Plutarch, "How to Tell a Flatterer from a Friend," trans. Babbitt, 1: 291–395.

25. Galen, *On the Passions and Errors of the Soul.*

26. For the other Foucauldian analyses of the relation between *parrēsia* and rhetoric, see HS, 350–51, 357, 365–69; HS (Eng), 368, 373, 381–86; GSA, 53–54; GSO, 53–54; CV, 14–15; CT, 13–14. See also the lecture at the University of Grenoble, *supra* pp. 21–24.

27. Plato, *Gorgias,* trans. Lamb, 395 (487b). For a more detailed study of the *Gorgias,* see GSA, 328–44; GSO, 357–74.

28. Plato, *Phaedrus,* trans. Hackforth, 505 (259e). For the argument according to which the problem of the *Phaedrus* is not the opposition between written and oral discourse, but to know whether or not this discourse is indexed to truth, see GSA, 301–8; GSO, 327–36. See also "Débat au Département de Français," in CCS, 158, 164.

29. See for example, Seneca, letter 75, *Epistles of Seneca,* 2: 135–47.

30. Quintilian, *Institutio Oratoria,* trans. Butler, 3: 388–89. See *supra,* p. 235, endnote 27.

31. Polybius, *Histories,* trans. Paton, 1: 369 (2.38.6).

32. In his Collège de France course *The Government of Self and Others,* Foucault speaks of "philosophical *parrēsia,*" notably when referring to Socrates, and he specifies that "this philosophical *parrēsia* does not necessarily or exclusively go through *logos,* through the great ritual of language in which one addresses the group or even an individual. After all, *parrēsia* may appear in the things themselves, it may appear in ways of doing things, it may appear in ways of being." See GSA, 295; GSO, 320. See also GSA, 296, 299, 315–16; GSO, 320–21, 326, 343–44, where Foucault presents the philosophic life as criss-crossed, penetrated, and sustained by an essential parrhesiastic function that is in fact a "manifestation of truth." This theme will be taken up and pushed to its logical conclusions during the Foucauldian analysis of Cynic *parrēsia* in *Courage of Truth.*

33. Plato, *Apology,* trans. Hugh Tredennick, *Collected Dialogues,* 16 (30a–c). For an analysis of Socratic *parrēsia* in the *Apology,* see GSA, 286–300; GSO, 310–21; CV, 68–84; CT, 74–80.

34. Plato, *Alcibiades,* trans. W. R. M. Lamb (Cambridge: Harvard University Press, 1927), 103–35 (104e–113c). Foucault never returns to this text in his lectures at Berkeley. He treats it rapidly in his lecture from February 16, 1983, in *The Government of Self and Others.* See GSA, 207–9; GSO, 225–28.

35. Philodemus, *Peri parrēsias.*

36. Seneca, "On Tranquility of Mind," trans. John W. Basore, in *Moral Essays,* 3 vols. (Cambridge: Harvard University Press, 1928–35), 2: 202–85.

37. On the "cultivation of the self," see notably HS, 173–74 *et passim;* HS (Eng.), 179–80 *et passim;* CCS, 81–98; and SS, 51–85; CS, 37–68.

38. Foucault proposes his first major analysis of what he calls the "critical attitude" in his lecture *What Is Critique?,* delivered to the Société française de Philosophie on May 27, 1978. In this lecture, the critical attitude is defined both in terms of an extension of Foucault's analysis of "governmentality" and

"counter-conducts" undertaken in his Collège de France course *Security, Territory, and Population,* and also through his reading of Kant's essay "What Is Enlightenment?" See CCS, 33–70. Between 1983 and 1984, Foucault returns several times to this text by Kant and elaborates the concept of a "historical (or historico-critical) ontology of ourselves." See GSA, 8–38; GSO, 25–40; CCS, 81–85; "What Is Enlightenment?" in DE, II, no. 351, pp. 1498–1507. See also *supra,* p. 68. In his lectures at the University of California at Berkeley, Foucault clearly delineates the tight relation between these ideas and his thoughts on ancient *parrēsia.* See *supra,* pp. 43–46, 57 endnote *, 63, 68; *infra,* p. 224. On this point, see also GSA, 322; GSO, 350; Daniele Lorenzini and Arnold I. Davidson, Introduction, in CCS, 25; Nancy Luxon, *Crisis of Authority: Politics, Trust, and Truth-Telling in Freud and Foucault* (Cambridge: Cambridge University Press, 2013), 164–206.

39. See Friedrich Nietzsche, *Thus Spoke Zarathustra,* ed. Adrian Del Caro and Robert Pippin (Cambridge: Cambridge University Press, 2006).

40. Foucault will return to and develop this discussion of "four fundamental modalities of truth-telling" in the first lecture for the course *The Courage of Truth.* See CV, 16–30; CT, 1–31.

41. Foucault expresses himself here in French. Ernest Renan was relieved of his chair at the Collège de France in 1863 following a scandal provoked by the publication of his *The Life of Jesus.*

42. See *supra,* p. 247, endnote 38.

OCTOBER 31, 1983

1. See *supra,* p. 231, endnote 15.

2. Euripides, *Phoenician Maidens,* trans. Way, 21–22 (ll. 387–94). For these lectures, Foucault uses the older, verse translation by Arthur S. Way. That translation has been retained here, with citations to a more modern translation when the meaning of a passage shifts. For a longer discussion of this translator's dilemma, please see the Translator's Note at the beginning of the volume.

3. Euripides, *Hippolytus,* trans. Arthur S. Way, in *Tragedies of Euripides in English Verse,* 1: 145–46 (ll. 419–30). A more recent translation of *Hippolytus* reads: "My friends, it is this very purpose that is bringing about my death, that I may not be convicted of bringing shame to my husband or to the children I gave birth to but rather that they may live in glorious Athens as free men, free of speech and flourishing, enjoying good repute where their mother is concerned. For it enslaves even a bold-hearted man when he is conscious of sins committed by his mother or father. One thing only, they say, competes in value with

life, the possession of a heart blameless and good. But as for the base among mortals, they are exposed, late or soon, by Time, who holds up to them, as to a young girl, a mirror. In their number may I never be found!" Euripides, *Hippolytus,* trans. David Kovacs, in *Children of Heracles, Hippolytus, Andromache, Hecuba* (Cambridge: Harvard University Press, 1995), 165–67 (ll. 420–30).

4. Euripides, *Bacchanals,* trans. Way, 400 (ll. 664–76).

5. This is the first and only time that Foucault adds a reading of *Electra* to his analysis of *parrēsia* in the tragedies of Euripides, and that he proposes a reflection on the "inverted" parrhesiastic pact that emerges between Clytemnestra and Electra.

6. Euripides, *Electra,* trans. Way, 233–35 (ll. 1012–48).

7. Euripides, *Electra,* trans. Way, 235 (ll. 1049–59). A modern translation renders the passage as: "Clytemnestra: If you so desire, speak and tell me in perfect liberty (*leg'ei ti chrēzeis kantithes parrēsia*) how it was unjust that your father was killed. . . . Electra: Remember, mother, the last words you said, giving me liberty to speak to you (*didousi pros se moi parrēsian*). Clytemnestra: That is what I say now, and I do not unsay it, my child. Electra: Will you hear me, mother, and then do me harm? Clytemnestra: No: it is a pleasure to accommodate myself to your mind." Euripides, *Electra,* trans. David Kovacs in *Suppliant Women, Electra, Heracles* (Cambridge: Harvard University Press, 1998), 267–69 (ll. 1049–59).

8. Euripides, *Electra,* trans. Way, 2: 235–37 (ll. 1060–99).

9. After this response, and in answer to another question about his second example of *parrēsia* in Euripides given earlier, Foucault talks through a few points regarding the English translation of *Hippolytus* with which he is working—one that he describes as a flamboyant and "very free one." The interlocutor presses Foucault on the use of "shame" (line 420) and "honest" (line 427); Foucault disputes the rendering of *gnōmēn dikaian kagathēn* as "an honest heart and good." This exchange has been omitted because only fragments are audible.

10. Foucault devotes himself to an analysis of *Ion*—which he considers to be "the tragedy of truth-telling"—during the lectures from January 19 and 26, 1983, at the Collège de France, and he returns to them at the beginning of the lecture of February 2, 1983. See GSA, 71–145; GSO, 75–158.

11. According to legend, Erechtheus was killed by either Zeus or Poseidon and was devoured by the earth.

12. The first performance of *Ion* is thought to be 413, and scholars date its writing (on stylistic grounds) to the decade 420–410 BCE.

13. In an analogous manner to his Collège de France course *The Govern-*

ment of Self and Others (see GSA, 78 ff.; GSO 83 ff.), Foucault proposes here a tight juxtaposition between the structure of *Ion* and that of *Oedipus the King* by Sophocles. *Oedipus* is the "alethurgical" tragedy par excellence that Foucault studied at least five other times in earlier years. See Michel Senellart, in GV, 42n2; GL, 43n2; and Frédéric Gros, in GSA, 89n11; GSO, 94n11.

14. Euripides, *Ion*, trans. Way, 284 (ll. 365–67). The modern translation for these two lines reads, "Ion: Will the god prophesy a thing he wants concealed? . . . Shame is what he feels at this matter. Do not show him up!" See Euripides, *Ion*, trans. David Kovacs in *Trojan Women, Iphigenia among the Taurians, Ion* (Cambridge: Harvard University Press, 1999), 365.

15. Euripides, *Ion*, trans. Way, 284 (ll. 375–80). The modern translation reads, "Ion: It would be equally foolish if, knowing they did not wish to do so, we were to try to get the gods to speak either by means of slaughtered sheep offered at altars or by bird omens. Whatever blessings we pursue by force, against the will of the gods, these we find are of no use. It is what they give us willingly that helps us." See Euripides, *Ion*, trans. Kovacs, 367.

16. Euripides, *Ion*, trans. Way, 352–53 (ll. 553–68).

17. Euripides, *Ion*, trans. Way, 292–93 (ll. 534–36). The Way translation reads: "Ion: What were the words of Phoebus? Xuthus: That the one who met me—Ion: What meeting? Xuthus: As I came out of the temple—Ion: What would be the result? Xuthus: That he would be my son (*Paid'emon pephukenai*)." A more modern translation reads: "Ion: But what did Phoebus say? Xuthus: That the one who met me . . . Ion: What meeting is this? Xuthus: . . . as I came out of this temple of the god . . . Ion: What would happen to him? Xuthus: . . . is my son." See Euripides, *Ion*, trans. Kovacs, 385.

18. Euripides, *Ion*, trans. Way, 291–98 (ll. 528–62).

19. Euripides, *Ion*, trans. Way, 298–302 (ll. 563–675).

20. See GSA, 79; GSO, 83: "I think we can recognize here a sort of echo of the famous scene of Laius and Oedipus, which you know, in many versions (not in that of Sophocles, but in many others), was a seduction scene."

21. Euripides, *Ion*, trans. Way, 293–94 (ll. 539–43): "Ion: Ha, what mother bare me to thee? Xuthus: Sooth, thereof can I say nought. Ion: Neither Phoebus told? Xuthus: For joy of this thing, that I never sought. Ion: Ah, a child of mother Earth! Xuthus: Nay, children spring not from the sod. Ion: How then thine am I? Xuthus: I know not. I refer it to the God (*anapherō eis ton theon*). Ion: Come, to other reasonings turn we (*logōn hapsometh' allōn*)."

22. Euripides, *Ion*, trans. Way, 294 (l. 544).

23. Foucault also speaks about different forms of truth, inquiry, and Oedipus in his 1973 lectures *Truth and Juridical Forms*, EW, 1: 1–89.

24. Euripides, *Ion*, trans. Way, 298–302 (ll. 563–75).

25. Euripides, *Ion*, trans. Way, 299 (ll. 589–94): "The glorious earth-born state, Athens, men say, hath naught of alien strain. I shall trust in, stained with a twofold taint—An outland father, and my bastard self. And, bearing this reproach, nor strong in friends, 'Nobody' shall be called—'Nobody's Son.'"

26. On this expression, and more generally on the meaning of the verb *chrēsthai*, see HS, 55–56; HS (Eng), 56–57 and GSA, 95, 144; GSO, 102, 157.

27. Euripides, *Ion*, trans. Way, 299 (ll. 595–606): "Then, if I press to Athens' highest ranks, / And seek a name, of them that fail shall I / Win hate (*tōn adunatōn*): with climbers aye climbs jealousy. / And noble souls, born guides of men (*chrēstoi dunamenoi te*), which yet / Are silent, meddling not with things of state (*ontes sophoi, sigōsi kou speudousin es ta pragmata*). / To them shall I be laughing-stock and fool, / Who, in a town censorious, go not softly. / Yea, if mid men of mark, which helm the state (*logō te chrōmenōn te tē polei*), / I win repute, I shall be hedged in more / By checking votes. Thus is it ever, father: / They which sway nations, and have won repute, / To young ambitions are the bitterest foes."

28. Euripides, *Ion*, trans. Way, 300 (ll. 621–28): "And power—this power men falsely praise so oft. / Winsome its face is, but behind the veil / Is torment. Who is happy, fortunate who / That, fearing violence, glancing aye askance, / Weareth out life ? Nay, rather would I live / Happy-obscure, than be exalted prince, / —One who must joy to have for friends the vile, / Who hates the good, and ever dreads to die."

29. Euripides, *Ion*, trans. Way, 668–75. The modern translation reads: "Ion: I will go! Now only one thing is missing from my lot. Unless I find my mother, my life will be no life at all (*abiōton*), father. If it is right to do so, I pray my mother may be Athenian, so that I may have free speech as my maternal inheritance (*ōs moi genētai mētrothen, parrēsia*)! For if a foreigner, even though nominally a citizen, comes into that pure-bred city, his tongue is enslaved and he has no freedom of speech (*kouk echei parrēsian*)." See *Ion*, trans. Kovacs, 403.

30. See GSA, 125; GSO 134: "In the text called *Rhetorica ad Herennium*, *licentia*, the Latin translation of *parrēsia*, is defined as that which someone addresses to persons he should fear and honor. And speaking on his own behalf for his right to people he should fear and honor, he reproaches these powerful people for an offense they have committed." See also Frédéric Gros in GSA, 135n6; GSO, 146n6.

31. Euripides, *Ion*, ll. 859–922. For this passage, Foucault uses a different translation than the one from Arthur S. Way; its source could not be identified and so a modern translation has been substituted.

32. Euripides, *Ion*, trans. Kovacs, 423–27 (ll. 859–922).

33. Euripides, *Ion*, trans. Way, 313–17 (ll. 925–969).

34. See Jean-Baptiste Racine, *Phaedra*, act 1, scene 3:

"PHAEDRA: You know that son of the Amazon, That prince oppressed for so long by me?
OENONE: Hippolytus! Great Gods!
PHAEDRA: You are the one who named him."

Foucault also refers to this play in GSA, 129, 148–49; GSO, 139, 161–62.

35. Foucault proposes an analysis of these other episodes at the end of the lecture of January 26, 1983, in the series *The Government of Self and Others*, GSA, 130–35; GSO, 140–45.

NOVEMBER 7, 1983

1. Foucault omits lines 907–13, generally considered to be an interpolation: "Whoso with understanding counsel well / Profit the state—ere long, if not straightway. / Thus ought we on each leader of men to look, and so esteem: for both be in like case, / The orator, and the man in office set." See *supra* p. 109 where Foucault returns to this passage.

2. Foucault cites from Euripides, *Orestes*, trans. Way, 3: 145–46 (ll. 884–930). The modern translation renders the passage as: "Messenger: When the Argive assembly had fully gathered, a herald got up and said, 'Who wishes to speak about whether Orestes should die for killing his mother, or be allowed to live?' At this Talthybius got up, who had helped your father destroy the Phrygians. He is subservient to whoever is in power (*hupo tois dunamenois ōn*), and so he spoke ambiguously (*elexe dichomutha*), greatly admiring your father but dispraising your brother by whirling to and fro words fair-seeming and base: Orestes, he said, was establishing a bad precedent toward parents. He kept turning an obsequious face toward Aegisthus' friends. That is what his kind are like. Heralds are always leaping over to join those in prosperity: whoever has power in the city and enjoys high office is their friend. After him king Diomedes spoke. He was opposed to killing either you or your brother but said that exiling you would satisfy piety's demands. The crowd murmured in response, some saying that the advice was good, others showing disapproval. Then there stood up a man with no check on his tongue (*athuroglossōs*), strong in his brashness (*ischuōn thrasei*); [he was an Argive but no Argive, suborned, relying on noise from the crowd and the obtuse license of his tongue (*ēnaskamenos thorubō te pisunos kamathei parrēsia*), persuasive enough to involve them

in the future in some misfortune. When someone of pleasing speech but without sense persuades the people, it is a great misfortune for the city. But those who always give good counsel with intelligence are useful to the city in the long run, if not immediately. One should look at the leader this way: the same thing applies to the public speaker as to the holder of offices;] he proposed putting you and Orestes to death by stoning. But it was Tyndareus who had supplied the arguments [for the man trying to kill you to deliver, like this]. Another man got up and made precisely the opposite proposal. He was not handsome to look at but a brave man, one who rarely had anything to do with the city or the market circle, a man who farmed with his own hands (*autourgos*), the sort who alone keep the land from destruction, yet clever enough to grapple in argument when he wanted: he has lived a life of integrity, above reproach. His proposal was that Orestes, son of Agamemnon, should be given a garland for being willing to avenge his father by killing a wicked and godless woman. This woman, he said, was depriving us of all this: there would be no more taking the sword in the hand, no more leaving home to go on campaign if the men left behind would then subvert domestic order by outrageously seducing the soldiers' wives. The better sort of people thought his proposal was good." Euripides, *Orestes*, trans. David Kovacs, in *Helen, Phoenician Women, Orestes* (Cambridge: Harvard University Press, 2002). Foucault lectures on this tragedy for the first time on February 2, 1983, for the course *The Government of Self and Others*, but he proposes a much more detailed analysis here. GSA, 150–155; GSO, 160–164.

3. Euripides, *Orestes*, trans. Way, 145 (l. 885).

4. Euripides, *Orestes*, trans. Way, 145 (l. 889).

5. The play *Les Troyennes* is usually translated in English as *The Trojan Women*.

6. Euripides, *The Daughters of Troy*, trans. Arthur S. Way, in *Tragedies of Euripides in English Verse* 2: 135 (l. 417).

7. Foucault cites from Euripides, *Daughters of Troy*, trans. Way, 2: 136 (ll. 424–30). The translation obscures the relations of inequality that thread through this scene. A more modern translation renders the passage as: "What a clever fellow this servant is! Why are they called 'heralds,' these creatures all mortals hate, when they are merely lackeys bustling about tyrants and cities? You claim that my mother will come to the palace of Odysseus. But where are the words of Apollo, communicated to me, that she will die here? I will not reproach her with the rest of her fate." Euripides, *Trojan Women*, in *Trojan Women, Iphigenia among the Taurians, Ion*, trans. Kovacs, 57 (ll. 424–30).

8. Euripides, *Suppliants*, trans. Arthur S. Way, in *Tragedies of Euripides in English Verse* 1: 381–82 (ll. 399–463).

9. Euripides, *Suppliants*, trans. Way, 1: 381 (ll. 403–8): "First, stranger, with false note thy speech began, / Seeking a despot here. Our state is ruled / Not of one only man: Athens is free. / Her people in the order of their course / Rule year by year, bestowing on the rich / Advantage none; the poor hath equal right."

10. Euripides, *Suppliants*, trans. Way, 382, (ll. 429–41): "No worse foe than the despot hath a state. / Under whom, first, can be no common laws, / But one rules, keeping in his private hands / The law: so is equality no more. / But when the laws are written, then the weak / And wealthy have alike but equal right. / Yea, even the weaker may fling back the scoff / Against the prosperous, if he be reviled; / And, armed with right, the less o'ercomes the great. / Thus Freedom speaks:—'What man desires to bring / Good counsel for his country to the people?' Who chooseth this, is famous: who will not, / Keeps silence. Can equality further go?"

11. Foucault cites from Euripides, *Orestes*, trans. Way, 3: 145 (ll. 889–93). The modern translation reads: "He is subservient to whoever is in power, and so he spoke ambiguously (*elexe dichomutha*), greatly admiring your father but dispraising your brother by whirling to and fro words fair-seeming and base: Orestes, he said, was establishing a bad precedent toward parents." Euripides, *Orestes*, trans. Kovacs, 513 (ll. 889–93).

12. Euripides, *Orestes*, trans. Way, 3: 145 (ll. 902–3).

13. Theognis, *Greek Elegiac Poetry*, ed. and trans. Douglas E. Gerber (Cambridge: Harvard University Press, 1999), 235 (1.421–24): "Many men do not have on their tongue a door that closes with a well-adjusted fit, and they care about much that does not concern them. Often it is better for the bad to be stored away within and better for the good to come out than the bad."

14. Plutarch, "Concerning Talkativeness," in *Moralia*, trans. Helmbold, 5: 403 (503C): "And yet Nature has built about none of our parts so stout a stockade as about the tongue, having placed before it as an outpost the teeth, so that when reason within tightens 'the reins of silence,' if the tongue does not obey or restrain itself, we may check its incontinence by biting it till it bleeds." Foucault also evokes Plutarch's "De garrulitate" in the March 3, 1982 lecture from the course *Hermeneutics of the Subject*. See HS, 324–26; HS (Eng), 341–42.

15. Plutarch, "Concerning Talkativeness," 403 (503C–D): "And those who believe that storerooms without doors and purses without fastenings are of no use to their owners, yet keep their mouths without lock or door, maintaining as perpetual an outflow as the mouth of the Black Sea, appear to regard speech as the least valuable of all things."

16. This detailed confrontation between *athurostōmia* and *parrēsia* is a singular example for Foucault.

17. Plutarch, "The Education of Children," trans. Frank C. Babbitt in *Moralia* 1: 53 (11B–C): "For Antigonus sent his chief cook, Eutropion, who had been an officer in his army, to Theocritus, and insisted that Theocritus should come to him and engage him in discussion. When Eutropion delivered his message to Theocritus, coming several times for the purpose, the latter said, 'I know very well that you want to serve me up raw to your Cyclops,' twitting the one for being disfigured and the other for being now a cook. 'Then you shall not keep your head on,' said Eutropion, 'but you shall pay the penalty for this reckless talk and madness of yours.' He thereupon reported the remark to the king, who sent and had Theocritus put to death."

18. Plato, *Letter VII*, 1584 (336b): "As it was, though, some divinity or some evil spirit broke loose with lawlessness, with ungodliness, and, worst of all, with the boldness of folly (*amathias*)—the soil in which all manner of evil to all men takes root and flourishes and later produces a fruit most bitter for those who sowed it. So folly a second time brought complete failure and disaster."

19. Xenophon, *Oeconomicus*, trans. E. C. Marchant and O. J. Todd, in *Memorabilia, Oeconomicus, Symposium, Apology* (Cambridge: Harvard University Press, 2013), 427–33 (5).

20. Xenophon, *Oeconomicus*, 481–91 (11).

21. Euripides, *Orestes*, trans. Way, 146 (l. 922).

22. On the "crisis" of democratic *parrēsia* at the turn of the fifth and fourth centuries BCE in Athens, see GSA, 164–68, 277–79; GSO, 181–84, 301–3; CV, 34–51; CT, 33–52. See also the November 14, 1983 lecture given at the University of California, Berkeley.

23. On the Foucauldian history of thought as opposed to a "history of ideas," see among other sources: CCS, 84–85; Foucault, "Preface to The History of Sexuality," in *The Foucault Reader*, ed. Paul Rabinow (New York: Pantheon Books, 1984), 333–39; "Polemics, Politics, and Problematizations," in *Foucault Reader*, 381–90; "Foucault," in DE, II, no. 345, 1450–51.

24. Actually, the issue is not with the Thirty—who will not take power until 404, after the defeat of Athens—but with the Four Hundred. This last group, following an antidemocratic coup d'état, put in place an oligarchic constitution in 411, but one that lasted only a few months.

25. This complex dynamic is described by Foucault in *Discipline and Punish*, notably about the French penal system. See SP, especially 75–105, 269–99; DP, 73–103, 257–92.

26. Euripides, *Ion*, trans. Way, 293 (l. 536).

27. In effect, Apollo is the illegitimate son of Zeus.

28. Thucydides, *History of the Peloponnesian War*, trans. Warner, 144–51 (35–46). Taking into account the context, it seems that Foucault is instead referring to the third speech given by Pericles (158–62 [59–64]). Thucydides introduces this speech with the following words: "After the second invasion of the Peloponnesians there had been a change in the spirit of the Athenians. Their land had been twice devastated, and they had to contend with the war and the plague at the same time. Now they began to blame Pericles for having persuaded them to go to war and to hold him responsible for all the misfortunes which had overtaken them; They became eager to make peace with Sparta, and actually sent ambassadors there, who failed to achieve anything. They were then in a state of utter hopelessness, and all their angry feelings turned against Pericles. Pericles himself saw well enough how bitterly they felt at the situation in which they found themselves; he saw, in fact, that they were behaving exactly as he had expected that they would. He therefore, since he was still general, summoned an assembly with the aim of putting fresh courage into them and of guiding their embittered spirits so as to leave them in a calmer and more confident frame of mind. Coming before them, he made the following speech . . ."

29. See for example GSA, 164–68, 176–80; GSO, 181–84, 192–96; CV, 34–51; CT, 33–52.

NOVEMBER 14, 1983

1. [Pseudo-]Xenophon, *The Constitution of the Athenians*, trans. E. C. Marchant and G. W. Bowersock, in *Scripta Minora* (Cambridge: Harvard University Press, 1925), 479 (1.6–9). For a deeper analysis of this text, see CV, 40–44; CT, 40–44.

2. Isocrates, "On the Peace," trans. George Norlin, in *Isocrates*, 2: 13–15 (13): "Whenever you take counsel regarding your private business you seek out as counsellors men who are your superiors in intelligence, but whenever you deliberate on the business of the state you distrust and dislike men of that character and cultivate, instead, the most depraved of the orators who come before you on this platform; and you prefer as being better friends of the people those who are drunk to those who are sober, those who are witless to those who are wise, and those who dole out the public money to those who perform public services at their own expense. So that we may well marvel that anyone can expect a state which employs such counsellors to advance to better things."

3. Isocrates, "On the Peace," trans. Norlin, 7–9 (3).

4. Isocrates, "On the Peace," trans. Norlin, 15 (14): "But I know that it is hazardous to oppose your views and that, although this is a free government, there exists no 'freedom of speech' (*parrēsia*) except that which is enjoyed in this Assembly by the most reckless orators, who care nothing for your welfare, and in the theatre by the comic poets."

5. Isocrates, "Areopagiticus," trans. George Norlin, in *Isocrates,* 2: 115–17 (20): "For those who directed the state in the time of Solon and Cleisthenes did not establish a polity which in name merely was hailed as the most impartial and the mildest of governments, while in practice showing itself the opposite to those who lived under it, nor one which trained the citizens in such fashion that they looked upon insolence as democracy, lawlessness as liberty, impudence of speech as equality, and licence to do what they pleased as happiness (*epaideue tous politas ōsth' hēgeisthai tēn mēn akolasian dēmokratian, tēn de paranomian eleutherian, tēn de parrēsian isonomian, tēn d'exousian tou tauta poiein eudaimonian*), but rather a polity which detested and punished such men and by so doing made all the citizens better and wiser."

6. Plato, *Republic,* trans. Shorey, 785 (557a–b): "And a democracy, I suppose, comes into being when the poor, winning the victory, put to death some of the other party, drive out others, and grant the rest of the citizens an equal share in both citizenship and offices—and for the most part these offices are assigned by lot.—Why, yes, he said, that is the constitution of democracy alike whether it is established by force of arms or by terrorism resulting in the withdrawal of one of the parties.—What, then, said I, is the manner of their life and what is the quality of such a constitution? For it is plain that the man of this quality will turn out to be a democratic sort of man.—It is plain, he said.—To begin with, are they not free? and is not the city chock-full of liberty and freedom of speech? and has not every man licence to do as he likes (*kai eleutherias ē polis mestē kai parrēsias gignetai, kai exousia en autē poiein ho ti tis bouletai*)?—So it is said, he replied.—And where there is such licence, it is obvious that everyone would arrange a plan for leading his own life in the way that pleases him (*dēlon oti idian ekastos an kataskeuēn tou hautou biou kataskeuazoito ēn autē, hētis hekaston areskoi*)."

7. Plato, *Republic,* trans. Shorey, 786 (557c–d): "'Possibly,' said I, 'this is the most beautiful of polities as a garment of many colors, embroidered with all kinds of hues, so this, decked and diversified with every type of character, would appear the most beautiful. And perhaps,' I said, 'many would judge it to be the most beautiful, like boys and women when they see bright-colored things.' 'Yes indeed,' he said. 'Yes,' said I, 'and it is the fit place, my good friend, in which to look for a constitution.' 'Why so?' 'Because, owing to this licence,

[the democratic city] includes all kinds [of constitutions], and it seems likely that anyone who wishes to organize a state, as we were just now doing, must find his way to a democratic city and select the model that pleases him, as if in a bazaar of constitutions, and after making his choice, establish his own.'"

8. See, for examples, Demosthenes, "The Third Philippic," trans. J. H. Vince, in *Orations* (Cambridge: Harvard University Press, 1930), 1: 227 (51.3–4): "I claim for myself, Athenians, that if I utter some home-truths with freedom (*an ti alēthōn meta parrēsias legō*), I shall not thereby incur your displeasure. For look at it in this way. In other matters you think it so necessary to grant general freedom of speech to everyone in Athens (*parrēsian epi men tōn allōn houtō koinēn oiesthe dein einai pasi tois en tē polei*) that you even allow aliens and slaves to share in the privilege, and many menials may be observed among you speaking their minds with more liberty than citizens enjoy in other states; but from your deliberations you have banished it utterly. Hence the result is that in the Assembly your self-complacency is flattered by hearing none but pleasant speeches, but your policy and your practice are already involving you in the gravest peril. Therefore, if such is your temper now, I have nothing to say; but if, apart from flattery, you are willing to hear something to your advantage, I am ready to speak." See also, "On Organization," 363 (15), and "The Third Olynthiac," 43–45, 61 (3, 32).

9. Aristotle, *Constitution of Athens*, trans. F. G. Canyon, in *Complete Works of Aristotle*, 2350 (16): "[Pisistratus] often made expeditions in person into the country to inspect it and to settle disputes between individuals, that they might not come into the city and neglect their farms. It was in one of the progresses that, as the story goes, Pisistratus has his adventure with the man of Hymettus, who was cultivating the spot afterwards known as 'Tax-free Farm.' He saw a man digging and working at a very stony piece of ground, and being surprised he sent his attendant to ask what he got out of this plot of land. 'Aches and pains,' said the man; 'and that's what Pisistratus ought to have his tenth of.' The man spoke without knowing who his questioner was; but Pisistratus was so pleased with his frank speech and his industry that he granted him exemption from all taxes." Foucault also references this text during his February 8, 1984 lecture from the course *The Courage of Truth*. See CV, 56; CT, 60.

10. Aristotle, *Nicomachean Ethics*, trans. Ross and Urmson, 1772–75 (1123a–1125a). Foucault evokes this text from Aristotle, one which links *megalopsuchia* (magnanimity, or a grandeur of the soul) to the practice of *parrēsia*, in the first lecture for the course *The Courage of Truth*, where he notably insists on the theme of courage: courage at once of the parrhesiast and of his interlocutor. See CV, 13–14; CT, 12.

11. Aristotle, *Nicomachean Ethics,* trans. Ross and Urmson 1774 (1124b): "[The proud man] does not run into trifling dangers, nor is he fond of danger, because he honors few things; but he will face great dangers (*ouk esti mikrokindunos oude philokindunos dia to oliga timan, megakindunos de*), and when he is in danger he is unsparing of his life, knowing that there are conditions on which life is not worth having."

12. Aristotle, *Nicomachean Ethics,* trans. Ross and Urmson, 1775 (1124b): "He must also be open in his hate and in his love (for to conceal one's feelings is a mark of timidity), and must care more for truth than for what people will think (*amelein tēs alētheias mallon ē tēs doxēs*), and must speak and act openly; for he is free of speech because he is contemptuous (*parrēsiastēs gar dia to kataphronētikos einai*), and he is given to telling the truth, except when he speaks with irony to the vulgar."

13. Plato, *Laches,* trans. W. R. M Lamb (Cambridge: Harvard University Press, 1924), 7, 9, 41 (178a, 179c, 189a). This is the first time that Foucault proposes an analysis of Socratic *parrēsia* while relying on a study of the *Laches*; the importance of this dialogue, in his eyes, lies above all in the fact that *bios* emerges here as a "principal element of the parrhesiastic game." In the Collège de France lectures *The Courage of Truth,* Foucault will take up and develop this analysis, by arguing that if the *Alcibiades* is the point of departure for the development of Socratic truth-telling that tends toward a "metaphysics of the soul," then the *Laches* is, by contrast, the point of departure for a truth-telling that tends toward a "stylistics of existence." In other words, the *Laches* marks, according to Foucault, the emergence of the theme "of the true life according to the principle and form of truth-telling," all the while pointing already toward the form that *parrēsia* will take with the Cynics. See CV, 147–53; CT, 159–166.

14. Plato, *Laches,* trans. Lamb, 81–83 (200e–201c):

> "SOCRATES: Why, how strange it would be, Lysimachus, to refuse to lend one's endeavours for the highest improvement of anybody! Now if in the debates that we have just held I had been found to know what our two friends did not know, it would be right to make a point of inviting me to take up this work: but as it is, we have all got into the same difficulty, so why should one of us be preferred to another? In my own opinion, none of us should; and this being so, perhaps you will allow me to give you a piece of advice. I tell you, gentlemen—and this is confidential—that we ought all alike to seek out the best teacher we can find, first for ourselves—for we need one—and then for our boys, sparing neither expense nor anything else we can do: but to leave ourselves as we now are, this

I do not advise. And if anyone makes fun of us for seeing fit to go to school at our time of life, I think we should appeal to Homer, who said that 'shame is no good mate for a needy man.' So let us not mind what anyone may say, but join together in arranging for our own and the boys' tuition (*koinē hēmōn autōn kai tōn meirakiōn epimeleian poiēsōmetha*).

LYSIMACHUS: I gladly approve of your suggestion, Socrates; and as I am the oldest, so I am the most eager to have lessons with the young ones. Now this is what I ask you to do: come to my house tomorrow at daybreak; be sure not to fail, and then we shall consult on this very matter. For the present, let us break up our meeting.

SOCRATES: I will not fail, Lysimachus, to come to you to-morrow, God willing."

15. Lysimachus was the son of Aristides, also called Aristides the Just, an Athenian statesman from the fifth century, and Melesias's father was Thucydides (not to be confused with the historian), who was one of the heads of the aristocratic faction.

16. Plato, *Laches*, trans. Lamb, 37–39 (187e–188c).

17. Foucault insists on the role played by Socrates as "touchstone" in the *Laches* in his February 22, 1984 lecture in *Courage of Truth*. English: CV, 133–43; CT, 143–53. See also footnote 26 from the Grenoble lecture presented earlier in this volume.

18. Plato, *Laches*, trans. Lamb, 37–41 (188c–89c).

19. The battle referenced here is the battle of Delium in 424 BC.

20. See Plato, *Gorgias*, trans. Lamb, 395–97 (486d–487b). See *supra* p. 235, endnote 26.

21. Plato, *Apology*, trans. Tredennick, 7–9, 15–17 (20e–23e, 29b–31c). Foucault deepens his analysis of the "Socratic mission" assigned to Socrates by the god at Delphi in the February 15, 1984 lecture of the course *The Courage of Truth*. See CV, 74–83; CT, 81–90.

22. It is not until fall 1983 that Foucault will become interested in the Cynics as a significant moment in the history of *parrēsia*—a "moment," however, that some months later will acquire in his eyes a much greater importance when he decides to consecrate the second half of his Collège de France lectures on the *Courage of Truth* to them. Until that moment, Foucault referred to Cynicism principally through his commentary on chapter 22 of book 3 of the *Discourses* of Epictetus, in which Epictetus sketches the portrait of a Cynic very much influenced by his own philosophical position. For different Foucauldian

commentaries on this text, see SV, 117–18; ST, 113–15; HS, 134, 423; HS (Eng), 138–39, 441; GSA, 318–20; GSO, 346–48; CV, 267–78; CT, 291–303; SS, 185–86; CS, 157–59.

23. Plato, *Laws*, trans. Taylor, 1400–1401 (835b–c): "There is no difficulty in discovering how to reduce these details and others of the kind to a legitimate order, nor again will a different arrangement of them cause much benefit or detriment to society. But there is a matter of vast moment, as to which it is truly hard to inspire conviction. The task, indeed, is one for God himself, were it actually possible to receive orders from him. As things are, it will probably need a bold man, a man who puts plain speaking before everything, to declare his real belief about the true interest of state and citizens (*os parrēsian diapherontōs timōn erei ta dokounta arist' einai polei kai politais*), and make the regulations the whole social system requires and demands in a corrupt age—a man who will oppose the passions at their strongest, and stand alone in his loyalty to the voice of truth without one creature on earth to second him." See also endnote 24 from the Grenoble lecture presented earlier.

24. For an interpretation of this principle, "know thyself," engraved on the pediment of the temple at Delphi, see HS, 5–6; HS (Eng), 3–4.

25. See HS, 19; HS (Eng), 17: "Aristotle is not the pinnacle of Antiquity but its exception." See also Foucault's conversation, *Discussion with Michel Foucault*, IMEC/Fonds Michel Foucault, D 250(8), p. 13, cited in CCS, 185n41.

26. Aristotle, *Nicomachean Ethics*, trans. Ross and Urmson, 1774 (1124b).

NOVEMBER 21, 1983

1. On the theme of "aesthetics of existence," see the following, among others: Foucault, "Débat au Département d'Histoire à Berkeley," in CCS, 143; "Débat au Département de Français," CCS, 154–56; "On the Genealogy of Ethics: An Overview of Work in Progress," in *Michel Foucault: Beyond Structuralism and Hermeneutics*, ed. Paul Rabinow and Hubert L. Dreyfus, 2nd ed. (Chicago: University of Chicago Press, 1983), 235; "Rêver de ses plaisirs: Sur l'Onirocritique d'Artémidore," in DE, II, no. 332, p. 1307; "An aesthetics of existence," interview with Alessandro Fontana, DE, II, no. 357, pp. 1550–51. See also CV, 149–51; CT, 161–63; UP, 103–107; UP (Eng), 89–93.

2. This manner of presenting the study of "parrhesiastic practices" at the heart of philosophy, and notably the "three principal forms of relations that are implicated in this new political *parrēsia*"—*parrēsia* in the context of community life, in the context of public life, in the context of individual relations—is unique to Foucault.

3. In France, the *écoles normales* are publicly funded schools for the training of primary and secondary school teachers.

4. Philodemus, *Peri parrēsias.*

5. Gigante, "Philodème," 196–217.

6. Foucault evokes this comparison between medicine, piloting, and the art of governing men in the March 10, 1982 lecture for the course *Hermeneutics of the Subject.* See HS, 386; HS (Eng), 402. In the February 15, 1978 lecture for the course *Security, Territory, and Population,* Foucault insists that the Greeks generally rejected the idea that political leaders should be like shepherds tending their flocks, and said that the model for political action, the art of governing men, was instead more like weaving. See STP, 149–50; STP (Eng), 145–46. See also Foucault, "'Omnes et Singulatim': Toward a Critique of Political Reason," in EW, 1: 298–325.

7. See Gregory Nazianzen, *Orations,* trans. Charles Gordon Brown, in *A Select Library of Nicene and Post-Nicene Fathers* (Grand Rapids: W. B. Eerdmans, 1893), 7: 208. See also STP, 154, 163n46, 196; STP (Eng), 150–51, 159n46, 192; GV, 51; GL, 52.

8. On the hierarchical structure that characterizes Epicurean schools, see HS, 131–33; HS (Eng), 135–37.

9. Philodemus, *Peri parrēsias,* ed. Olivieri, 17 (fragment 36).

10. On the "mode of tradition" that was very particular to Cynicism, founded on stories, anecdotes, and examples that transmit models of comportment and matrices of attitudes, and that Foucault calls an "existential tradition" as opposed to a "doctrinal tradition," see CV, 193–94; CT, 208–10.

11. Farrand Sayre, *Diogenes of Sinope: A Study of Greek Cynicism* (Baltimore: J. H. Furst, 1938).

12. Lucian, "The Runaways," trans. A. M. Harmon (Cambridge: Harvard University Press, 1936), 5: 73 (16): "Consequently, every city is filled with such upstarts, particularly with those who enter the names of Diogenes, Antisthenes, and Crates as their patrons and enlist in the army of the dog."

13. Julian, "To the Uneducated Cynics," trans. W. C. Wright (Cambridge: Harvard University Press, 1913), vol. 2.

14. Lucian, "The Passing of Peregrinus," trans. A. M. Harmon (Cambridge: Harvard University Press, 1936), vol. 5. For an analysis of the figure of Peregrinus, see CV, 167, 180–81, 233–34; CT, 181, 195, 254.

15. On Cynicism as the "essence of philosophical heroism," see CV, 194–95; CT, 210–211.

16. In fall 1983, Foucault organizes his analysis of Cynical *parrēsia* in a rather different way than he will a few months later at the Collège de France. In par-

ticular, he gives a good deal of importance to the analysis of discursive parrhesiastic practices (exhortation and provocative dialogue), and gives little place to the discussion of "scandalous behaviors." In *The Courage of Truth*, by contrast, Cynical *parrēsia* is presented primarily as an attitude, an ethos, a fully fledged manner of living—and its discursive practices recede to the background. Foucault also refers to the scandalous gesture of Cynic philosophy in UP, 64–5; UP (Eng), 54–55.

17. Epictetus, *Discourses as Reported by Arrian*, trans. Oldfather, 3: 131–69 (22).

18. Dio Chrysostom, "The Fourth Discourse on Kingship," trans. J. W. Cohoon, in *Dio Chrysostom*, vol. 1 (Cambridge: Harvard University Press, 1932), 169–233.

19. Dio Chrysostom, "The Ninth, or Isthmian, Discourse," trans. J. W. Cohoon, in *Dio Chrysostom*, 1: 409–11(10–14).

20. Dio Chrysostom, "The Ninth, or Isthmian, Discourse," trans. Cohoon, 415 (22).

21. C. P. Jones, *The Roman World of Dio Chrysostom* (Cambridge: Harvard University Press, 1978).

22. Dio Chrysostom, "The Seventh, or Euboean, Discourse," trans. J. W. Cohoon, in *Dio Chrysostom*, 1: 285–373.

23. Foucault analyzes, in a less detailed manner, the story by Dio Chrysostom about the meeting between Diogenes and Alexander, in his March 21, 1984 lecture for the course *The Courage of Truth*. See CV, 252–55; CT, 275–78.

24. Dio Chrysostom, "Fourth Discourse on Kingship," trans. Cohoon, 171–73 (9–10): "if he expected to keep the Macedonians and the other Greeks submissive [he] must time and again curry the favour of their rulers and the general populace by words and gifts (*logois te kai dōrois*); whereas Diogenes cajoled no men by flattery, but told everybody the truth (*alla talēthē pros apantas legōn*) . . ."

25. Dio Chrysostom, "Fourth Discourse on Kingship," trans. Cohoon, 175 (14–15): "So the king came up to him as he sat there and greeted him, whereat the other looked up at him with a terrible glare like that of a lion and ordered him to step aside a little, for Diogenes happened to be warming himself in the sun. Now Alexander was at once delighted with the man's boldness and composure in not being awestruck in his presence. For it is somehow natural for the courageous to love the courageous, while cowards eye them with misgiving and hate them as enemies, but welcome the base and like them. And so to the one class truth and frankness (*alētheia kai parrēsia*) are the most agreeable things in the world, to the other, flattery and deceit. The latter lend a willing ear

to those who in their intercourse seek to please, the former, to those who have regard for the truth."

26. Foucault does not return to this heated debate between the provocative dialogue of Diogenes and the Socratic dialogue during his Collège de France course *Courage of the Truth*. There the analysis of the meeting between Diogenes and Alexander focuses largely on the theme of the Cynic-king. See CV, 252–55; CT, 275–78.

27. By "ignore," Foucault could also have in mind the French meaning of the word, "to be ignorant of."

28. Plato, *Gorgias*, trans. Lamb, 461–62 (505c–d).

29. Dio Chrysostom, "Fourth Discourse on Kingship," trans. Cohoon, 197 (64).

30. Dio Chrysostom, "Fourth Discourse on Kingship," trans. Cohoon, 197 (63–64).

31. Dio Chrysostom, "Fourth Discourse on Kingship," trans. Cohoon, 195–97 (59).

32. Dio Chrysostom, "Fourth Discourse on Kingship," trans. Cohoon, 175 (15).

33. Dio Chrysostom, "Fourth Discourse on Kingship," trans. Cohoon, 203 (76).

34. Dio Chrysostom, "Fourth Discourse on Kingship," trans. Cohoon, 177 (18–20): "'But tell me this: are you the Alexander whom they call a bastard?' At this the king flushed and showed anger, but he controlled himself and regretted that he had deigned to enter into conversation with a man who was both rude and an imposter, as he thought. Diogenes, however, marking his embarrassment, would fain change his throw just like men playing at dice. So when the king said, 'What gave you the idea of calling me a bastard?' he replied, 'What gave it? Why, I hear that your own mother says this of you. Or is it not Olympias who said that Philip is not your father, as it happens, but a dragon or Ammon or some god or other or demigod or wild animal? And yet in that case you would certainly be a bastard.'

Thereupon Alexander smiled and was pleased as never before, thinking that Diogenes, so far from being rude, was the most tactful of men and the only one who really knew how to pay a compliment."

35. See Dio Chrysostom, *Quatrième discours: Sur la royauté*, in *Les Cyniques grecs*, trans. Léonce Paquet (Paris: Le Livre de Poche, 1992), 257. The editor for this volume describes the myth: "It speaks of strange creatures, half-woman, half-animal, who seduced sailors with their beautiful faces as they sailed along the coasts of Libya, and later devoured them under cover of night."

36. Dio Chrysostom, "Fourth Discourse on Kingship," trans. Cohoon, 203 (73–74).

37. Dio Chrysostom, "Fourth Discourse on Kingship," trans. Cohoon, 203 (77–78).

38. Dio Chrysostom, "Fourth Discourse on Kingship," trans. Cohoon, 179 (24–25).

39. Dio Chrysostom, "Fourth Discourse on Kingship," trans. Cohoon, 179 (25).

40. Dio Chrysostom, "Fourth Discourse on Kingship," trans. Cohoon, 181 (26–31).

41. In his Collège de France course *The Courage of Truth,* Foucault will insist quite a bit on the public and theatrical character of Cynic life. See CV, 159–61, 169, 231–35; CT, 172–74, 183, 251–54.

42. Aristotle, *Rhetoric,* trans. Rhys Roberts, in *Complete Works of Aristotle,* 2252 (1411a24): "Diogenes the Dog called taverns 'the mess-rooms of Attica.'"

43. On the figure of Demetrius, see HS, 137–38, 221–22; HS (Eng), 142–43, 231–32; CV, 179–81; CT, 193–95.

44. Dio Chrysostom, "Fourth Discourse on Kingship," trans. Cohoon, 207–9 (83–84).

45. François Vandenbroucke, "Démon en Occident," in *Dictionnaire de spiritualité* (Paris: Beauchesne, 1957), 3: 212–38.

46. Hadot, *Philosophy as a Way of Life.*

NOVEMBER 30, 1983

1. Plutarch, "How to Tell a Flatterer from a Friend," trans. Babbitt, 291–395. For another Foucauldian analysis of this text, see *supra*, pp. 19–20, 26–29.

2. Plutarch, "How to Tell a Flatterer from a Friend," trans. Babbitt, 265–67 (48F–49B): "It is because of this self-love that everybody is himself his own foremost and greatest flatterer, and hence finds no difficulty in admitting the outsider to witness with him and to confirm his own conceits and desires. For the man who is spoken of with opprobrium as a lover of flatterers is in high degree a lover of self, and, because of his kindly feeling toward himself, he desires and conceives himself to be endowed with all manner of good qualities; but although the desire for these is not unnatural, yet the conceit that one possesses them is dangerous and must be carefully avoided. Now if Truth is a thing divine, and, as Plato puts it, the origin 'of all good for gods and all good for men,' then the flatterer is in all likelihood an enemy to the gods and particularly to the Pythian god. For the flatterer always takes a position over against

the maxim 'Know thyself,' by creating in every man deception towards himself and ignorance both of himself and of the good and evil that concerns himself; the good he renders defective and incomplete, and the evil wholly impossible to amend."

3. Plutarch, "How to Tell a Flatterer from a Friend," trans. Babbitt, 281 (52A–B): "In the first place, it is necessary to observe the uniformity and permanence of his tastes, whether he always takes delight in the same things, and commends always the same things, and whether he directs and ordains his own life according to one pattern, as becomes a free-born man and a lover of congenial friendship and intimacy; for such is the conduct of a friend. But the flatterer, since he has no abiding-place of character to dwell in, and since he leads a life not of his own choosing but another's, moulding and adapting himself to suit another, is not simple, not one, but variable and many in one, and, like water that is poured into one receptacle after another, he is constantly on the move from place to place, and changes his shape to fit his receiver."

4. For a discussion of the problem of self-deception and the inconstancy of mind in early Christianity, see GV, 289–301; GL, 294–307; OHS, 78–81; ABHS, 65–68; "Discussion of 'Truth and Subjectivity,'" in OHS, 120; ABHS, 105–6; "Sexuality and Solitude," EW, 1: 182–83.

5. Galen, *On the Passions and Errors of the Soul,* trans. Harkins, 27–69. For another Foucauldian analysis of this text, see above, *supra* pp. 17–18, 20, 24, 27–28.

6. Galen, *On the Passions and Errors of the Soul,* trans. Harkins, 30–31: "As Aesop says, we have two sacks suspended from our necks; the one in front is filled with the faults of others; the one behind is filled with our own. This is the reason why we see the faults of others but remain blind to those which concern ourselves. All men admit the truth of this and, furthermore, Plato gives the reason for it. He says that the lover is blind in the case of the object of his love. If, therefore, each of us loves himself most of all, he must be blind in his own case."

7. Galen, *On the Passions and Errors of the Soul,* trans. Harkins, 31–33: "Since errors come from false opinion while the passions arise by an irrational impulse, I thought the first step was for a man to free himself from his passions; for these passions are probably the reason why we fall into false opinions. And there are passions of the soul which everybody knows: anger, wrath, fear, grief, envy, and violent lust. In my opinion, excessive vehemence in loving or hating anything is also a passion; I think the saying 'moderation is best' is correct, since no immoderate action is good. How, then, could a man cut out these passions if he did not first know that he had them? But as we said, it is impossible to know them, since we love ourselves to excess. Even if this saying will

not permit you to judge yourself, it does allow that you can judge others whom you neither love nor hate. Whenever you hear anyone in town being praised by many because he flatters no man, associate with that man and judge from your own experience whether he is the sort of man they say he is. First, if you see him going continually to the homes of the wealthy, the powerful, or even monarchs, be sure that you have heard falsely that this man always speaks the truth, for such adulation leads to lies. Second, be equally sure that his reputation is false if you see him greeting these people by name, visiting them, and even dining with them. Whoever has chosen such a life, not only does not speak the truth, but he is wholly evil, because he loves some or all of the following: wealth, rule, honors, reputation. When a man does not greet the powerful and wealthy by name, when he does not visit them, when he does not dine with them, when he lives a disciplined life, expect that man to speak the truth; try, too, to come to a deeper knowledge of what kind of man he is (and this comes about through long association). If you find such a man, summon him and talk with him one day in private; ask him to reveal straightway whatever of the above-mentioned passions he may see in you. Tell him you will be most grateful for this service and that you will look on him as your deliverer more than if he had saved you from an illness of the body. Have him promise to reveal it whenever he sees you affected by any of the passions I mentioned. If, after several days, although he has obviously been spending time with you, he tells you nothing, reproach him and again urge him, still more earnestly than before, to reveal immediately whatever he sees you doing as the result of passion. If he tells you that he has said nothing because he has seen you commit no passionate act during this time, do not immediately believe him, nor think that you have suddenly become free from fault, but consider that the truth is one or the other of the following. First, the friend whom you have summoned has either been negligent and has not paid attention to you, or he remains silent because he is afraid to reproach you, or because he does not wish to be hated, knowing as he does that it is usual, as I might say, with all men to hate those who speak the truth. Second, if he has not remained silent for these reasons, perhaps he is unwilling to help you and says nothing for this or some other reason which we cannot find it in ourselves to praise."

8. On the Greek idea of *askēsis*, see SV, 35–6; ST, 32–33; HS, 301–6, 398; HS (Eng), 315–21, 416–17; UP, 84–90; UP (Eng), 72–77.

9. See Musonius Rufus, "Which Is More Effective, Theory or Practice?," trans. Cora E. Lutz, in *Musonius Rufus 'The Roman Socrates'* (New Haven: Yale University Press, 1947), 49–53. See also HS, 302–3; HS (Eng), 316–17.

10. Seneca, "De ira"/"On Anger," trans. John W. Basore, in *Moral Essays*.

For other Foucauldian analyses of this passage from *De ira*, see CV, 235–41; CT, 258–61; OHS, 42–45; ABHS, 28–32; MFDV, 94–97; WDTT, 97–100; HS, 157, 461–64; HS (Eng), 162–63, 481–84; SS, 77–79; CS, 60–62; "Technologies of the Self," 32–34.

11. Cicero, *On Old Age*, trans. W. A. Falconer (Cambridge, MA: Harvard University Press, 1923), 47 (38): "I follow the practice of the Pythagoreans and run over in my mind every evening all that I have said, heard, or done during the day."

12. Plato, *Republic*, trans. Shorey, 798–99 (571d–572b): "But when, I suppose, a man's condition is healthy and sober, and he goes to sleep after arousing his rational part and entertaining it with fair words and thoughts, and attaining to clear self-consciousness, while he has neither starved nor indulged to repletion his appetitive part, so that it may be lulled to sleep and not disturb the better part by its pleasure or pain, but may suffer that in isolated purity to examine and reach out towards and apprehend some of the things unknown to it, past, present or future, and when he has in like manner tamed his passionate part, and does not after a quarrel fall asleep with anger still awake within him, but if he has thus quieted the two elements in his soul and quickened the third, in which reason resides, and so goes to his rest, you are aware that in such case he is most likely to apprehend truth, and the visions of his dreams are least likely to be lawless."

13. Seneca, letter 108, *Epistles of Seneca*, 3: 228–53.

14. Foucault refers to Quintus Sextius the Elder, a Stoic philosopher from the first century BCE.

15. Seneca, "De Ira," trans. Basore, 341 (3.36).

16. Foucault is referring to Kenneth James Dover (1920–2010), who was particularly known for having written *Greek Homosexuality* (New York: Bloomsbury, 2016 [1978]). Foucault wrote a review of this book that was published in the June 1, 1982 issue of *Libération*. See "Des caresses d'hommes considérées comme un art," in DE, II, no. 314, pp. 1134–36. See also "Entretien avec M. Foucault," with Jean-Pierre Joecker, Michèle Ouerd, and Alain Sanzio, in DE, II, no. 311, pp. 1105–14.

17. Seneca, "On Tranquility of Mind," trans. Basore, 2: 202–85. For other Foucauldian analyses of this text, see GV, 235; GL, 239–40; OHS, 46–50; ABHS, 32–36; MFDV, 97–101; WDTT, 100–103; HS, 86, 126–29, 150–51; HS (Eng), 89, 131–34, 157.

18. Seneca, "On Tranquility of Mind," trans. Basore, 203 (1.1–2).

19. Seneca, "On Tranquility of Mind," trans. Basore, 203–5 (1.3–4).

20. Seneca, "On Tranquility of Mind," trans. Basore, 211–13 (1.18): "I know

that these mental disturbances of mine are not dangerous and give no promise of a storm; to express what I complain of in apt metaphor, I am distressed, not by a tempest, but by sea-sickness. Do you, then, take from me this trouble, whatever it be, and rush to the rescue of one who is struggling in full sight of land."

21. Seneca, "On Tranquility of Mind," trans. Basore, 1, 4–15, pp. 205–11. For lack of time, Foucault only reads aloud the first paragraph or so from this passage; since he comments on the passage in its entirety, it is reproduced in full here.

22. Seneca, "On Tranquility of Mind," trans. Basore, 209 (1.10–13).

23. Seneca, "On Tranquility of Mind," trans. Basore, 209–11 (1.13–15).

24. Foucault uses the English word "topic," which is a false cognate for the French word *topique* that more closely aligns with *topos*, which indicates a convention or motif.

25. When raising an analogous problem, in his analysis of "On Tranquility of Mind," given at both Berkeley and Dartmouth in October and November 1980 respectively, Foucault insists on "the force of the truth." That is to say, on that truth which is necessary precisely in order to transform the theoretical principles and practical rules that Serenus already knows into "a victorious force," thus assuring him *tranquillitas*. See OHS, 47–49; ABHS, 32–35.

26. Regarding the examination of representations in Epictetus, see HS, 285–86; HS (Eng), 298–99; "L'herméneutique du sujet," in DE, II, no. 323, p. 1183; "The Hermeneutics of the Subject," in EW, 1: 103–4; "Technologies of the Self," 37–38; "Débat au Département de Français," in CCS, 166–70.

27. Epictetus, *Discourses as Reported by Arrian*, trans. Oldfather, 3: 85–87 (12.15): "For, just as Socrates used to tell us not to live a life unsubjected to examination, so we ought not to accept a sense-impression unsubjected to examination, but should say, 'Wait, allow me to see who you are and whence you come' (just as the night-watch say, 'Show me your tokens')."

28. Epictetus, *Discourses as Reported by Arrian*, trans. Oldfather, 1: 135–37 (20.7–10): "Therefore, the first and greatest task of the philosopher is to test the impressions and discriminate between them, and to apply none that has not been tested. You all see in the matter of coinage, in which it is felt that we have some interest, how we have even invented an art, and how many means the tester (*argurognōmōn*) employs to test the coinage—sight, touch, smell, finally hearing; he throws the denarius down and then listens to the sound, and is not satisfied with the sound it makes on a single test, but, as a result of his constant attention to the matter, he catches the tune, like a musician."

29. John Cassian, "The First Conference of Abba Moses: On the Goal

and the End of the Monk," trans. Boniface Ramsey, in *The Conferences* (New York: Paulist Press, 1997), 59–63 (20–22). For an analysis of these metaphors as used by Cassian, see GV, 294–96; GL, 298–302; OHS, 79–82; ABHS, 66–69; MFDV, 147–48; WDTT, 149–50; HS, 286–87; HS (Eng), 299–300; "Le combat de la chasteté," in DE, II, no. 312, pp. 1124–25; "The Battle for Chastity," in EW, 1: 185–86; "Technologies of the Self," 45–47.

30. See GV, 293; GL, 297; "L'herméneutique du sujet," in DE, II, no. 323, p. 1183; "The Hermeneutics of the Subject" in EW, 1: 104.

31. This sophism is attributed to Chrysippus by Diogenes Laërtius. See Diogenes Laërtius, *Lives and Opinions of Eminent Philosophers*, trans. R. D. Hicks (Cambridge: Harvard University Press, 1925), 2: 297 (7. 187, Chrysippus): "If you say something, it passes through your lips: now you say wagon, consequently a wagon passes through your lips."

32. Epictetus, *Discourses as Reported by Arrian*, trans. Oldfather, 3: 61 (8.1–3): "As we exercise ourselves to meet the sophistical interrogations, so we ought also to exercise ourselves daily to meet the impressions of our senses, because these too put interrogations to us. So-and-so's son is dead. Answer, 'That lies outside the sphere of the moral purpose, it is not an evil.' His father has disinherited So-and-so; what do you think of it? 'That lies outside the sphere of the moral purpose, it is not an evil.' Caesar has condemned him. 'That lies outside the sphere of the moral purpose, it is not an evil.' He was grieved at all this. 'That lies within the sphere of the moral purpose, it is an evil.' He has borne up under it manfully. 'That lies within the sphere of the moral purpose, it is a good.'"

33. See for example "Débat au Département de Français," CCS, 166–70; "On the Genealogy of Ethics: An Overview of a Work in Progress," 249–50.

34. Epictetus, *Discourses as Reported by Arrian*, trans. Oldfather, 3: 33 (3.14–16). Foucault may be paraphrasing a slightly different translation.

35. As Foucault explains on many occasions, and especially clearly in an interview published in January 1984, in Stoicism "the problem is to learn by the teaching of a certain number of truths, of doctrines, some of which are fundamental principles and others rules of conduct. It is a question of having these principles tell you in each situation, and in some way spontaneously, how you should behave . . . You will have become the *logos* or the *logos* will have become you." See "The Ethics of the Concern for Self as a Practice of Freedom," in EW, 1: 286. See also "Self Writing," in EW, 1: 206–7; HS, 308–9; HS (Eng), 322–23.

36. The passage in Plutarch to which Foucault refers is to be found not in the treatise "On Tranquility of Mind" (*Peri Euthumias*), but in the treatise "On

the Control of Anger," *Moralia*, trans. Helmbold, 6: 93 (452F–453A): "A good plan, as it seems to me, Fundanus, is that which painters follow: they scrutinize their productions from time to time before they finish them. They do this because, by withdrawing their gaze and by inspecting their work often, they are able to form a fresh judgement, and one which is more likely to seize upon any slight discrepancy, such as the familiarity of uninterrupted contemplation will conceal. Since, therefore, it is impossible for a man to contemplate himself from time to time by getting apart from himself and interrupting his consciousness of himself by breaking its continuity (and this is what, more than anything else, makes every man a poorer judge of himself than of others), the next best course would be for him to inspect his friends from time to time and likewise to offer himself to them, not to see if he is grown old suddenly or if his body is better or worse, but for them to examine both his behaviour and his character to learn whether time has added some excellence or taken away some vice."

37. On the distinction between the "analytics of the truth" (what Foucault also calls a "formal ontology of the truth") and the critical tradition of Western philosophy (to which Foucault usually makes reference when speaking about "the historical ontology of the present"), see "What Is Enlightenment?" in EW, 1: 318–19, as well as GSA, 21–22; GSO, 20–21; CCS, 84.

38. For more on problematization, see among others: "Polemics, Politics, and Problematizations," 389–90; "Le souci de la vérité," in DE, II, no. 350, pp. 1488–89; UP, 16–19; UP (Eng), 10–13.

39. See UP, 85; UP (Eng), 73: "The doctrine and practice of the Cynics . . . accorded a good deal of importance to *askēsis*; indeed, the Cynic life as a whole could be seen as a sort of continuous exercise." Also see CV, 191–93; CT, 206–9. A study of Cynic *askēsis* can also be found in Marie-Odile Goulet-Cazé, *L'ascèse cynique: Un commentaire de Diogène Laërce VI 70–71* (Paris: Vrin, 1986).

40. For an extensive analysis of authorship and critique in Foucault, see Nancy Luxon, *Crisis of Authority: Politics, Trust, and Truth-Telling in Freud and Foucault* (Cambridge: Cambridge University Press, 2013).

INDEX OF NAMES